LOEB CLASSICAL LIBRARY
FOUNDED BY JAMES LOEB 1911

EDITED BY
JEFFREY HENDERSON

EARLY GREEK PHILOSOPHY
III

LCL 526

EARLY GREEK PHILOSOPHY

VOLUME III

EARLY IONIAN THINKERS

PART 2

EDITED AND TRANSLATED BY
ANDRÉ LAKS AND GLENN W. MOST

IN COLLABORATION WITH
GÉRARD JOURNÉE

AND ASSISTED BY
LEOPOLDO IRIBARREN

HARVARD UNIVERSITY PRESS
CAMBRIDGE, MASSACHUSETTS
LONDON, ENGLAND
2016

Copyright © 2016 by the President and Fellows
of Harvard College
All rights reserved

First published 2016

LOEB CLASSICAL LIBRARY® is a registered trademark
of the President and Fellows of Harvard College

Library of Congress Control Number 2015957358
CIP data available from the Library of Congress

ISBN 978-0-674-99691-5

*Composed in ZephGreek and ZephText by
Technologies 'N Typography, Merrimac, Massachusetts.
Printed on acid-free paper and bound by
The Maple-Vail Book Manufacturing Group*

CONTENTS

EARLY IONIAN THINKERS, PART 2
    8. Xenophanes   3
    9. Heraclitus   114

EARLY IONIAN THINKERS
PART 2

8. XENOPHANES [XEN.]

Xenophanes was born in Colophon, a Greek city of Ionia, between 570 and 560 BC, according to the most plausible chronology; he himself states that he lived until a very advanced age (**P1, D61**). A rhapsode by profession, he employs various poetic forms (dactylic hexameter, elegiac couplet, perhaps iambic trimeter), and he discusses a variety of subjects (customs, morality, theology, natural phenomena, human understanding), often in a free and polemical tone. This makes him difficult to classify as an author (his fragments also form part of the corpus of Greek elegiac poets). Aristotle's negative judgment of him (**R12**) certainly had lasting repercussions upon the reception of his thought: if it is true that he was legitimated philosophically by a construction that turned him into Parmenides' teacher and the ancestor of the Eleatic line of descent (**R1–R3**), the presentation of his doctrine also suffered from a massive Eleatization, which, even if it was prompted by Xenophanes' view of divinity as one, nonetheless greatly distorted it (**R5–R11**). His spirit was an enlightened one, and his lasting influence can be perceived for example in the critique of traditional theology in Book 2 of Plato's *Republic*.

EARLY GREEK PHILOSOPHY III

BIBLIOGRAPHY

Editions

B. Gentili and C. Prato, eds. *Poetarum elegiacorum testimonia et fragmenta* (Leipzig, 1979–1985; 2nd ed. 1988–2002), vol. 1, pp. 144–83.

E. Heitsch, ed. *Xenophanes. Fragmente* (Munich, 1983).

J. Lesher, ed. *Xenophanes of Colophon. Fragments* (Toronto, 1992).

M. L. West, ed. *Iambi et elegi Graeci ante Alexandrum cantati* (2nd ed. Oxford, 1989–1992), vol. 2, pp. 184–91.

Studies

J. Wiesner. *Ps.-Aristoteles MXG: Der historische Wert des Xenophanesreferats* (Amsterdam, 1974).

OUTLINE OF THE CHAPTER

P

Family, City, Chronology (P1–P7)
Teachers (P8–P9)
Xenophanes in Western Greece (P10–P14)
   Xenophanes and Parmenides (P10–P11)
   Xenophanes and Empedocles (P12)
   Xenophanes and Hieron (P13)
   Sold as a Slave? (P14)
Character (P15)
Apothegms (P16–P22)

XENOPHANES

D

Writings (D1–D6)
  Meters and Subjects (D1)
  His Satires, Known Under the Title Mockeries *(Silloi) (D2–D5)*
  Xenophanes, an Admirer of Thales (THAL. R1)
  A Traditional Title: On Nature *(D6)*
From Xenophanes' Poem(s) in Dactylic Hexameters (D7–D59)
  The Gods (D7–D21)
    Mistaken Beliefs about the Gods . . . (D7–D15)
      . . . Propagated by the Ancient Greek Poets (D7–D11)
      . . . or Deriving from Self-Projections (D12–D14)
      Belief in Divination Is Mistaken (D15)
    Correct Beliefs about the Gods (D16–D20)
      God Is Unlike Humans in Shape and Action (D16–D19)
      A Doxographical Summary of Xenophanes' Theology (D20)
    An Anonymous Fragment Sometimes Attributed to Xenophanes (D21)
  Natural Phenomena (D22–D48)
    Three Doxographical Summaries Deriving Probably from Theophrastus (D22–D24)
    Earth and Water as Origins (D25–D27)
    Clouds as Cosmological Principles (D28–D40)
      The Sun and Moon Are Clouds (D28–D35)
        The Nature of the Sun and Moon (D28–D29)

The Course and Effects of the Sun (D30–D33)
Disappearances of the Sun (D34–D35)
The Heavenly Bodies and Other Luminous Celestial Phenomena Are Clouds (D36–D38)
The Rainbow Too Is a Cloud (D39)
Lightning (D40)
The Earth (D41–D45)
The Sea (D46)
The Soul (D47–D48)
Epistemological Considerations (D49–D53)
Other Fragments from Poems in Dactylic Hexameters (D54–D58)
From Xenophanes' Poem(s) in Elegiac Couplets (D59–D69)
Social Norms (D59–D63)
From a Poem about Old Age and Death? (D64–D67)
References to Other Poets (D68–D69)
An Isolated Word in Uncertain Meter (D70)

R

First Mentions and Allusions
In Heraclitus (HER. D20)
Parodies and Allusions in Epicharmus (DRAM. T2–T3)
Imitations in Euripides (DRAM. T72–T73)
Xenophanes as the Initiator of the Eleatic Line of Descent of Greek Philosophy (R1–R3)
The Eleatization of Xenophanes (R4–R11)
Peripatetic Criticisms (R12–R14)

XENOPHANES

The Skeptical Tradition (R15–R23)
 Xenophanes' Special Role in Timon of Phlius' Mockeries (Silloi) *(R15–R16)*
 Was Xenophanes Skeptical or Dogmatic? (R17–R22)
An Epicurean Criticism of Xenophanes' Theology (R23)
A Problem of Interpretation: Does Everything Come from Earth According to Xenophanes? (R24–R26)
 Aristotle's Report (R24)
 The Disagreement of the Traditions (R25–R26)
Judgments on Xenophanes' Poetry (R27–R29)
Xenophanes in The Assembly of the Philosophers *(R30)*

XENOPHANES [21 DK]

P

Family, City, Chronology (P1–P7)

P1 (< A1) Diog. Laert. 9.18–20

[18] Ξενοφάνης Δεξίου ἤ, ὡς Ἀπολλόδωρος [*FGrHist* 244 F68a], Ὀρθομένους, Κολοφώνιος [. . .]. οὗτος ἐκπεσὼν τῆς πατρίδος ἐν Ζάγκλῃ τῆς Σικελίας[1] διέτριβε[2] καὶ ἐν Κατάνῃ. [. . .] καί, ὡς Σωτίων φησί [Frag. 28 Wehrli], κατ᾽ Ἀναξίμανδρον[3] ἦν. [. . .] μακροβιώτατός τε γέγονεν, ὥς που καὶ αὐτός φησιν· [19] [. . . = **D66**]. [. . .] [20] καὶ ἤκμαζε κατὰ τὴν ἑξηκοστὴν Ὀλυμπιάδα.

[1] post Σικελίας lac. ind. Diels ‹διέτριβε καὶ τῆς εἰς Ἐλέαν ἀποικίας κοινωνήσας ἐδίδασκεν ἐκεῖ›   [2] δὲ post διέτριβε habent BP[1]: om. F, del. P[4]   [3] Ἀναξιμένην Croenert

P2 (< A6) Ps.-Luc. *Long.* 20

Ξενοφάνης δὲ ὁ Δεξίνου μὲν υἱὸς [. . .] ἐβίωσεν ἔτη ἓν καὶ ἐνενήκοντα.

XENOPHANES

P

Family, City, Chronology (P1–P7)

P1 (< A1) Diogenes Laertius

[18] Xenophanes, from Colophon, son of Dexius or, as Apollodorus says, of Orthomenes [. . .]. After he had been exiled from his fatherland, he spent time in Zancle in Sicily and in Catania.[1] [. . .] And, as Sotion says, he lived at the time of Anaximander. [. . .] and he lived to a very great age, as he himself says somewhere: [19] [. . . = **D66**]. [. . .] [20] and he reached full maturity in the 60th Olympiad [540/36].

[1] Diels completes this possibly lacunose sentence as follows: "After he had been exiled from his fatherland, he spent time in Zancle in Sicily, ⟨and having participated in the colony sent to Elea, he taught there;⟩ and he spent time in Catania too."

P2 (< A6) Ps.-Lucian, *Long-lived Men*

Xenophanes, the son of Dexinus [. . .] lived for ninety-one years.

P3 (A7) Cens. *Die nat.* 15.3

[. . .] Xenophanes Colophonius maior annorum centum fuit.

P4 (< A8) Clem. Alex. *Strom.* 1.64.2

[. . . = **R3**] Ξενοφάνης ὁ Κολοφώνιος [. . .], ὅν φησι Τίμαιος [*FGrHist* 566 F92] κατὰ Ἱέρωνα τὸν Σικελίας δυνάστην καὶ Ἐπίχαρμον τὸν ποιητὴν γεγονέναι, Ἀπολλόδωρος [*FGrHist* 244 F68c] δὲ κατὰ τὴν τεσσαρακοστὴν[1] Ὀλυμπιάδα γενόμενον παρατετακέναι ἄχρι τῶν Δαρείου τε καὶ Κύρου χρόνων.

[1] πεντηκοστὴν Ritter, cf. Diog. Laert. 9.20, sed τεσσ. Sext. Emp. *Adv. Math.* 1.257

P5 (cf. A9) Eus. *Chron.* (Hier., Cyr.)

a Hier. *Chron.* 103b2

[ad Ol. 56][1] Xenofanes Colofonius clarus habetur.

[1] Ol. 56 *OM*: Ol. 56.2 *AL*: Ol. 57.2 *B*

b Hier. *Chron.* 103b23

[ad Ol. 60][1] Simonides lyricus et Phocylides clari habentur et Xenophanes physicus [. . .].

[1] Ol. 59.4 *Mac. PM*: Ol. 60.1 *N*: Ol. 60.2 *OL*: Ol. 61.3 *B*

XENOPHANES

P3 (A7) Censorinus, *The Birthday*

Xenophanes of Colophon lived more than one hundred years.

P4 (< A8) Clement of Alexandria, *Stromata*

[. . .] Xenophanes of Colophon [. . .], who, Timaeus says, lived at the time of Hieron, the ruler of Sicily, and of Epicharmus the poet; but Apollodorus [scil. says] that he was born during the 40th Olympiad (620/16) and that his life lasted until the times of Darius and Cyrus.

P5 (cf. A9) Eusebius, *Chronicle*

a

(Jerome) 56th Olympiad [= 556/52]: Xenophanes of Colophon is considered well known.

b

(Jerome) 60th Olympiad [= 540/36]: Simonides the lyric poet and Phocylides are considered well known and Xenophanes the natural philosopher [. . .].

c Cyrill. Alex. *Jul.* 1.15

πεντηκοστῇ ἐννάτῃ Ὀλυμπιάδι Ἴβυκος ὁ μελοποιὸς καὶ Φερεκύδης ὁ ἱστοριογράφος καὶ Φωκυλίδης καὶ Ξενοφάνης [. . .] γεγόνασι.

P6 (A10, 14.8) Ps.-Iamb. *Theol.*, p. 52.18–22

φ′ γὰρ καὶ ιδ′ ἔτη ἔγγιστα ἀπὸ τῶν Τρωικῶν ἱστορεῖται μέχρι Ξενοφάνους τοῦ φυσικοῦ καὶ τῶν Ἀνακρέοντός τε καὶ Πολυκράτους χρόνων καὶ τῆς ὑπὸ Ἁρπάγου τοῦ Μήδου Ἰώνων πολιορκίας καὶ ἀναστάσεως, ἣν Φωκεῖς φυγόντες Μασσαλίαν ᾤκησαν [. . . cf. **PYTH. a P5**].

P7 (< A33) (Ps.-?) Hippol. *Ref.* 1.14.1

Ξενοφάνης δὲ ὁ Κολοφώνιος Ὀρθομένους υἱός. οὗτος ἕως Κύρου διέμεινεν [. . . = **R20**].

Teachers (P8–P9)

P8 (< A1) Diog. Laert. 9.18

διήκουσε δὲ κατ' ἐνίους μὲν οὐδενός, κατ' ἐνίους δὲ Βότωνος Ἀθηναίου ἤ, ὥς τινες, Ἀρχελάου.

XENOPHANES

c

(Cyril) 59th Olympiad [= 544/40]: Ibycus the lyric poet, Pherecydes the historian, Phocylides, Xenophanes [. . .] were alive.

P6 (A10, 14.8) Ps.-Iamblichus, *The Theology of Arithmetic*

For nearly 514 years are recorded from the Trojan War until Xenophanes the natural philosopher, the times of Anacreon and Polycrates, and the siege and removal of the Ionians by Harpagus the Mede; the Phocians who fled this founded Marseille [. . .].[1]

[1] A very rough synchronism that refers globally to the first half of the sixth century BC and seems to be based on a date for the fall of Troy that differs from Eratosthenes' (1184 BC).

P7 (< A33) (Ps.-?) Hippolytus, *Refutation of All Heresies*

Xenophanes of Colophon, son of Orthomenes. He lived until the time of Cyrus [. . .].

Teachers (P8–P9)

P8 (< A1) Diogenes Laertius

According to several authors he did not study with anyone, according to several ones with Boton of Athens or, according to some, with Archelaus.[1]

[1] Boton is otherwise unknown, and Archelaus is chronologically impossible.

P9 (< A2) Diog. Laert. 9.21

[. . . = **P11**] τοῦτον Θεόφραστος ἐν τῇ Ἐπιτομῇ [Frag. 227D FHS&G] Ἀναξιμάνδρου φησὶν ἀκοῦσαι.

Xenophanes in Western Greece (P10–P14)
Xenophanes and Parmenides (P10–P11)

P10 (< A30) Arist. *Metaph.* A5 986b22

[. . . = **R2**] ὁ γὰρ Παρμενίδης τούτου λέγεται μαθητής [. . .].

P11 (< A2) Diog. Laert. 9.21

Ξενοφάνους δὲ διήκουσε Παρμενίδης Πύρητος Ἐλεάτης [. . . = **P9**].

Xenophanes and Empedocles (P12)

P12 (A5) Diog. Laert. 8.56

Ἕρμιππος δὲ [Frag. 26 Wehrli] οὐ Παρμενίδου, Ξενοφάνους δὲ γεγονέναι ζηλωτήν, ᾧ καὶ συνδιατρῖψαι καὶ μιμήσασθαι τὴν ἐποποιίαν.

XENOPHANES

P9 (< A2) Diogenes Laertius

[. . .] Theophrastus says of him in his *Epitome* that he studied with Anaximander [cf. **PARM. P6a**].

Xenophanes in Western Greece (P10–P14)
Xenophanes and Parmenides (P10–P11)

P10 (< A30) Aristotle, *Metaphysics*

[. . .] for Parmenides is said to have been his pupil [. . .].

P11 (< A2) Diogenes Laertius

Parmenides, son of Pyres, from Elea, studied with Xenophanes [. . .].

Xenophanes and Empedocles (P12)

P12 (A5) Diogenes Laertius

Hermippus [scil. says] that he [i.e. Empedocles] was a follower not of Parmenides but of Xenophanes, with whom he also spent some time[1] and whose epic verse he imitated [. . .] [cf. **EMP. P14**].

[1] If we suppose that Xenophanes died ca. 460 BC at about one hundred years of age and that Empedocles was born ca. 484, this claim is not completely impossible chronologically, but it does remain very unlikely.

EARLY GREEK PHILOSOPHY III

Xenophanes and Hieron (P13)

P13 (A11) Plut. *Reg. et imp. apophth.* 4 175C

πρὸς δὲ Ξενοφάνην τὸν Κολοφώνιον εἰπόντα μόλις οἰκέτας δύο τρέφειν "ἀλλ' Ὅμηρος," εἶπεν, "ὃν σὺ διασύρεις, πλείονας ἢ μυρίους τρέφει τεθνηκώς."

Sold as a Slave? (P14)

P14 (< A1) Diog. Laert. 9.20

δοκεῖ δὲ πεπρᾶσθαι ὑπὸ <. . . καὶ λελύσθαι ὑπὸ>[1] τῶν Πυθαγορικῶν Παρμενίσκου καὶ Ὀρεστάδου, καθά φησι Φαβωρῖνος ἐν Ἀπομνημονευμάτων πρώτῳ [Frag. 46 Amato].

[1] <. . . καὶ λελύσθαι ὑπὸ> Diels, alii aliter

Character (P15)

P15 (< A1) Diog. Laert. 9.20

φησὶ δὲ Δημήτριος ὁ Φαληρεὺς ἐν τῷ Περὶ γήρως [Frag. 83 Wehrli] καὶ Παναίτιος ὁ Στωικὸς ἐν τῷ Περὶ εὐθυμίας [Frag. 45 van Straaten] ταῖς ἰδίαις χερσὶ θάψαι τοὺς υἱεῖς αὐτόν, καθάπερ καὶ Ἀναξαγόραν.

XENOPHANES

Xenophanes and Hieron (P13)

P13 (A11) Plutarch, *Sayings of Kings and Commanders*

To Xenophanes of Colophon, who said he could scarcely maintain two household slaves, he [i.e. Hieron] said, "But Homer, on whom you heap scorn, maintains more than ten thousand, dead though he is."

Sold as a Slave? (P14)

P14 (< A1) Diogenes Laertius

He is thought to have been sold into slavery by <. . . and ransomed by> the Pythagoreans Parmeniscus and Orestades, according to what Favorinus says in Book 1 of his *Memoirs*.[1]

[1] A similar story is reported of Plato (cf. Diogenes Laertius 3.19–20).

See also **P1, P17, P22, R2–R4**

Character (P15)

P15 (< A1) Diogenes Laertius

Demetrius of Phalerum in his *On Old Age,* and Panaetius the Stoic in his *On Cheerfulness,* say that he buried his sons with his own hands, just like Anaxagoras [cf. **ANAXAG. P38–P40**].

EARLY GREEK PHILOSOPHY III

Apothegms (P16–P22)

P16 (< A12) Arist. *Rhet.* 2.23 1399b6–8

[. . .] Ξενοφάνης ἔλεγεν ὅτι ὁμοίως ἀσεβοῦσιν οἱ γενέσθαι φάσκοντες τοὺς θεοὺς τοῖς ἀποθανεῖν λέγουσιν· ἀμφοτέρως γὰρ συμβαίνει μὴ εἶναι τοὺς θεούς ποτε.

P17 (< A13) Arist. *Rhet.* 2.23 1400b5–8

[. . .] Ξενοφάνης Ἐλεάταις ἐρωτῶσιν εἰ θύωσι τῇ Λευκοθέᾳ καὶ θρηνῶσιν ἢ μή, συνεβούλευεν, εἰ μὲν θεὸν ὑπολαμβάνουσιν, μὴ θρηνεῖν, εἰ δ' ἄνθρωπον, μὴ θύειν.

P18 (A14) Arist. *Rhet.* 1.15 1377a19–21

καὶ τὸ τοῦ Ξενοφάνους ἁρμόττει, ὅτι οὐκ ἴση πρόκλησις αὕτη ἀσεβεῖ πρὸς εὐσεβῆ, ἀλλ' ὁμοία καὶ εἰ ἰσχυρὸς ἀσθενῆ πατάξαι ἢ πληγῆναι προκαλέσαιτο.

P19 (A16) Plut. *Vit. pud.* 5 530E–F

μὴ δυσωπηθῇς μηδὲ δείσῃς σκωπτόμενος· ἀλλ'

XENOPHANES

Apothegms (P16–P22)

P16 (< A12) Aristotle, *Rhetoric*

[. . .] Xenophanes used to say that those who say the gods are born are just as impious as those who say they die,[1] for in both cases the result is that there is a certain time when the gods do not exist.

[1] The apothegm is inspired by Xenophanes' theology, especially his criticism of the Homeric gods; cf. **D7–D14.**

P17 (< A13) Aristotle, *Rhetoric*

[. . .] when the Eleans asked Xenophanes whether they should sacrifice to Leucothea and mourn her or not, he advised them that if they thought she was a goddess they should not mourn her, and if they thought she was human they should not sacrifice to her.[1]

[1] Plutarch records a version of this saying three times, each time substituting the Egyptians for the Eleans and Egyptian divinities for Leucothea: *Amat.* 18.12 763D; *Is. et Os.* 70 379B; *Superstit.* 13 171E; see also Ps.-Plutarch *Apophth. Lac.* 26 228E.

P18 (A14) Aristotle, *Rhetoric*

And the saying of Xenophanes is fitting, that it is unfair for an impious man to challenge a pious man to an oath, for it is just like a strong man challenging a weak one to hit him or be hit.

P19 (A16) Plutarch, *On Being Ashamed*

Do not be discountenanced or frightened when you are

ὥσπερ Ξενοφάνης Λάσου τοῦ Ἑρμιονέως μὴ βουλόμενον αὐτῷ συγκυβεύειν δειλὸν ἀποκαλοῦντος ὁμολόγει[1] καὶ πάνυ δειλὸς εἶναι πρὸς τὰ αἰσχρὰ καὶ ἄτολμος.

[1] ὡμολόγει mss., corr. Matthaei

P20 (A17) Plut. *Comm. not.* 46 1084E

ὁ μὲν οὖν Ξενοφάνης διηγουμένου τινὸς ἐγχέλεις ἑωρακέναι ἐν ὕδατι θερμῷ ζώσας "οὐκοῦν," εἶπεν, "ἐν ψυχρῷ αὐτὰς ἑψήσομεν."

P21 (< A1) Diog. Laert. 9.19

ἔφη δὲ καὶ τὰ πολλὰ ἥσσω νοῦ εἶναι. καὶ τοῖς τυράννοις ἐντυγχάνειν ἢ ὡς ἥκιστα ἢ ὡς ἥδιστα.

P22 (< A1) Diog. Laert. 9.20

Ἐμπεδοκλέους δὲ εἰπόντος αὐτῷ ὅτι ἀνεύρετός ἐστιν ὁ σοφός, "εἰκότως," ἔφη· "σοφὸν γὰρ εἶναι δεῖ τὸν ἐπιγνωσόμενον τὸν σοφόν."

mocked, but [scil. do] just like Xenophanes when Lasus of Hermione called him a coward when he refused to play dice with him: agree that you really are very cowardly and pusillanimous—with regard to shameful things.

P20 (A17) Plutarch, *On Common Conceptions*

When someone said that he had seen eels living in hot water, Xenophanes said, "Well then, we shall boil them in cold water."

P21 (< A1) Diogenes Laertius

He said that most things are inferior to mind; and that he met with tyrants as rarely (*hêkista*) or as agreeably (*hêdista*) as possible.

P22 (< A1) Diogenes Laertius

When Empedocles said to him that the sage had not been discovered, he said, "That is just as one would expect: for the man who will be able to recognize the sage has to be a sage."[1]

[1] In certain gnomologies, this apothegm is attributed to Empedocles himself.

See also **P13**

XENOPHANES [21 DK]

D

Writings (D1–D6)
Meters and Subjects (D1)

D1 (< A1) Diog. Laert. 9. 18, 20

[18] γέγραφε δὲ ἐν ἔπεσι καὶ ἐλεγείας καὶ ἰάμβους καθ' Ἡσιόδου καὶ Ὁμήρου, ἐπικόπτων αὐτῶν τὰ περὶ θεῶν εἰρημένα. ἀλλὰ καὶ αὐτὸς ἐρραψῴδει τὰ ἑαυτοῦ. [. . .] [20] ἐποίησε δὲ καὶ Κολοφῶνος κτίσιν καὶ τὸν εἰς Ἐλέαν τῆς Ἰταλίας ἀποικισμὸν ἔπη δισχίλια.

His Satires, Known Under the Title Mockeries
(Silloi) *(D2–D5)*

D2 (> A20) Strab. 14.1.28

[. . .] καὶ Ξενοφάνης ὁ φυσικός, ὁ τοὺς Σίλλους ποιήσας διὰ ποιημάτων.

D3 (> A22) Procl. *In Hes. Op.* 286

καὶ τί δεῖ τούτους λέγειν, ὅπου γε καὶ Ξενοφάνης[1] διὰ

[1] Ξενοφάνην Pertusi

XENOPHANES

D

Writings (D1–D6)
Meters and Subjects (D1)

D1 (< A1) Diogenes Laertius

[18] He wrote in dactylic hexameters, elegiac couplets, and iambs against Hesiod and Homer, deriding what they said about the gods. But he himself also performed as a rhapsode his own compositions. [. . .] [20] He also composed poetry on the foundation of Colophon and on the colonization of Elea in Italy, two thousand verses.

His Satires, Known Under the Title Mockeries
(Silloi) (D2–D5)

D2 (A20) Strabo, *Geography*

[. . .] and Xenophanes the natural philosopher, who composed *Mockeries* in verses.

D3 (> A22) Proclus, *Commentary on Hesiod's* Works and Days

And why do we need to speak of these [scil. celebrated polemicists: Archilochus, Hipponax, Timocrates, and Me-

23

EARLY GREEK PHILOSOPHY III

δή τινα πρὸς τοὺς κατ' αὐτὸν φιλοσόφους καὶ ποιητὰς μικροψυχίαν Σίλλους ἀτόπους συνθεῖναι[2] <λέγεται>[3] κατὰ πάντων φιλοσόφων καὶ ποιητῶν.

[2] συνθεῖναι AQR: ἐκθεῖναι ZB   [3] <λέγεται> Gaisford

D4 (A23) Schol. ABT ad *Il*. 2.212b

ἤδη δὲ οὐ Ξενοφάνει, ἀλλ' Ὁμήρῳ πρώτῳ Σίλλοι πεποίηνται, ἐν οἷς αὐτόν[1] τε τὸν Θερσίτην σιλλαίνει καὶ ὁ Θερσίτης τοὺς ἀρίστους.

[1] αὐτός Diels

D5 (A24) Ar. Did. in Stob. 2.1.17

Ξενοφάνους πρώτου λόγος ἦλθεν εἰς τοὺς Ἕλληνας ἄξιος γραφῆς, ἅμα παιδιᾷ τάς τε τῶν ἄλλων τόλμας ἐπιπλήττοντος καὶ τὴν αὐτοῦ παριστάντος εὐλάβειαν ὡς ἄρα θεὸς μὲν οἶδε τὴν ἀλήθειαν, δόκος δ' ἐπὶ πᾶσι τέτυκται [**D49.4b**].

Xenophanes, an Admirer of Thales

See **THAL. R1**

A Traditional Title: On Nature *(D6)*

D6

a (cf. ad B30) Schol. Genav. ad *Il*. 21.196

Ξενοφάνης ἐν τῷ Περὶ φύσεως [. . . = **D46**].

trodorus], when Xenophanes ⟨is said⟩ to have composed absurd *Mockeries* against all the philosophers and poets because of a certain mean-spiritedness he felt toward contemporary philosophers and poets?

D4 (A23) Scholia on Homer's *Iliad*

Mockeries were composed already first of all not by Xenophanes but by Homer; in them he mocks (*sillainei*) Thersites himself and Thersites mocks the best men [cf. *Il.* 2.211–42].

D5 (A24) Arius Didymus in Stobaeus, *Anthology*

Xenophanes was the first author of a discourse worthy of mention that came to the Greeks playfully rebuking the audacities of other people and at the same time demonstrating his own piety, on the idea that god knows the truth, **"but opinion extends over all men."**[1]

[1] The translation here reflects what seems to be Arius Didymus' understanding of this phrase, which differs from the one we provide at **D49**.

Xenophanes, an Admirer of Thales

See **THAL. R1**

A Traditional Title: On Nature *(D6)*

D6

a (cf. ad B30) Geneva Scholia on Homer's *Iliad*

Xenophanes in his *On Nature:* [. . .].

b (< B39) Pollux *Onom.* 6.46

[. . . = **D57**] ἐν τῷ Περὶ φύσεως Ξενοφάνους [. . .].

c (< A36) Stob. 1.10.12

γράφει γὰρ ἐν τῷ Περὶ φύσεως [. . . = **D27**].

*From Xenophanes' Poem(s) in Dactylic
Hexameters (D7–D59)
The Gods (D7–D21)
Mistaken Beliefs about the Gods. . . (D7–D15)
. . . Propagated by the Ancient Greek Poets
(D7–D11)*

D7 (< A19) Diog. Laert. 2.46

[. . .] ἀποθανόντι δὲ Ξενοφάνης ὁ Κολοφώνιος [sc. Ὁμήρῳ ἐφιλονείκει] [. . .].

D8 (B11) Sext. Emp. *Adv. Math.* 9.193

πάντα θεοῖς ἀνέθηκαν Ὅμηρός θ' Ἡσίοδός τε
ὅσσα παρ' ἀνθρώποισιν ὀνείδεα καὶ ψόγος
   ἐστίν,
κλέπτειν μοιχεύειν τε καὶ ἀλλήλους ἀπατεύειν.

XENOPHANES

b (< B39) Pollux, *Onomasticon*

[. . .] in Xenophanes' *On Nature* [. . .].

c (< A36) Stobaeus, *Anthology*

For he writes in his *On Nature:* [. . .].

> *From Xenophanes' Poem(s) in Dactylic*
> *Hexameters (D7–D59)*[1]
> *The Gods (D7–D21)*
> *Mistaken Beliefs about the Gods. . . (D7–D15)*
> *. . . Propagated by the Ancient Greek Poets*
> *(D7–D11)*

[1] Some of the fragments in this section are only one verse long or take the form of paraphrases; in principle they could come from elegiac poems instead, but they have been placed here because of the affinity of their subject matter.

D7 (< A19) Diogenes Laertius

[. . .] and Xenophanes of Colophon [scil. rivaled with Homer] after his death [. . .].

D8 (B11) Sextus Empiricus, *Against the Natural Philosophers*

> **Homer and Hesiod have attributed to the gods all things**
> **That among men are sources of blame and censure:**
> **Thieving, committing adultery, and deceiving each other.**

D9 (B12) Sext. Emp. *Adv. Math.* 1.289

Ὅμηρος δὲ καὶ Ἡσίοδος κατὰ τὸν Κολοφώνιον Ξενοφάνη

ὡς πλεῖστ' ἐφθέγξαντο θεῶν ἀθεμίστια ἔργα,
κλέπτειν μοιχεύειν τε καὶ ἀλλήλους ἀπατεύειν.

1 ὅς πλεῖστα ἐφθέγξατο mss., corr. Fabricius

D10 (B10) Hdn. π. διχρ., p. 16.20

ἐξ ἀρχῆς καθ' Ὅμηρον ἐπεὶ μεμαθήκασι πάντες

D11 (B13) Aul. Gell. *Noct.* 3.11.2

alii Homerum quam Hesiodum maiorem natu fuisse scripserunt, in quis Philochorus et Xenophanes, alii minorem [. . .].

    . . . *or Deriving from Self-Projections (D12–D14)*

D12 (B14) Clem. Alex. *Strom.* 5.109.1 (et al.)

ἀλλ' οἱ βροτοὶ δοκοῦσι γεννᾶσθαι θεούς,
τὴν σφετέρην δ' ἐσθῆτα ἔχειν φωνήν τε δέμας τε.

1 incertum utrum v. 1 trimeter iambicus sit an potius hexameter dactylicus mancus: ita Eus. *PE* 13.13.36 (ex Clem.), Theod. *Cur.* 3.72: ἀλλὰ βροτοὶ δοκοῦσι θεοὺς γεννᾶσθαι Clem.: ἀλλὰ βρότοι δοκέουσι θεοὺς γεννᾶσθαι ⟨ὁμοίως⟩ Bergk

XENOPHANES

D9 (B12) Sextus Empiricus, *Against the Professors*

According to Xenophanes of Colophon, Homer and Hesiod

> **Sang of many lawless deeds committed by the gods:**
> **Thieving, committing adultery, and deceiving each other.**[1]

[1] The second line is identical with the third line of the preceding fragment and is not mentioned in Sextus' explanation after his quotation here; its presence here may be due to scribal error or an inopportune authorial reminiscence, but it cannot be excluded that the verse was deliberately repeated by Xenophanes.

D10 (B10) Herodian, *On Syllables with Double Value*

> **Since from the beginning all have learned according to Homer**

D11 (B13) Aulus Gellius, *Attic Nights*

Some have written that Homer was older than Hesiod, among them Philochorus and Xenophanes, others that he was younger [. . .].

. . . or Deriving from Self-Projections (D12–D14)

D12 (B14) Clement of Alexandria, *Stromata*

> **But mortals think that gods are born**
> **And have clothing, voice, and bodily frame just like theirs.**[1]

[1] The first line is transmitted as an iambic trimeter.

EARLY GREEK PHILOSOPHY III

D13 (B16) Clem. Alex. *Strom.* 7.22.1

Αἰθίοπές τε ⟨θεοὺς σφετέρους⟩ σιμοὺς μέλανάς
τε
Θρῆκές τε γλαυκοὺς καὶ πυρρούς ⟨φασι
πέλεσθαι⟩.

1 ⟨θεοὺς σφετέρους⟩ Diels   σιμοὺς μέλανας τε Diels:
μέλανας σιμούς τε mss.   2 Θρῆκές Diels: Θρᾷκες mss.
γλαυκοὺς καὶ πυρροὺς Diels: πυρροὺς καὶ γλαυκούς mss.
⟨φασι πέλεσθαι⟩ Diels

D14 (B15) Clem. Alex. Strom. 5.109.1 (et al.)

ἀλλ' εἰ χεῖρας ἔχον βόες ⟨ἵπποι τ'⟩ ἠὲ λέοντες,
ἢ γράψαι χείρεσσι καὶ ἔργα τελεῖν ἅπερ
ἄνδρες,
ἵπποι μέν θ' ἵπποισι, βόες δέ τε βουσὶν ὁμοίας
καί ⟨κε⟩ θεῶν ἰδέας ἔγραφον καὶ σώματ'
ἐποίουν
5   τοιαῦθ' οἷόν περ καὐτοὶ δέμας εἶχον ἕκαστοι.

1 εἰ χεῖρας ἔχον Eus. *PE* 13.13.36 (ex Clem.): εἴ τοι χεῖρας
εἶχον mss.   ⟨ἵπποι τ'⟩ Diels   ἠὲ λέοντες Clem. et
Theod. *Cur.* 3.72 KBL: ἢ ἐλέφαντες Theod. MSCV   2 ἢ
Clem. Eus. Theod.: ὡς Heise   3 ὁμοίας Theod.: ὅμοιοι
Clem. Eus.   4 ⟨κε⟩ Sylburg   5 ἕκαστοι Herwerden:
ὁμοῖον Clem. Theod.: ὅμοιον Eus.

XENOPHANES

D13 (B16) Clement of Alexandria, *Stromata*

The Ethiopians ⟨say that their gods are⟩ **snub-nosed and dark-skinned,**
And the Thracians that they have blue eyes and red hair.

D14 (B15) Clement of Alexandria, *Stromata*

But if oxen, ⟨horses⟩ **or lions had hands**
Or could draw with their hands and create works like men,
Then horses would draw the shapes of gods like horses, and oxen like oxen,
And they would make the same kinds of bodies
As each one possessed its own bodily frame.

EARLY GREEK PHILOSOPHY III

Belief in Divination Is Mistaken (D15)

D15

a (A52) Aët. 5.1.2 (Ps.-Plut.) [περὶ μαντικῆς]

Ξενοφάνης καὶ Ἐπίκουρος ἀναιροῦσι τὴν μαντικήν.

b (< A52) Cic. *Div.* 1.5

[. . .] Colophonius Xenophanes unus, qui deos esse diceret, divinationem funditus sustulit; reliqui vero omnes praeter Epicurum [. . .] divinationem probaverunt.

Correct Beliefs about the Gods (D16–D20)
God Is Unlike Humans in Shape and
Action (D16–D19)

D16 (B23) Clem. Alex. *Strom.* 5.109.1

εὖ γοῦν καὶ Ξενοφάνης ὁ Κολοφώνιος, διδάσκων ὅτι εἷς καὶ ἀσώματος ὁ θεός, ἐπιφέρει·

εἷς θεός, ἔν τε θεοῖσι καὶ ἀνθρώποισι μέγιστος,
οὔτε δέμας θνητοῖσιν ὁμοίιος οὔτε νόημα.

2 οὔτε prius Sylburg: οὔ τι ms.   οὔτε alt. Diels: οὐδὲ ms.

D17 (B24) Sext. Emp. *Adv. Math.* 9.144

οὖλος ὁρᾷ, οὖλος δὲ νοεῖ, οὖλος δέ τ' ἀκούει.

XENOPHANES

Belief in Divination Is Mistaken (D15)

D15

a (A52) Aëtius

Xenophanes and Epicurus abolish divination.

b (< A52) Cicero, *On Divination*

[...] Xenophanes of Colophon is the only one [scil. among the most ancient philosophers] to have said that the gods exist, but to have abolished divination completely; all the others approved of divination, except for Epicurus [...].

Correct Beliefs about the Gods (D16–D20)
God Is Unlike Humans in Shape and Action (D16–D19)

D16 (B23) Clement of Alexandria, *Stromata*

Xenophanes of Colophon, who teaches that god is one and bodiless, does well when he asserts,

> **One god, among both gods and humans the greatest,**
> **Neither in bodily frame similar to mortals nor in thought.**

D17 (B24) Sextus Empiricus, *Against the Natural Philosophers*

> **As a whole he sees, as a whole he thinks, and as a whole he hears.**[1]

[1] Sextus cites this line without naming its author; the attribution to Xenophanes is based essentially upon doxographical notices (cf. in particular **D20** and **R6[6]**).

EARLY GREEK PHILOSOPHY III

D18 (B25) Simpl. *In Phys.*, p. 23.20

ἀλλ' ἀπάνευθε πόνοιο νόου φρενὶ πάντα
κραδαίνει.

D19 (B26) Simpl. *In Phys.*, p. 23.11–12

αἰεὶ δ' ἐν ταὐτῷ μίμνει κινούμενος οὐδέν,
οὐδὲ μετέρχεσθαί μιν ἐπιπρέπει ἄλλοτε ἄλλῃ.

1 ἀεὶ mss., corr. Karsten   κινούμενος E^aF: κινούμενον DE

A Doxographical Summary of
Xenophanes' Theology (D20)

D20 (< A1) Diog. Laert. 9.19

[. . . = **D24, R8a**] ὅλον δὲ ὁρᾶν καὶ ὅλον ἀκούειν, μὴ μέντοι ἀναπνεῖν· σύμπαντά τε εἶναι νοῦν καὶ φρόνησιν καὶ ἀίδιον [. . .].

An Anonymous Fragment Sometimes
Attributed to Xenophanes (D21)

D21 (Frag. dub. 47 Gentili-Prato) Philop. *Aetern.*, p. 582.21–23 Rabe (et al.)

πάντα θεοῦ πλήρη, πάντῃ δὲ οἵ εἰσιν ἀκουαί

1 θεοῦ Philop. *Aetern.*, Olymp. *In Alc.*, p. 30 Westerink: θεῶν Philop. *In An.*, p. 188.26   πάντῃ Philop.: πάντα Olymp.

XENOPHANES

D18 (B25) Simplicius, *Commentary on Aristotle's* Physics

**But without any toil, by the organ of his mind
(*noou phrêni*)[1] he makes all things tremble.**

[1] Xenophanes uses *noou* as a qualifying, explanatory genitive in order to make clear that in the case of his god the cognitive organ (*phrên*) is not the usual one, which is connected with human psychic states such as emotions and passions.

D19 (B26) Simplicius, *Commentary on Aristotle's* Physics

**He always stays in the same place, not moving at all,
And it is not fitting that he travel now to one place, now to another.**

*A Doxographical Summary of
Xenophanes' Theology (D20)*

D20 (< A1) Diogenes Laertius

[. . .] as a whole he sees and as a whole he hears, but he does not breathe; he is completely mind and thought and is eternal [. . .].

*An Anonymous Fragment Sometimes
Attributed to Xenophanes (D21)*

D21 (≠ DK) Philoponus, *Commentary on Aristotle's* On the Soul

All things are full of god, his ears are everywhere

καὶ διὰ πετράων καὶ ἀνὰ χθόνα καί τε δι' αὐτοῦ
ἀνέρος ὅττι κέκευθεν ἐνὶ στήθεσσι νόημα.

Natural Phenomena (D22–D48)
Three Doxographical Summaries Deriving
Probably from Theophrastus (D22–D24)

D22 (< A33) (Ps.-?) Hippol. *Ref.* 1.14.3–6

[3] τὸν δὲ ἥλιον ἐκ μικρῶν πυριδίων ἀθροιζομένων γίνεσθαι καθ' ἑκάστην ἡμέραν· τὴν δὲ γῆν ἄπειρον εἶναι καὶ μήτε ὑπ' ἀέρος μήτε ὑπὸ τοῦ οὐρανοῦ περιέχεσθαι. καὶ ἀπείρους ἡλίους εἶναι καὶ σελήνας, τὰ δὲ πάντα εἶναι ἐκ γῆς. [4] οὗτος τὴν θάλασσαν ἁλμυρὰν ἔφη διὰ τὸ πολλὰ μίγματα συρρέειν ἐν αὐτῇ· [. . .] [5] ὁ δὲ Ξενοφάνης μῖξιν τῆς γῆς πρὸς τὴν θάλασσαν γίνεσθαι δοκεῖ καὶ τῷ χρόνῳ ὑπὸ τοῦ ὑγροῦ λύεσθαι, φάσκων τοιαύτας ἔχειν ἀποδείξεις, ὅτι ἐν μέσῃ γῇ καὶ ὄρεσιν εὑρίσκονται κόγχαι· καὶ ἐν Συρακούσαις δὲ ἐν ταῖς λατομίαις λέγει εὑρῆσθαι τύπον ἰχθύος καὶ φωκῶν,[1] ἐν δὲ Πάρῳ τύπον δάφνης[2] ἐν τῷ βάθει τοῦ λίθου, ἐν δὲ Μελίτῃ[3] πλάκας συμπάντων τῶν θαλασσίων.[4] [6] ταῦτα δέ φησι γενέσθαι ὅτε

---

[1] καὶ φωκῶν mss.: καὶ φυκῶν Th. Gomperz: secl. Marcovich (cf. ad 4) [2] ἀφύης Gronovius [3] Μελίτῃ Karsten: μελίτῳ LB: μηλίτῳ O [4] πλάκας ⟨φωκῶν καὶ⟩ Marcovich

XENOPHANES

And through stones, along the whole earth, and in man
Himself, whatever be the thought that he [i.e. man] hides in his chest.[1]

[1] The attribution to Xenophanes, proposed by Lebedev in F. Capasso et al., *Studi di filosofia preplatonica* (Naples, 1985), pp. 13–15, remains very uncertain. For the phrase "all things are full of gods" (which is also transmitted instead of "all things are full of god"), cf. **THAL. D10.**

Natural Phenomena (D22–D48)
Three Doxographical Summaries Deriving
Probably from Theophrastus (D22–D24)

D22 (< A33) (Ps.-?) Hippolytus, *Refutation of All Heresies*

[3] [scil. he says] that the sun comes about every day out of small fires that are collected together, that the earth is unlimited and is surrounded neither by air nor by the heavens; and that there in an unlimited number of suns and moons, and that all things come from earth. [4] He said that the sea is salty because of the many mixtures that flow together in it. [. . .] [5] Xenophanes thinks that the land is mixed with the sea and that with time it is dissolved by moisture, saying that he has the following proofs: that shells are found inland and on mountains, and he says that in Syracuse the outlines of fishes and seals are found in quarries, in Paros the outline of coral in the depths of the stone, and on Malta marble slabs [scil. containing] all kinds of sea creatures. [6] He says that all this came about

πάντα ἐπηλώθησαν πάλαι, τὸν δὲ τύπον ἐν τῷ πηλῷ ξηρανθῆναι. ἀναιρεῖσθαι δὲ τοὺς ἀνθρώπους πάντας, ὅταν ἡ γῆ κατενεχθεῖσα εἰς τὴν θάλασσαν πηλὸς γένηται· εἶτα πάλιν ἄρχεσθαι τῆς γενέσεως, καὶ ταύτην[5] πᾶσι τοῖς κόσμοις γίνεσθαι μεταβολήν.[6]

[5] ταύτην Diels: τοῦτο mss.: οὕτω Karsten   [6] μεταβολήν Diels: καταβάλλειν mss.: καταβολήν Roeper

D23 (cf. A32) Ps.-Plut. *Strom.* 4 (Eus. *PE* 1.8.4)

[. . . = **R9**] ἀποφαίνεται δὲ καὶ τῷ χρόνῳ καταφερομένην συνεχῶς καὶ κατ' ὀλίγον τὴν γῆν εἰς τὴν θάλασσαν χωρεῖν. φησὶ δὲ καὶ τὸν ἥλιον ἐκ μικρῶν καὶ πλειόνων πυριδίων[1] ἀθροίζεσθαι. [. . .] ἀποφαίνεται δὲ καὶ τὴν γῆν ἄπειρον εἶναι καὶ κατὰ πᾶν μέρος μὴ περιέχεσθαι ὑπὸ ἀέρος· γίνεσθαι δὲ ἅπαντα ἐκ γῆς, τὸν δὲ ἥλιόν φησι καὶ τὰ ἄλλα ἄστρα ἐκ τῶν νεφῶν γίνεσθαι.

[1] πυριδίων Toupius: πυρίων mss.: πυριῶν prop. Mourelatos (per litt.)

D24 (< A1) Diog. Laert. 9.19

τὰ νέφη συνίστασθαι τῆς ἀφ' ἡλίου ἀτμίδος ἀναφερομένης καὶ αἰρούσης αὐτὰ εἰς τὸ περιέχον. [. . . = **R8a, D20**] πρῶτός τε ἀπεφήνατο ὅτι πᾶν τὸ γινόμενον φθαρτόν ἐστι καὶ ἡ ψυχὴ πνεῦμα.

when everything was covered by mud long ago and the outline in the mud dried out. And that all human beings are destroyed when the earth deposited in the sea becomes mud; and that then generation begins again, and that this change happens in all the worlds.

D23 (cf. A32) Ps.-Plutarch, *Stromata*

[. . .] He asserts that earth is deposited continually and little by little, and with time it goes into the sea. And he says that the sun is produced by the collecting together of many small fires. [. . .] And he asserts that the earth is unlimited and is not surrounded by the air in every part; and that everything comes about from earth; but he says that the sun and the other heavenly bodies come to be from clouds.

D24 (< A1) Diogenes Laertius

The clouds are formed when the vapor caused by the sun lifts them up and raises them up to what surrounds [scil. the earth]. [. . .] He was the first to assert that everything that comes about is perishable and that the soul is breath.

EARLY GREEK PHILOSOPHY III

Earth and Water as Origins (D25–D27)

D25 (< A29, B29) Philop. *In Phys.*, p. 125.30; Simpl. *In Phys.*, p. 189.1

γῆ καὶ ὕδωρ πάντ' ἔσθ' ὅσα γίνοντ' ἠδὲ
φύονται.

πάντ' ἔσθ' ὅσα Philop.: πᾶν ἔστ' ὅσα Simpl. E: πάντα θ' ὅσσα Simpl. F: πᾶν ὅσα τε Simpl. D: πάνθ' ὅσσα Simpl. ed. Ald.   γίνοντ' (γίνονται mss.) ἠδὲ φύονται Simpl.: φύοντ' ἠδὲ γίνονται Philop.

D26 (B33) Sext. Emp. *Adv. Math.* 9.361, 10.314 (et al.)

πάντες γὰρ γαίης τε καὶ ὕδατος ἐκγενόμεσθα.

γὰρ om. (Ps.-?) Hippol. *Ref.* 10.7

D27 (A36, B27) Sext. Emp. *Adv. Math.* 10.313

ἐκ γαίης γὰρ πάντα, καὶ εἰς γῆν πάντα
τελευτᾷ.

Clouds as Cosmological Principles (D28–D40)
The Sun and Moon Are Clouds (D28–D35)
The Nature of the Sun and Moon (D28–D29)

D28 (A40) Aët. 2.20.3 (Stob. 1.25.1a–b, cf. Ps.-Plut., Theod. 4.21, Eus. *PE* 15.23) [περὶ οὐσίας ἡλίου]

a

Ξενοφάνης ἐκ νεφῶν πεπυρωμένων εἶναι τὸν ἥλιον.[1]

XENOPHANES

Earth and Water as Origins (D25–D27)

D25 (< A29, B29) Philoponus and Simplicius, *Commentary on Aristotle's* Physics

> **Earth and water are everything that comes into being and grows.**[1]

[1] In the manuscripts of Simplicius, the line is erroneously attributed to Anaximenes.

D26 (B33) Sextus Empiricus, *Against the Natural Philosophers*

> **For all of us came about from earth and water.**

D27 (A36, B27) Sextus Empiricus, *Against the Natural Philosophers*

> **For from earth come all these** [or: all] **things, and into earth all end up.**

Clouds as Cosmological Principles (D28–D40)
The Sun and Moon Are Clouds (D28–D35)
The Nature of the Sun and Moon (D28–D29)

D28 (A40) Aëtius

a

Xenophanes: the sun is made out of clouds that have been ignited.

---

[1] Ξενοφάνης . . . τὸν ἥλιον habet Stob. 1a, om. Plut., sed cf. Theod.

b

Ξενοφάνης[1] ἐκ πυριδίων μὲν τῶν συναθροιζομένων[2] ἐκ[3] τῆς ὑγρᾶς ἀναθυμιάσεως, συναθροιζόντων δὲ τὸν ἥλιον.[4]

[1] Ξενοφάνης Plut.: Θεόφραστος ἐν τοῖς Φυσικοῖς γέγραφεν Stob. 1b: Ξενοφάνης ⟨ὡς⟩ Θεόφραστος ἐν τοῖς Φυσικοῖς γέγραφεν Mansfeld et Runia   [2] μὲν τῶν συναθροιζομένων Stob.: τῶν συναθροιζομένων μὲν Plut.   [3] ἐκ Plut.: om. Stob.   [4] post ἥλιον hab. ἢ νέφος πεπυρωμένον Plut., ἐκ νεφῶν πεπυρωμένων Eus. (cf. Stob. 1a)

D29 (A43) Aët. 2.25.4 (Ps.-Plut. 2. 28. 1; Stob. 2.29.5)

a [περὶ οὐσίας σελήνης]

Ξενοφάνης νέφος εἶναι πεπιλημένον.[1]

[1] πεπιλημένον Π: πεπυρωμένον m: πεπυρωλημένον M: πεπυρωμένον πεπιλημένον Mansfeld et Runia

b [περὶ φωτισμῶν σελήνης]

[. . .] Ξενοφάνης [. . .] ἴδιον αὐτὴν ἔχειν φῶς.

c [περὶ ἐκλείψεως σελήνης]

Ξενοφάνης καὶ τὴν μηνιαίαν ἀπόκρυψιν κατὰ σβέσιν.

XENOPHANES

b

Xenophanes: [scil. the sun is made] out of little fires that are collected together out of the moist exhalation, and these form the sun by being collected together.[1]

[1] The version in Stobaeus attributes this explanation to Theophrastus. J. Mansfeld and D. T. Runia, *Aëtiana,* vol. 2 (Leiden, 2009), p. 530, suggest that the source said, "Xenophanes, as Theophrastus says in his *Physics,* . . . "

D29 (A43) Aëtius

a

Xenophanes: [scil. the moon is] a compressed cloud.

b

[. . .] Xenophanes, [. . .]: it [i.e. the moon] possesses its own light.

c

Xenophanes: the monthly disappearance too [scil. of the moon comes about] by extinguishing.

EARLY GREEK PHILOSOPHY III

The Course and Effects of the Sun (D30–D33)

D30 (B31) Heracl. *Alleg.* 44.5

ἠέλιός θ' ὑπεριέμενος γαῖάν τ' ἐπιθάλπων

D31 (< A41a) Aët. 2.24.9 (Stob.) [περὶ ἐκλείψεως ἡλίου]

[. . . = **D35**] ὁ δ' αὐτὸς τὸν ἥλιον εἰς ἄπειρον μὲν προιέναι, δοκεῖν δὲ κυκλεῖσθαι διὰ τὴν ἀπόστασιν.

D32 (A46) Aët. 3.4.4 (Stob.) [περὶ νεφῶν ὁμίχλης ὑετῶν δρόσου χιόνος πάχνης χαλάζης]

Ξενοφάνης· ἀπὸ[1] τῆς τοῦ ἡλίου θερμότητος ὡς ἀρκτικῆς αἰτίας τἀν[2] τοῖς μεταρσίοις συμβαίνειν· ἀνελκομένου γὰρ ἐκ τῆς θαλάττης τοῦ ὑγροῦ τὸ γλυκὺ διὰ τὴν λεπτομέρειαν διακρινόμενον νέφη τε[2] συνιστάνειν ὀμιχλούμενον καὶ καταστάζειν ὄμβρους ὑπὸ πιλήσεως καὶ διατμίζειν τὰ πνεύματα· γράφει γὰρ διαρρήδην "πηγὴ δ' ἐστὶ θάλασσ' ὕδατος" [**D46.1a**].

[1] κἂν ms., corr. Karsten   [2] τὸ ms., corr. Karsten

D33 (A42) Aët. 2.30.8 (Stob.) [περὶ ἐμφάσεως αὐτῆς (scil. τῆς σελήνης)]

Ξενοφάνης τὸν μὲν ἥλιον χρήσιμον εἶναι πρὸς τὴν τοῦ κόσμου καὶ τὴν τῶν ἐν αὐτῷ ζῴων γένεσίν τε καὶ διοίκησιν, τὴν δὲ σελήνην παρέλκειν.

XENOPHANES

The Course and Effects of the Sun (D30–D33)

D30 (B31) Heraclitus, *Homeric Allegories*

The sun, rushing over the earth and warming it

D31 (< A41a) Aëtius

[. . .] The same man [i.e. Xenophanes]: the sun proceeds onward infinitely but it seems to move in a circle because of the distance.

D32 (A46) Aëtius

Xenophanes: what happens in the upper regions [i.e. in the atmosphere] has as efficient cause the warmth of the sun. For when the moisture is drawn up from the sea, the sweet part is separated out because of its fineness, condenses to form clouds, drips down as rain because of compression, and exhales the winds. For he writes explicitly, **"the sea is the source of water."**

D33 (A42) Aëtius

Xenophanes: the sun is useful for the generation and organization of the world and of the living beings in it, but the moon is irrelevant.

EARLY GREEK PHILOSOPHY III

Disappearances of the Sun (D34–D35)

D34 (A41) Aët. 2.24.4 (Ps.-Plut.) [περὶ ἐκλείψεως ἡλίου]

Ξενοφάνης κατὰ σβέσιν· ἕτερον δὲ πάλιν πρὸς ταῖς ἀνατολαῖς γίνεσθαι· παριστόρηκε δὲ καὶ ἔκλειψιν ἡλίου ἐφ᾽ ὅλον μῆνα καὶ πάλιν ἔκλειψιν ἐντελῆ, ὥστε τὴν ἡμέραν νύκτα φανῆναι.

D35 (< A41a) Aët. 2.24.9 (Stob.; cf. Ps.-Plut.) [περὶ ἐκλείψεως ἡλίου]

Ξενοφάνης· πολλοὺς εἶναι ἡλίους καὶ σελήνας κατὰ τὰ[1] κλίματα τῆς γῆς καὶ ἀποτομὰς καὶ ζώνας. κατὰ δέ τινα καιρὸν ἐκπίπτειν[2] τὸν δίσκον εἴς τινα ἀποτομὴν τῆς γῆς οὐκ οἰκουμένην[3] ὑφ᾽ ἡμῶν καὶ οὕτως ὡσπερεὶ κενεμβατοῦντα ἔκλειψιν ὑποφαίνειν[4] [. . . = **D31**].

[1] τὰ om. Plut.   [2] ἐμπίπτειν Plut.   [3] οἰκουμένης Stob.   [4] ὑποφαίνειν Stob. Plut. M: ὑπομένειν Plut. mΠ

The Heavenly Bodies and Other Luminous Celestial Phenomena Are Clouds (D36–D38)

D36 (A38) Aët. 2.13.14 (Theod., Ach. Tat.) [τίς ἡ οὐσία τῶν ἄστρων, πλανητῶν καὶ ἀπλανῶν]

a Theod. *Cur.* 4.19

Ξενοφάνης δὲ ἐκ νεφῶν μὲν λέγει πεπυρωμένων ξυνίστασθαι, σβεννυμένους δὲ μεθ᾽ ἡμέραν νύκτωρ πάλιν ἀναζωπυρεῖσθαι, καθάπερ τοὺς ἄνθρακας.

XENOPHANES

Disappearances of the Sun (D34–D35)

D34 (A41) Aëtius

Xenophanes: [scil. the eclipses of the sun come about] by extinguishing,[1] and a different one comes about in turn in the east. He has also reported in passing an eclipse of the sun that lasted a whole month and again a total eclipse, of which the effect was that the day appeared to be night.

[1] This chapter of Aëtius is about eclipses, but this explanation bears rather on sunset. The important point for Xenophanes seems to have been disappearance in general.

D35 (< A41a) Aëtius

Xenophanes: there are many suns and moons according to the latitudes, sections, and zones of the earth, and sometimes the disk falls down onto some section of the earth uninhabited by us, and in this way, as though its fall left behind an empty space, it makes an eclipse appear [...].

The Heavenly Bodies and Other Luminous Celestial Phenomena Are Clouds (D36–D38)

D36 (A38) Aëtius

a

Xenophanes says that [scil. the heavenly bodies] come about out of clouds that have been ignited; they are extinguished by day and are kindled again at night like coals.

b Ach. Tat. *Introd. Arat.* 11

Ξενοφάνης δὲ λέγει τοὺς ἀστέρας ἐκ νεφῶν συνεστάναι ἐμπύρων καὶ σβέννυσθαι καὶ ἀνάπτεσθαι ὡσανεὶ ἄνθρακας, καί, ὅτε μὲν ἅπτονται, φαντασίαν ἡμᾶς ἔχειν ἀνατολῆς, ὅτε δὲ σβέννυνται, δύσεως.

D37 (A44) Aët. 3.2.11 (Ps.-Plut.) [περὶ κομητῶν καὶ διαττόντων καὶ δοκίδων]

Ξενοφάνης· πάντα τὰ τοιαῦτα νεφῶν πεπυρωμένων συστήματα ἢ κινήματα.

D38 (A39) Aët. 2.18.1 (Ps.-Plut.) [περὶ τῶν ἀστέρων τῶν καλουμένων Διοσκούρων]

Ξενοφάνης· τοὺς ἐπὶ τῶν πλοίων φαινομένους οἷον ἀστέρας νεφέλια εἶναι κατὰ τὴν ποιὰν κίνησιν παραλάμποντα.

The Rainbow Too Is a Cloud (D39)

D39 (B32) Schol. BLT Eust. ad *Il.* 11.27b

ἥν τ' Ἶριν καλέουσι, νέφος καὶ τοῦτο πέφυκε,
πορφύρεον καὶ φοινίκεον καὶ χλωρὸν ἰδέσθαι.

XENOPHANES

b

Xenophanes says that the heavenly bodies have come about out of clouds that have been ignited, and that they are extinguished and are kindled again like coals, and that, when they are kindled, we have the impression of a rising, and when they are extinguished, that of a setting.

D37 (A44) Aëtius

Xenophanes: all things of this sort [i.e. comets, shooting stars, and other luminous phenomena] are groups or motions of clouds that have been ignited.

D38 (A39) Aëtius

Xenophanes: the phenomena similar to stars that appear on boats [i.e. St. Elmo's fire] are small clouds that gleam because of their particular kind of motion.

The Rainbow Too Is a Cloud (D39)

D39 (B32) Scholia on Homer's *Iliad*

> **And what they call Iris, this too by nature is a cloud,**
> **Purple, red and greenish yellow to look on.**

Lightning (D40)

D40 (A45) Aët. 3.3.6 (Stob.) [περὶ βροντῶν ἀστραπῶν κεραυνῶν πρηστήρων τυφώνων]

Ξενοφάνης· ἀστραπὰς γίνεσθαι λαμπρυνομένων τῶν νεφῶν κατὰ τὴν κίνησιν.

The Earth (D41–D45)

D41 (B28) Ach. Tat. *Intr. Arat.* 4

γαίης μὲν τόδε πεῖραρ· ἄνω παρὰ ποσσὶν ὁρᾶται
ἠέρι προσπλάζον, τὸ κάτω δ' ἐς ἄπειρον
ἱκνεῖται.

1 πεῖραρ Maass: πεῖραν V: πεῖρας M   2 ἠέρι Diels: καὶ ῥεῖ mss.: αἰθέρι Karsten

D42 (< A47) Aët. 3.9.4 (Ps.-Plut.) [περὶ γῆς καὶ τίς ἡ ταύτης οὐσία καὶ πόσαι]

Ξενοφάνης· ἐκ τοῦ κατωτέρω μέρους εἰς ἄπειρον βάθος[1] ἐρριζῶσθαι, ἐξ ἀέρος δὲ καὶ πυρὸς συμπαγῆναι.

[1] βάθος AE: μέρος Mm: del. Diels

D43 (< A47) Aët. 3.11.2 (Ps.-Plut.; cf. Eus. *PE* 15.57.2) [περὶ θέσεως γῆς]

[. . . = **THAL. R24**] Ξενοφάνης πρώτην· εἰς ἄπειρον γὰρ[1] ἐρριζῶσθαι.

[1] γὰρ Eus.: om. Plut.

XENOPHANES

Lightning (D40)

D40 (A45) Aëtius

Xenophanes: lightning flashes come about because of the illumination of clouds in motion.

The Earth (D41–D45)

D41 (B28) Achilles Tatius, *Introduction to Aratus'* Phaenomena

> **This is the limit of the earth: above, one sees it at our feet**
> **Pressing against the air; but below, it stretches down to the unlimited.**

D42 (< A47) Aëtius

Xenophanes: [scil. the earth] is rooted from its lower part down to an unlimited depth and is made out of solidified air and fire.

D43 (< A47) Aëtius

[. . .] Xenophanes: [scil. the earth] is first, for it is rooted in the unlimited.[1]

[1] This statement has led to an error in the doxographic tradition; see Stobaeus 1.22.3b (2) (**DOX. T17**).

EARLY GREEK PHILOSOPHY III

D44 (B37) Hdn. *Mon. Lex.* 2, p. 936.19

καὶ μὲν ἐνὶ σπεάτεσσί τεοις καταλείβεται ὕδωρ.

μὲν Diels: μὴν ms.

D45 (A48) Ps.-Arist. *Mir. ausc.* 37 833a15–17

τὸ δ' ἐν τῇ Λιπάρᾳ ποτὲ καὶ ἐκλιπεῖν Ξενοφάνης φησὶν ἐπ' ἔτη ἑκκαίδεκα, τῷ δὲ ἑβδόμῳ ἐπανελθεῖν.

The Sea (D46)

D46 (B30) Crates in Schol. Genav. in *Il.* 21.196

Ξενοφάνης ἐν τῷ Περὶ φύσεως·

> πηγὴ δ' ἐστὶ θάλασσ' ὕδατος, πηγὴ δ' ἀνέμοιο·
> οὔτε γὰρ ἐν νέφεσιν ⟨γίνοιτό κε ἲς ἀνέμοιο
> ἐκπνείοντος⟩ ἔσωθεν ἄνευ πόντου μεγάλοιο
> οὔτε ῥοαὶ ποταμῶν οὔτ' αἰθ⟨έρος⟩ ὄμβριον
>   ὕδωρ,
> 5 ἀλλὰ μέγας πόντος γενέτωρ νεφέων ἀνέμων τε
> καὶ ποταμῶν ∪ ∪ | – ∪ ∪ | – ∪ ∪ | – ∪ ∪ | – –

1 θάλασσ' Nicole: θάλασση ms.   2–3 suppl. Diels: ⟨πνοιαί κ' ἀνέμοιο φύοιντο ἐκπνείοντος⟩ Diels olim [=1891], alii aliter   3 ἄνα πόντοιο ms., corr. Nicole   4 αἰθέρος Nicole: αἰθ#### cum ras. ms.   5 νεφελῶν Nicole

XENOPHANES

D44 (B37) Herodian, *On Particular Usages*

And in some caves, water drips down.

D45 (A48) Ps.-Aristotle, *On Marvelous Things Heard*

Xenophanes says that the [scil. fire] in Lipari once ceased for sixteen years and resumed in the seventeenth.

The Sea (D46)

D46 (B30) Geneva Scholia on Homer's *Iliad* (derived from Crates of Mallos)

Xenophanes in his *On Nature*:

The sea is the source of water and the source of the wind.
For neither would in the clouds ⟨**the force of the wind come about,**
That blows out⟩ **from within, without the great sea,**
Nor the streams of rivers, nor the rainy water of the air:
But the great sea is the begetter of clouds, winds,
And rivers . . .

The Soul (D47–D48)

D47 (A50) Macr. *In Somn.* 1.14.20

[. . .] Xenophanes ex terra et aqua [. . .].

D48 (A51) Tert. *An.* 43.2

[. . .] Anaxagoras cum Xenophane defetiscentiam [. . .].

Epistemological Considerations (D49–D53)

D49 (B34) Sext. Emp. *Adv. Math.* 7.49, 7.110 (cf. 7.51), 8.326 (et al.)

καὶ τὸ μὲν οὖν σαφὲς οὔτις ἀνὴρ γένετ' οὐδέ
  τις ἔσται
εἰδὼς ἀμφὶ θεῶν τε καὶ ἄσσα λέγω περὶ πάντων·
εἰ γὰρ καὶ τὰ μάλιστα τύχοι τετελεσμένον
  εἰπών,
αὐτὸς ὅμως οὐκ οἶδε· δόκος δ' ἐπὶ πᾶσι
  τέτυκται.

1 γένετ' Plut. *Aud. poet.* 2 17D: ἴδεν Sext. Emp. (οἶδεν Sext. Emp. 7.49 NA, Diog. Laert. 9.72 BF, εἶδεν Diog. Laert. P)

XENOPHANES

The Soul (D47–D48)

D47 (A50) Macrobius, *Commentary on Cicero's* Dream of Scipio

[. . .] Xenophanes: [scil. the soul is composed] out of earth and water [. . .].[1]

[1] This is doubtless an illegitimate inference based on **D26** (cf. **D25**).

D48 (A51) Tertullian, *On the Soul*

[. . .] Anaxagoras together with Xenophanes [scil. say that sleep is] exhaustion [. . .].

Epistemological Considerations (D49–D53)

D49 (B34) Sextus Empiricus, *Against the Logicians*

And thus there has never been any man, nor will there ever be one,
Who knows what is clear about the gods and whatever I say about all things.
For even if he happened most to say something perfect,
He himself nonetheless does not know: opinion is set upon all things.

D50 (B35) Plut. *Quaest. conv.* 9.14 746B

ταῦτα δεδοξάσθω μὲν ἐοικότα τοῖς ἐτύμοισι

δεδοξάσθω Wilamowitz: δεδοξάσθαι mss.: δεδόξασται Karsten

D51 (B36) Hdn. π. διχρ., p. 16.22

ὁππόσα δὴ θνητοῖσι πεφήνασιν εἰσοράασθαι

D52 (B38) Hdn. *Mon. Lex.* 2, p. 946.23

εἰ μὴ χλωρὸν ἔφυσε θεὸς μέλι, πολλὸν
    ἔφασκον
γλύσσονα σῦκα πέλεσθαι. ∪ | – ∪ ∪ | – ∪ ∪ | – –

1 πολλὸν Lehrs: πολλῶν mss.   ἔφασκον mss.: ἔφασκ' ἄν coni. Diels

D53 (B18) Stob. 1.8.2; 3.29.41

οὔτοι ἀπ' ἀρχῆς πάντα θεοὶ θνητοῖσ' ὑπέδειξαν,
ἀλλὰ χρόνῳ ζητοῦντες ἐφευρίσκουσιν ἄμεινον.

2 ἐφευρίσκουσιν 3.29.41: ἐφεύρεσκον 1.8.2 F: ἐφεύρισκον 1.8.2 P

XENOPHANES

D50 (B35) Plutarch, *Table Talk*

> Then let this be accepted as opinions similar to
> real things

D51 (B36) Herodian, *On Syllables with Double Value*

> All the things that appear[1] to mortals to look
> upon

[1] Or "all the things that they [scil. the gods] reveal."

D52 (B38) Herodian, *On Particular Usages*

> If god had not created the yellow honey, they
> would say that
> Figs are much sweeter.

D53 (B18) Stobaeus, *Anthology*

> The gods have not indicated all things to
> mortals from the beginning,
> But in time, by searching, they find something
> more that is better.

EARLY GREEK PHILOSOPHY III

Other Fragments from Poems in Dactylic Hexameters (D54–D58)

D54 (B22) Athen. *Deipn.* 2.44 54E

Ξενοφάνης ὁ Κολοφώνιος ἐν παρῳδίαις·[1]

    πὰρ πυρὶ χρὴ τοιαῦτα λέγειν χειμῶνος ἐν ὥρῃ
    ἐν κλίνῃ μαλακῇ κατακείμενον, ἔμπλεον ὄντα,
    πίνοντα γλυκὺν οἶνον, ὑποτρώγοντ' ἐρεβίνθους·
    τίς πόθεν εἶς ἀνδρῶν, πόσα τοι ἔτε' ἐστί,
        φέριστε;
5   πηλίκος ἦσθ' ὅθ' ὁ Μῆδος ἀφίκετο; | – ∪ ∪ | – –

1 παρῳδαις mss., corr. Menagius   4 ἔτη mss., corr. Diels

D55 (B17) Schol. in Aristoph. *Equit.* 408b

βάκχους [. . .] καὶ τοὺς κλάδους οὓς οἱ μύσται φέρουσι. μέμνηται δὲ Ξενοφάνης ἐν Σίλλοις οὕτως·

    ἑστᾶσιν δ' ἐλάτης ⟨βάκχοι⟩ πυκινὸν περὶ δῶμα.

ἐλάτης ΓΘ: ἐλάτη VE: ἐλάται Musurus   ⟨βάκχοι⟩ Wachsmuth

D56 (B21a) Schol. in *Il.* 7 (P.Oxy. 1087 Col. 2.40–41)

τὸ Ἔρυ|κος παρὰ Ξεν[ο]φάνει ἐν ε' Σίλλων [. . .].

XENOPHANES

Other Fragments from Poems in Dactylic Hexameters (D54–D58)

D54 (B22) Athenaeus, *Deipnosophists*

Xenophanes of Colophon in his parodies [i.e. doubtless the *Mockeries*]:

> **Beside the fire, during the winter, one should say these sorts of thing,**
> **Reclining on a soft couch, having eaten one's fill,**
> **Drinking sweet wine and nibbling chickpeas:**
> **"Who are you among men and from where? How old are you, my good man?**
> **How old were you when the Mede came?"**

D55 (B17) Scholia on Aristophanes' *Knights*

bakkhoi [. . .] and the branches that mystic initiates carry. Xenophanes mentions them in his *Mockeries:*

> **Around the sturdy house stand ⟨*bakkhoi*⟩ of fir.**

D56 (B21a), Scholia on Homer's *Iliad*

The word **Erukos** [scil. to designate Mt. Eryx in Sicily] is found in Xenophanes in Book 5 of his *Mockeries*.

D57 (B39) Pollux *Onom.* 6.46

[...] **κέρασον** τὸ δένδρον ἐν τῷ Περὶ φύσεως Ξενοφάνους εὑρών.

D58 (B41) Tzetz. *In Dion. Perieg.* 940 et Comm. ad Tzetz.

σιλλογράφος δέ τις τὸ σι μακρὸν γράφει,
τῷ ῥῶ, δοκεῖ μοι, τοῦτο μηκύνας τάχα.

σιλλογράφος νῦν ὁ Ξενοφάνης ἐστὶ καὶ ὁ Τίμων καὶ ἕτεροι [Testim. 15 Di Marco].

*From Xenophanes' Poem(s) in
Elegiac Couplets (D59–D69)
Social Norms (D59–D63)*

D59 (B1) Athen. *Deipn.* 11.7 462C

νῦν γὰρ δὴ ζάπεδον καθαρὸν καὶ χεῖρες ἁπάντων
 καὶ κύλικες· πλεκτοὺς δ' ἀμφιτιθεῖ στεφάνους,
ἄλλος δ' εὐῶδες μύρον ἐν φιάλῃ παρατείνει·
 κρατὴρ δ' ἕστηκεν μεστὸς εὐφροσύνης·
5 ἄλλος δ' οἶνος ἕτοιμος, ὃς οὔποτέ φησι προδώσειν,

2 ἀμφιτιθεῖ Dindorf: ἀμφιτιθεὶς mss.   5 οἶνος ἕτοιμος corr. Musurus: οἶνος ἐστὶν ἕτοιμος mss.

XENOPHANES

D57 (B39) Pollux, *Onomasticon*

[...] having found ***kerason*** (i.e. "cherry tree") for the tree in Xenophanes' *On Nature*.

D58 (B41) Tzetzes, *Commentary on Dionysius Periegetes* (and a commentary on Tzetzes)

> A certain writer of *Mockeries* writes the *si-* (scil. of
>   ***siros***, i.e. "storage pit") long,
> Lengthening it perhaps, I suppose, because of the *r*.

Xenophanes is a writer of *Mockeries,* and also Timon, and others.

From Xenophanes' Poem(s) in
Elegiac Couplets (D59–D69)
Social Norms (D59–D63)

D59 (B1) Athenaeus, *Deipnosophists*

For now the floor is truly purified, and the
    hands of all,
  And the wine cups. One person puts plaited
      garlands on us,
Another proffers fragrant ointment in a saucer.
    The mixing bowl stands full of good cheer,
And other wine, which promises never to betray, 5
    is ready,

μείλιχος ἐν κεράμοισ' ἄνθεος ὀσδόμενος·
ἐν δὲ μέσοισ' ἁγνὴν ὀδμὴν λιβανωτὸς ἵησι·
ψυχρὸν δ' ἐστὶν ὕδωρ καὶ γλυκὺ καὶ
καθαρόν.
πάρκεινται δ' ἄρτοι ξανθοὶ γεραρή τε τράπεζα
10 τυροῦ καὶ μέλιτος πίονος ἀχθομένη·
βωμὸς δ' ἄνθεσιν ἂν τὸ μέσον πάντῃ
πεπύκασται,
μολπῇ δ' ἀμφὶς ἔχει δώματα καὶ θαλίη.
χρὴ δὲ πρῶτον μὲν θεὸν ὑμνεῖν εὔφρονας ἄνδρας
εὐφήμοις μύθοις καὶ καθαροῖσι λόγοις·
15 σπείσαντας δὲ καὶ εὐξαμένους τὰ δίκαια
δύνασθαι
πρήσσειν (ταῦτα γὰρ ὦν ἐστι προχειρότε-
ρον),
οὐχ ὕβρις πίνειν ὁπόσον κεν ἔχων ἀφίκοιο
οἴκαδ' ἄνευ προπόλου, μὴ πάνυ γηραλέος.
ἀνδρῶν δ' αἰνεῖν τοῦτον ὃς ἐσθλὰ πιὼν
ἀναφαίνῃ,
20 ὥς οἱ μνημοσύνη, καὶ τόνος ἀμφ' ἀρετῆς.
οὔτι μάχας διέπειν Τιτήνων οὐδὲ Γιγάντων
οὐδέ ⟨τι⟩ Κενταύρων, πλάσματα τῶν
προτέρων,

15 δὲ Bergk: τε mss.   17 ὕβρις Musurus: ὕβρεις mss.   δ' post πίνειν habent mss., del. Bergk   19 ἀναφαίνῃ Hermann: ἀναφαίνει mss.   20 ὥς οἱ Koraïs: ωση A: ὡς ἡ E   τὸν ὃς mss.: τόνος Diels   21 διέπειν A: διέπει E: διέπων Fränkel

62

XENOPHANES

    Honey-sweet in the clay jars, scented of flowers.
In the middle, incense sends up a sacred aroma.
    The water is cold, sweet, and pure.
Blond loaves of bread lie nearby and a majestic table
    Laden with cheese and rich honey.　　　　　　10
An altar is in the middle, decorated everywhere with flowers;
    On all sides song and festive joy fill the house.
First, cheerful [or: sensible] men should sing hymns to the god
    With words of good omen and pure speech.
Then, after having made libation and prayed to be able to act　　15
    Justly—for this is more appropriate (?)—
It is not presumptuous to drink so much that one can still go home
    Without a servant as guide, unless one is too old.
Praise that man who after drinking reveals noble thoughts,
    According to his memory, and him who [scil. speaks] about excellence;　　20
And do not recount the battles of Titans or of Giants
    Or of Centaurs, inventions of earlier men,

---

22 ⟨τι⟩ Meineke: αὖ Bergk: τὰ Hermann: τε Ludwig πλάσματα τῶν προτέρων Schweighaüser: πλασμάτων προτέρων mss.

EARLY GREEK PHILOSOPHY III

ἢ στάσιας σφεδανάς, τοῖς οὐδὲν χρηστὸν
  ἔνεστι,
θεῶν ‹δὲ› προμηθείην αἰὲν ἔχειν ἀγαθήν.

23 σφεδανάς Osann: φενδόνας mss.   24 ‹δὲ› Scaliger
ἀγαθόν Hermann

D60 (B5) Athen. *Deipn.* 11.18 782A

οὐδέ κεν ἐν κύλικι πρότερον κεράσειέ τις οἶνον
ἐγχέας, ἀλλ' ὕδωρ καὶ καθύπερθε μέθυ.

2 ἐγχεύας mss., corr. Casaubon

D61 (B2) Athen. *Deipn.* 10.6 413F

ἀλλ' εἰ μὲν ταχυτῆτι ποδῶν νίκην τις ἄροιτο
ἢ πενταθλεύων, ἔνθα Διὸς τέμενος
πὰρ Πίσαο ῥοῇσ' ἐν Ὀλυμπίῃ, εἴτε παλαίων
ἢ καὶ πυκτοσύνην ἀλγινόεσσαν ἔχων,
5   εἴτε τὸ δεινὸν ἄεθλον ὃ παγκράτιον καλέουσιν,
ἀστοῖσίν κ' εἴη κυδρότερος προσορᾶν
καί κε προεδρίην φανερὴν ἐν ἀγῶσιν ἄροιτο
καί κεν σῖτ' εἴη δημοσίων κτεάνων

5 εἴτε τὸ Wakefield: εἴτέτι ms.   6 προσορᾶν Iacobs: προσεραν ms.   8 σῖτ' εἴη Diels: σιτειη ms.: σίτησιν Kaibel

Or fierce civil strife, in which there is no profit
　　at all:
　　　But always have good forethought about the
　　　　gods.

D60 (B5) Athenaeus, *Deipnosophists*

Nor when mixing in the wine cup would one
　　　first pour in
　　Wine, but instead water and then on top of it
　　　pure wine.

D61 (B2) Athenaeus, *Deipnosophists*

But if someone were to carry off victory by
　　　swiftness of foot
　　Or in the pentathlon, where the precinct of
　　　Zeus lies
Beside the streams of the Pisa in Olympia, or by
　　　wrestling,
　　Or because he knows the art of painful
　　　boxing
Or the frightful discipline that they call the　　　　5
　　　pankration:
　　Then he would be more glorious to look
　　　upon for his fellow citizens,
And he would get a conspicuous seat of honor in
　　　the competitions,
　　And his food would come out of the people's
　　　expense

ἐκ πόλεως καὶ δῶρον ὅ οἱ κειμήλιον εἴη·
    εἴτε καὶ ἵπποισιν, ταῦτά κε πάντα λάχοι,
οὐκ ἐὼν ἄξιος ὥσπερ ἐγώ. ῥώμης γὰρ ἀμείνων
    ἀνδρῶν ἠδ' ἵππων ἡμετέρη σοφίη.
ἀλλ' εἰκῇ μάλα τοῦτο νομίζεται, οὐδὲ δίκαιον
    προκρίνειν ῥώμην τῆς ἀγαθῆς σοφίης.
οὔτε γὰρ εἰ πύκτης ἀγαθὸς λαοῖσι μετείη
    οὔτ' εἰ πενταθλεῖν οὔτε παλαισμοσύνην,
οὐδὲ μὲν εἰ ταχυτῆτι ποδῶν, τόπερ ἐστὶ πρότιμον
ῥώμης ὅσσ' ἀνδρῶν ἔργ' ἐν ἀγῶνι πέλει,
τοὔνεκεν ἂν δὴ μᾶλλον ἐν εὐνομίῃ πόλις εἴη.
    σμικρὸν δ' ἄν τι πόλει χάρμα γένοιτ' ἐπὶ τῷ,
εἴ τις ἀεθλεύων νικῷ Πίσαο παρ' ὄχθας·
    οὐ γὰρ πιαίνει ταῦτα μυχοὺς πόλεως.

10 κε πάντα Schweighaüser: κ' εἰπάντα ms.   15 λαοῖσι μετείη Stephanus: λαοῖσιν ἔτ' εἴη ms.

D62 (B3) Athen. *Deipn.* 12.31 526A

ἁβροσύνας δὲ μαθόντες ἀνωφελέας παρὰ Λυδῶν,

XENOPHANES

From the city, and he would receive a gift that would be an heirloom for him,
   Or else if with horses, he would get all these things—   10
But he would not be worthy as I am. For better than strength
   Of men or horses is our wisdom.
But this custom is quite haphazard, and it is not just
   To prefer strength to good wisdom.
For neither if there were a good boxer among the people,   15
   Nor someone good at the pentathlon or at wrestling
Nor if in swiftness of foot (which is most honored
   Of all the competitions for strength in the games of men),
Would the city because of him [or: this] be in a better state of lawfulness.
   The city would derive little pleasure from him,   20
If someone wins in the competitions besides the banks of the Pisa,
   For this does not fatten the city's store chambers.

D62 (B3) Athenaeus, *Deipnosophists*

After they [scil. the Colophonians] had learned about useless luxuries from the Lydians,

ὄφρα τυραννίης ἦσαν ἄνευ στυγερῆς,
ἤεσαν εἰς ἀγορὴν παναλουργέα φάρε' ἔχοντες,
οὐ μείους ὥσπερ χίλιοι εἰς ἐπίπαν,
5   αὐχαλέοι, χαίτῃσιν †ἀγάλλομεν† εὐπρεπέεσσιν
ἀσκητοῖσ' ὀδμὴν χρίμασι δευόμενοι.

1 ἀφροσύνας ms., corr. Schneider   2 ησσα | νευ ms., corr. Dindorf   5 χαίτῃσιν ἀγάλλομεν· Casaubon: χαίτης ἐν ἀγάλμασιν Hermann: χαίτῃσιν ἀγάλμενοι Wilamowitz: alii alia

D63 (< B4) Pollux *Onom.* 9.83

[. . .] Λυδοί, καθά φησι Ξενοφάνης [scil. πρῶτοι ἔκοψαν νόμισμα].

From a Poem about Old Age and Death? (D64–D67)

D64 (B7) Diog. Laert. 8.36

περὶ δὲ τοῦ ἄλλοτε ἄλλον αὐτὸν [scil. Πυθαγόρας] γεγενῆσθαι Ξενοφάνης ἐν ἐλεγείᾳ προσμαρτυρεῖ, ἧς ἀρχή·

νῦν αὖτ' ἄλλον ἔπειμι λόγον, δείξω δὲ κέλευθον.

ὁ δὲ περὶ αὐτοῦ φησιν οὕτως ἔχει·

XENOPHANES

> As long as they were free from hateful
>   tyranny,
> They would go forth to the agora wearing
>   mantles all purple,
> Not less than a thousand all in all,
> Boastful, †we pride ourselves† on their well-   5
>   ordered locks,
> Drenched with perfume from refined
>   ointments.

D63 (< B4) Pollux, *Vocabulary*

[. . .] the Lydians, according to what Xenophanes says, [scil. were the first to mint coins].

*From a Poem about Old Age and
Death? (D64–D67)*

D64 (B7) Diogenes Laertius

About the fact that he [i.e. Pythagoras] became a different person at different times, Xenophanes provides testimony in his elegiac poem that begins,

> Now I will pass over to another story, and I shall
>   show the path.

What he says about him is as follows:

καί ποτέ μιν στυφελιζομένου σκύλακος
   παριόντα
φασὶν ἐποικτῖραι καὶ τόδε φάσθαι ἔπος·
"παῦσαι μηδὲ ῥάπιζ', ἐπεὶ ἦ φίλου ἀνέρος ἐστί
ψυχή, τὴν ἔγνων φθεγξαμένης ἀίων."

2 φασὶν B: φασί γ' PΦ: φασὶ γοῦν F

D65 (B20) Diog. Laert. 1.111

βιοὺς [. . . scil. Ἐπιμενίδης], ὡς [. . .] Ξενοφάνης ὁ Κολοφώνιος ἀκηκοέναι φησί, τέτταρα πρὸς τοῖς πεντήκοντα καὶ ἑκατόν.

D66 (B8) Diog. Laert. 9.19

ἤδη δ' ἑπτά τ' ἔασι καὶ ἑξήκοντ' ἐνιαυτοί
   βληστρίζοντες ἐμὴν φροντίδ' ἀν' Ἑλλάδα
   γῆν·
ἐκ γενετῆς δὲ τότ' ἦσαν ἐείκοσι πέντε τε πρὸς
   τοῖς,
εἴπερ ἐγὼ περὶ τῶνδ' οἶδα λέγειν ἐτύμως.

D67 (B9) *Etym. Gen.* ad γῆρας 42 Calame

ἀνδρὸς γηρέντος πολλὸν ἀφαυρότερος

XENOPHANES

> And they say that when he was once passing by
> a puppy that was being mistreated,
> He took pity and said these words:
> "Stop beating it, since this is truly the soul
> Of a dear friend whom I recognized on
> hearing him cry out."

D65 (B20) Diogenes Laertius

As Xenophanes of Colophon says he heard [scil. Epimenides] lived for 154 [scil. years].

D66 (B8) Diogenes Laertius

> Already seven and sixty years have been tossing about
> My thought throughout the land of Greece;
> And at that time there had already been twenty-five more since my birth,
> If I myself know how to speak truly about these things.

D67 (B9) *Etymologicum Genuinum*

> Much more feeble than an old man

EARLY GREEK PHILOSOPHY III

References to Other Poets (D68–D69)

D68 (< B21) Schol. in Aristoph. *Pac.* 697

ὁ Σιμωνίδης διεβέβλητο ἐπὶ φιλαργυρίᾳ [. . .] ὅθεν Ξενοφάνης **κίμβικα** αὐτὸν προσαγορεύει.

D69 (B6) Athen. *Deipn.* 9.6, 368F

> πέμψας γὰρ κωλῆν ἐρίφου σκέλος ἤραο πῖον
>   ταύρου λαρινοῦ, τίμιον ἀνδρὶ λαχεῖν,
> τοῦ κλέος Ἑλλάδα πᾶσαν ἐφίξεται οὐδ'
>   ἀπολήξει,
> ἔστ' ἂν ἀοιδάων ᾖ γένος Ἑλλαδικῶν.

3 ἀφίξεται mss., corr. Karsten

An Isolated Word in Uncertain Meter (D70)

D70 (< B40) *Etym. Gen.* B.338

βρόταχος, τὸν βάτραχον Ἴωνες, [. . .] καὶ παρὰ Ξενοφάνει.[1]

[1] Ξενοφά(νει) A: Ξενοφ(ῶν)τ(ι) B

XENOPHANES

References to Other Poets (D68–D69)

D68 (< B21) Scholia on Aristophanes' *Peace*

Simonides was accused of being avaricious [. . .] for this reason Xenophanes calls him a **"skinflint."**

D69 (B6) Athenaeus, *Deipnosophists*

> **You sent the thighbone of a kid goat, but you received the rich leg**
> **Of a fatted bull, an honored piece to obtain for a man**
> **Whose fame will reach through all of Greece and will not cease**
> **As long as the race of Greek songs will live.**[1]

[1] The absence of context makes the point unclear, but it has often been thought that this is an ironic swipe at a fellow poet (perhaps Simonides, cf. **D68**).

An Isolated Word in Uncertain Meter (D70)

D70 (< B40) *Etymologicum Genuinum*

brotakhos: *botrakhros* [i.e. "frog"] in Ionic [. . .] and in Xenophanes.

XENOPHANES [21 DK]

R

*First Mentions and Allusions
In Heraclitus*

See **HER. D20**

Parodies and Allusions in Epicharmus

See **DRAM. T2–T3**

Imitations in Euripides

See **DRAM. T72–T73**

*Xenophanes as the Initiator of the Eleatic Line of
Descent of Greek Philosophy (R1–R3)*

R1 (< A29) Plat. *Soph.* 242d

[ΞΕ.] τὸ δὲ παρ' ἡμῖν[1] Ἐλεατικὸν ἔθνος, ἀπὸ Ξενοφάνους τε καὶ ἔτι πρόσθεν ἀρξάμενον, ὡς ἑνὸς ὄντος τῶν πάντων καλουμένων οὕτω διεξέρχεται τοῖς μύθοις.

[1] ἡμῖν Paris. 1808 (et Theod. *Cur.* 2.17): ἡμῶν BTW

XENOPHANES

R

First Mentions and Allusions In Heraclitus

See **HER. D20**

Parodies and Allusions in Epicharmus

See **DRAM. T2–T3**

Imitations in Euripides

See **DRAM. T72–T73**

Xenophanes as the Initiator of the Eleatic Line of Descent of Greek Philosophy (R1–R3)

R1 (< A29) Plato, *Sophist*

[The stranger from Elea:] Our Eleatic tribe, which begins with Xenophanes and even earlier, explain in their stories that what are called 'all things' is one [cf. **DOX. T4**].

EARLY GREEK PHILOSOPHY III

R2 (< A30) Arist. *Metaph.* A5 986b21–22

Ξενοφάνης δὲ πρῶτος τούτων ἐνίσας [. . . = **P10, R12**].

R3 (< A8) Clem. Alex. *Strom.* 1.64.2

τῆς δὲ Ἐλεατικῆς ἀγωγῆς Ξενοφάνης ὁ Κολοφώνιος κατάρχει [. . . = **D4**].

The Eleatization of Xenophanes (R4–R11)

R4 (< A31) Simpl. *In Phys.*, p. 22.26–23.14 (= Theophr. [Frag. 224 FHS&G]

μίαν δὲ τὴν ἀρχὴν ἤτοι ἓν τὸ ὂν καὶ πᾶν καὶ οὔτε πεπερασμένον οὔτε ἄπειρον οὔτε κινούμενον οὔτε ἠρεμοῦν Ξενοφάνην τὸν Κολοφώνιον τὸν Παρμενίδου διδάσκαλον ὑποτίθεσθαί φησιν ὁ Θεόφραστος ὁμολογῶν ἑτέρας εἶναι μᾶλλον ἢ τῆς περὶ φύσεως ἱστορίας τὴν μνήμην τῆς τούτου δόξης.

τὸ γὰρ ἓν τοῦτο καὶ πᾶν τὸν θεὸν ἔλεγεν ὁ Ξενοφάνης· ὃν ἕνα μὲν δείκνυσιν ἐκ τοῦ πάντων κράτιστον εἶναι. πλειόνων γάρ, φησίν, ὄντων ὁμοίως ὑπάρχειν ἀνάγκη πᾶσι τὸ κρατεῖν· τὸ δὲ πάντων κράτιστον καὶ ἄριστον θεός.

ἀγένητον δὲ ἐδείκνυεν ἐκ τοῦ δεῖν τὸ γινόμενον ἢ ἐξ ὁμοίου ἢ ἐξ ἀνομοίου γίνεσθαι· ἀλλὰ τὸ μὲν ὅμοιον

---

[1] It has often been doubted that Theophrastus could have been the author of a doxography that, probably combining the

XENOPHANES

R2 (< A30) Aristotle, *Metaphysics*

Xenophanes, the first of those [scil. together with Parmenides and Melissus] to have taught the One [. . .].

R3 (< A8) Clement of Alexandria, *Stromata*

Xenophanes of Colophon is the founder of the Eleatic school [. . .].

The Eleatization of Xenophanes (R4–R11)

R4 (< A31) Theophrastus in Simplicius, *Commentary on Aristotle's* Physics

Theophrastus says that Xenophanes of Colophon, the teacher of Parmenides, supposes that the principle is one, or that what is and the whole are one, and that it is neither limited nor unlimited, nor moving nor at rest; and he [i.e. Theophrastus] agrees that recording this man's opinion belongs to a different field of research rather than to the one concerning nature.[1]

For Xenophanes said of this one and whole that it is god. He demonstrated that he is one on the basis of the fact that he is the strongest of all: for, he says, if there were more than one, ruling would necessarily belong to all of them in a similar way; but god is the strongest and best of all.

He demonstrated that he is ungenerated on the basis of the fact that what comes about must come about either

Platonic tradition of Xenophanes' Eleatic filiation (cf. **R1**) with the naiveté noted by Aristotle (in **R12**), attributes theses to Xenophanes that he certainly never maintained.

ἀπαθές φησιν ὑπὸ τοῦ ὁμοίου· οὐδὲν γὰρ μᾶλλον γεννᾶν ἢ γεννᾶσθαι προσήκει τὸ ὅμοιον ἐκ τοῦ ὁμοίου· εἰ δὲ ἐξ ἀνομοίου γίνοιτο, ἔσται τὸ ὂν ἐκ τοῦ μὴ ὄντος. καὶ οὕτως ἀγένητον καὶ ἀίδιον ἐδείκνυ.

οὔτε δὲ ἄπειρον οὔτε πεπερασμένον εἶναι, διότι ἄπειρον μὲν τὸ μὴ ὂν ὡς οὔτε ἀρχὴν ἔχον οὔτε μέσον οὔτε τέλος, περαίνειν δὲ πρὸς ἄλληλα τὰ πλείω.

παραπλησίως δὲ καὶ τὴν κίνησιν ἀφαιρεῖ καὶ τὴν ἠρεμίαν. ἀκίνητον μὲν γὰρ εἶναι τὸ μὴ ὄν· οὔτε γὰρ ἂν εἰς αὐτὸ ἕτερον οὔτε αὐτὸ πρὸς ἄλλο ἐλθεῖν· κινεῖσθαι δὲ τὰ πλείω τοῦ ἑνός· ἕτερον γὰρ εἰς ἕτερον μεταβάλλειν,[1] ὥστε καὶ ὅταν ἐν ταὐτῷ μένειν λέγῃ καὶ μὴ κινεῖσθαι [. . . = **D19**], οὐ κατὰ τὴν ἠρεμίαν τὴν ἀντικειμένην τῇ κινήσει μένειν αὐτό φησιν, ἀλλὰ κατὰ τὴν ἀπὸ κινήσεως καὶ ἠρεμίας ἐξῃρημένην μονήν [. . . = **R5**].

[1] μεταβάλλειν Usener post Karsten: μεταβάλλει mss.

R5 (< A31) Simpl. *In Phys.*, p. 23.14–20

[. . . = **R4**] Νικόλαος δὲ ὁ Δαμασκηνὸς ὡς ἄπειρον καὶ ἀκίνητον λέγοντος αὐτοῦ τὴν ἀρχὴν ἐν τῇ Περὶ θεῶν [Frag. 1 Drossaart Lulofs] ἀπομνημονεύει, Ἀλέξανδρος δὲ ὡς πεπερασμένον αὐτὸ καὶ σφαιροειδές· ἀλλ᾽ ὅτι

---

[1] The attribution, found frequently in the doxography, of sphericity to Xenophanes' god goes back perhaps to Aristotle, if

from what is similar or from what is dissimilar. But he says that what is similar cannot be affected by what is similar, for it is not more appropriate for the similar to generate than to be generated out of what is similar. And if it came about from the dissimilar, then being would come from not-being. And in this way he demonstrated that he is ungenerated and eternal.

And that he is neither unlimited nor limited, since on the one hand unlimited is what does not exist, as it has neither a beginning nor a middle nor an end, and on the other hand what makes a limit with regard to one another is a plurality of things.

In the same way he abolishes both motion and rest. For immobile is what does not exist, for neither could something else go toward it nor could it go toward something else; and what moves is a plurality of things more than one, for one thing exchanges its place with another. So that when he says that he stays in the same place and does not move [. . . = **D19**], he says that it stays at rest not in the sense of that rest which is opposed to motion, but in the sense of motionlessness deprived of motion and rest [. . .].

R5 (< A31) Simplicius, *Commentary on Aristotle's* Physics

[. . .] Nicolaus of Damascus asserts in his *On Gods* that he [i.e. Xenophanes] says that the principle is unlimited and motionless, while Alexander says that it is limited and spherical.[1] But it is clear from what has been said earlier

it is admitted that Xenophanes conceived his god by referring to the totality of the world (cf. **R12**) and that the world is spherical (what is not the case for Xenophanes, cf. **D22 [3]** and **D31**).

μὲν οὔτε ἄπειρον οὔτε πεπερασμένον αὐτὸ δείκνυσιν,
ἐκ τῶν προειρημένων δῆλον· πεπερασμένον δὲ καὶ
σφαιροειδὲς αὐτὸ διὰ τὸ πανταχόθεν ὅμοιον λέγειν.
καὶ πάντα νοεῖν δέ φησιν αὐτὸ λέγων [. . . = **D18**].

R6 (< A28) Ps.-Arist. *MXG* 3.1–11 977a13–b19

[1] ἀδύνατόν φησιν εἶναι, εἴ τι ἔστι, γενέσθαι, τοῦτο
λέγων [977a14] ἐπὶ τοῦ θεοῦ· ἀνάγκη γὰρ ἤτοι ἐξ
ὁμοίου ἢ ἐξ ἀνομοίου [a15] γενέσθαι τὸ γενόμενον·
δυνατὸν δὲ οὐδέτερον· οὔτε γὰρ ὅμοιον ὑφ᾽ ὁμοίου
προσήκειν τεκνωθῆναι μᾶλλον ἢ τεκνῶσαι (ταὐτὰ
γὰρ ἅπαντα τοῖς γε ἴσοις καὶ ὁμοίως ὑπάρχειν πρὸς
ἄλληλα) οὔτ᾽ ἂν ἐξ ἀνομοίου τἀνόμοιον γενέσθαι. [2]
εἰ γὰρ γίγνοιτο ἐξ ἀσθενεστέρου τὸ ἰσχυρότερον ἢ ἐξ
ἐλάττονος τὸ [a20] μεῖζον ἢ ἐκ χείρονος τὸ κρεῖττον,
ἢ τοὐναντίον τὰ χείρω ἐκ τῶν κρειττόνων, τὸ οὐκ ὂν
ἐξ ὄντος[1] ἂν γενέσθαι, ὅπερ ἀδύνατον. ἀίδιον μὲν οὖν
διὰ ταῦτα εἶναι τὸν θεόν.

[3] εἰ δ᾽ ἔστιν ὁ θεὸς [a23] ἁπάντων κράτιστον, ἕνα
φησὶν αὐτὸν προσήκειν εἶναι. εἰ γὰρ δύο ἢ πλείους
εἶεν, οὐκ ἂν ἔτι κράτιστον καὶ βέλτιστον αὐτὸν [a25]
εἶναι πάντων. ἕκαστος γὰρ ὢν θεὸς τῶν πολλῶν
ὁμοίως ἂν τοιοῦτος εἴη. τοῦτο γὰρ θεὸν καὶ θεοῦ δύναμιν εἶναι, κρατεῖν, ἀλλὰ μὴ κρατεῖσθαι, καὶ πάντων

multa menda quae praesertim in ms. R exhibentur omittimus   [1] ὄντος ‹ἢ τὸ ὂν ἐξ οὐκ ὄντος› Brandis: τὸ ὂν ἐξ
οὐκ ὄντος Gomperz

that he demonstrates that it is neither unlimited nor limited, but that he says that it is limited and spherical since it is similar in every direction. And he says that it thinks all things, saying [... = **D18**].

R6 (< A28) Ps.-Aristotle, *On Melissus, Xenophanes, and Gorgias*

[1] He says that is it impossible, if something exists, for it to come about, saying this with regard to god. For it is necessary that what comes about come about either from what is similar or from what is dissimilar. But neither of these is possible. For it is suitable neither that what is similar be engendered by what is similar any more than that it engender it (for, at least for things that are equal, all things are the same, and with regard to one another they are in a similar way) nor could the dissimilar come about out of what is dissimilar. [2] For if the stronger came about from the weaker or the larger from the smaller or the better (*kreitton*) from the worse, or if inversely worse things came about from better ones, then what is not would come about from what is—which is impossible. For these reasons god is eternal.

[3] But if god is the strongest (*kratiston*) of all things, he says that it is suitable that he be one. For if there were two or more, he would no longer be the strongest and best of them all. For each of the many ones, being a god, would be like this in the same way. For this is what a god and the power of a god is, to dominate (*kratein*) and not to be dominated, and to be the strongest of all. So that to the

κράτιστον² εἶναι. ὥστε καθὸ μὴ κρείττων, κατὰ τοσοῦτον μὴ εἶναι θεόν. [4] πλειόνων οὖν ὄντων, εἰ μὲν
εἶεν τὰ μὲν ἀλλήλων κρείττους τὰ δὲ [a30] ἥττους, οὐκ
ἂν εἶναι θεούς· πεφυκέναι γὰρ τὸ θεῖον μὴ κρατεῖσθαι. [5] ἴσων δὲ ὄντων, οὐκ ἂν ἔχειν θεοῦ³ φύσιν,
⟨ὃν⟩⁴ δεῖν εἶναι⁵ κράτιστον· τὸ δὲ ἴσον οὔτε βέλτιον
οὔτε χεῖρον εἶναι τοῦ ἴσου. ὥστ᾽ εἴπερ εἴη τε καὶ
τοιοῦτον εἴη θεός, ἕνα μόνον εἶναι τὸν θεόν. οὐδὲ γὰρ
οὐδὲ πάντα δύνασθαι ἂν ἃ βούλοιτο. οὐ [a35] γὰρ ἂν
δύνασθαι πλειόνων ὄντων· ἕνα ἄρα εἶναι μόνον.

[6] ἕνα δ᾽ [a36] ὄντα ὅμοιον εἶναι πάντῃ, ὁρῶντα καὶ
ἀκούοντα⁶ τάς τε ἄλλας αἰσθήσεις ἔχοντα πάντῃ· εἰ
γὰρ μή, κρατεῖν ἂν καὶ κρατεῖσθαι ὑπ᾽ ἀλλήλων τὰ
μέρη θεοῦ ὄντα,⁷ ὅπερ ἀδύνατον.

[7] πάντῃ δ᾽ ὅμοιον ὄντα σφαιροειδῆ εἶναι· οὐ γὰρ
τῇ μὲν τῇ [977b1] δ᾽ οὐ τοιοῦτον εἶναι, ἀλλὰ πάντῃ.

[8] ἀίδιον δὲ ὄντα καὶ ἕνα [b2] καὶ⁸ σφαιροειδῆ οὔτε
ἄπειρον οὔτε πεπεράνθαι. ἄπειρον μὲν ὃ μὴ ὂν εἶναι·
τοῦτο γὰρ οὔτε μέσον οὔτε ἀρχὴν καὶ τέλος οὔτ᾽ ἄλλο
οὐδὲν μέρος ἔχειν, τοιοῦτον δὲ εἶναι τὸ ἄπειρον· οἷον
[b5] δὲ τὸ μὴ ὄν, οὐκ ἂν εἶναι τὸ ὄν· περαίνειν δὲ πρὸς
ἄλληλα, εἰ πλείω εἴη. τὸ δὲ ἓν οὔτε τῷ οὐκ ὄντι οὔτε
τοῖς πολλοῖς ὡμοιῶσθαι· ἓν γὰρ οὐκ ἔχειν,⁹ πρὸς ὅτι
περανεῖ.

---

² πάντα κρατεῖσθαι mss., corr. Karsten   ³ θεὸν mss.,
corr. Bonitz   ⁴ ⟨ὂν⟩ Diels   ⁵ θεοῦ φύσιν ⟨οὐδένα· τὸν
μὲν γὰρ θεὸν τὴν φύσιν⟩ δεῖν εἶναι Apelt

XENOPHANES

degree that he is not stronger, he is not god either. [4] So on the hypothesis that they are a plurality, if they were stronger in some regards but less so in others, they would not be gods; for what is divine has the nature of not being dominated. [5] And if they were equal, they would not have the nature of god, who must be the strongest; but what is equal is neither better nor worse than what is equal. So that if god really exists and if he is like this, god is only one. For [scil. otherwise] he would not be able to do all the things he wanted to do; for he would not be able to, if they were a plurality. So he is only one.

[6] Being one, he is similar everywhere, and he sees and hears and possesses the other senses everywhere. For otherwise, his parts, being [scil. parts] of a god, would dominate and be dominated by each other—which is impossible.

[7] Being similar everywhere, he is spherical in shape: for he is not this here but not there, but everywhere.

[8] Being eternal, one, and spherical in shape, he is not any more unlimited than he is limited. For unlimited is what does not exist; for this possesses neither a middle nor a beginning nor an end nor any other part, and the unlimited is like this. But what exists could not be what does not exist. And things would not limit one another unless they were a plurality. But the one is similar neither to what does not exist nor to what is a plurality. For the one does not possess anything against which it is limited.

---

⁶ ὁρᾶν τε καὶ ἀκουεῖν mss., corr. Wendland Diels ⁷ ὄντα del. ⁸ καὶ ⟨ὅμοιον καὶ⟩ Wendland ⁹ ἔχει mss., corr. Bonitz

[9] τὸ δὴ τοιοῦτον [b8] ἕν, ὃν τὸν θεὸν εἶναι λέγει, οὔτε κινεῖσθαι οὔτε ἀκίνητον εἶναι· ἀκίνητον μὲν γὰρ εἶναι τὸ μὴ ὄν· οὔτε γὰρ ἂν [b10] εἰς αὐτὸ ἕτερον οὔτ' ἐκεῖνο εἰς ἄλλο ἐλθεῖν. κινεῖσθαι δὲ τὰ πλείω ὄντα ἑνός· ἕτερον γὰρ εἰς ἕτερον δεῖν κινεῖσθαι. εἰς μὲν οὖν τὸ μὴ ὂν οὐδὲν ἂν κινηθῆναι· [10] τὸ γὰρ μὴ ὂν [b13] οὐδαμῇ εἶναι. εἰ δὲ εἰς ἄλληλα μεταβάλλοι, πλείω ἂν τὸ ὂν[10] εἶναι ἑνός. διὰ ταῦτα δὴ κινεῖσθαι μὲν ἂν τὰ δύο ἢ πλείω [b15] ἑνός, ἠρεμεῖν δὲ καὶ ἀκίνητον εἶναι τὸ οὐδέν. [11] τὸ δὲ ἓν οὔτε ἀτρεμεῖν οὔτε κινεῖσθαι· οὔτε γὰρ τῷ μὴ ὄντι οὔτε τοῖς πολλοῖς ὅμοιον εἶναι.

κατὰ πάντα δὲ οὕτως ἔχοντα[11] τὸν θεόν, ἀίδιόν τε καὶ ἕνα, ὅμοιόν τε καὶ σφαιροειδῆ ὄντα, οὔτε ἄπειρον οὔτε πεπερασμένον οὔτε ἠρεμοῦντα[12] οὔτε κινητὸν[13] εἶναι. [. . . = **R14**]

[10] ἂν τὸ ὄν (vel ἕν) Karsten: αὐτὸν mss.   [11] ἔχεις vel ἔχοις mss., corr. Diels post Apelt   [12] ἠρεμεῖν mss., corr. Diels   [13] ἀκίνητον mss., corr. Fülleborn

R7 (A37) Aët. 2.4.11 (Stob.) [εἰ ἄφθαρτος ὁ κόσμος]

Ξενοφάνης Παρμενίδης Μέλισσος ἀγένητον καὶ ἀίδιον καὶ ἄφθαρτον τὸν κόσμον.

R8

a (< A1) Diog. Laert. 9.19

[. . . = **D24**] οὐσίαν θεοῦ σφαιροειδῆ, μηδὲν ὅμοιον ἔχουσαν ἀνθρώπῳ [= **D20**].

[9] But a one like this, which he says is god, neither moves nor is immobile. For immobile is what does not exist; for neither could something else go toward it nor could it go toward something else. And what moves are things that are more than one; for it is necessary that one thing move toward another. So nothing could move toward what does not exist; [10] for what does not exist exists nowhere. But if things exchange places with one another, then what exists would be more than one. For these reasons two things or more than one could move, while what could rest and be immobile is nothing. [11] But the one does not rest any more than it moves; for it is similar neither to what does not exist nor to what are many.

And god being in this way in all these regards, he is eternal and one, similar and spherical, is neither unlimited nor limited, neither resting nor in motion. [. . .]

R7 (A37) Aëtius

Xenophanes, Parmenides, Melissus: the world is ungenerated, eternal, and indestructible.

R8

a (< A1) Diogenes Laertius

[. . .] the substance of god is spherical, and it possesses nothing similar to a human [. . .].

b (> A4) Cic. *Acad.* 2.118

Xenophanes paulo etiam antiquior unum esse omnia, neque id esse mutabile, et id esse deum neque natum umquam et sempiternum, conglobata figura.

R9 (cf. A32) Ps.-Plut. *Strom.* 4 (Eus. *PE* 1.8.4)

Ξενοφάνης δὲ ὁ Κολοφώνιος, ἰδίαν τινὰ ὁδὸν πεπορευμένος καὶ παρηλλαχυῖαν πάντας τοὺς προειρημένους, οὔτε γένεσιν οὔτε φθορὰν ἀπολείπει, ἀλλ' εἶναι λέγει τὸ πᾶν ἀεὶ ὅμοιον. εἰ γὰρ γίγνοιτο τοῦτο, φησίν, ἀναγκαῖον πρὸ τούτου μὴ εἶναι· τὸ μὴ ὂν δὲ οὐκ ἂν γένοιτο οὐδ' ἂν τὸ μὴ ὂν ποιῆσαι τι οὔτε ὑπὸ τοῦ μὴ ὄντος γένοιτ' ἄν τι. ἀποφαίνεται δὲ καὶ τὰς αἰσθήσεις ψευδεῖς καὶ καθόλου σὺν αὐταῖς καὶ αὐτὸν τὸν λόγον διαβάλλει. [. . . = **D23**] ἀποφαίνεται δὲ καὶ περὶ θεῶν ὡς οὐδεμιᾶς ἡγεμονίας ἐν αὐτοῖς οὔσης· οὐ γὰρ ὅσιον δεσπόζεσθαί τινα τῶν θεῶν· ἐπιδεῖσθαί τε μηδενὸς αὐτῶν μηδένα μηδ' ὅλως· ἀκούειν δὲ καὶ ὁρᾶν καθόλου καὶ μὴ κατὰ μέρος [. . .].

R10 (< A49) Aristocl. *Philos.* 7 (Eus. *PE* 14.17.1)

οἴονται γὰρ δεῖν τὰς μὲν αἰσθήσεις καὶ τὰς φαντασίας καταβάλλειν, αὐτῷ δὲ μόνῳ τῷ λόγῳ πιστεύειν· τοιαῦτα γάρ τινα πρότερον μὲν Ξενοφάνης καὶ Παρ-

XENOPHANES

b (> A4) Cicero, *Prior Academics*

Xenophanes, who is even a little earlier [scil. than Anaxagoras, said] that all things are one, and that this does not change, and that it is a god who is never born and is eternal, of a spherical shape.

R9 (cf. A32) Ps.-Plutarch, *Stromata*

Xenophanes of Colophon went his own way, one that differed from all of those we mentioned earlier [i.e. Thales, Anaximander, Anaximenes]: he accepts neither generation nor destruction, but says that the whole is always similar. For, he says, if it were generated, then necessarily it would not have existed earlier; but what does not exist could not come about, nor could what does not exist make anything nor could anything come about from the action of what does not exist. And he asserts that the senses are deceptive, and in general he also slanders, together with them, reason itself.[1] [. . .] And he asserts about the gods that there is no supremacy among them, for it would not be in conformity with piety for one of the gods to be subject to a master; and that none stands in need of any of them or of anything at all; and that he hears and sees as a whole and not in some part [. . .].

[1] This last phrase goes in the direction of the Skeptical interpretation (cf. **R15–R23**); contrast **R10**.

R10 (< A49) Aristocles, *On Philosophy*

For they [i.e. the philosophers Aristocles is about to mention] think that perceptions and representations (*phantasiai*) must be rejected and that trust must be placed in reason alone. For Xenophanes, Parmenides, Zeno, and

μενίδης καὶ Ζήνων καὶ Μέλισσος ἔλεγον [. . .]. ὅθεν ἠξίουν οὗτοί γε τὸ ὂν ἓν εἶναι καὶ τὸ ἕτερον μὴ εἶναι, μηδὲ γεννᾶσθαί τι μηδὲ φθείρεσθαι μηδὲ κινεῖσθαι τὸ παράπαν.

R11 (< A36) Theod. *Cur.* 4.5

Ξενοφάνης [. . .], ὁ τῆς Ἐλεατικῆς αἱρέσεως ἡγησάμενος, ἓν εἶναι τὸ πᾶν ἔφησε, σφαιροειδὲς καὶ πεπερασμένον, οὐ γενητόν, ἀλλ᾽ ἀίδιον καὶ πάμπαν ἀκίνητον. πάλιν δ᾽ αὖ τῶνδε τῶν λόγων ἐπιλαθόμενος, ἐκ τῆς γῆς φῦναι ἅπαντα εἴρηκεν. αὐτοῦ γὰρ δὴ τόδε τὸ ἔπος ἐστίν· [. . . = **D27**].

Peripatetic Criticisms (R12–R14)

R12 (< A30) Arist. *Metaph.* A5 986b18–27

Παρμενίδης μὲν γὰρ ἔοικε τοῦ κατὰ τὸν λόγον ἑνὸς ἅπτεσθαι, Μέλισσος δὲ τοῦ κατὰ τὴν ὕλην (διὸ καὶ ὁ μὲν πεπερασμένον ὁ δ᾽ ἄπειρόν φησιν εἶναι αὐτό)· Ξενοφάνης δὲ [. . . cf. **P10, R2**] οὐθὲν διεσαφήνισεν, οὐδὲ τῆς φύσεως τούτων οὐδετέρας ἔοικε θιγεῖν, ἀλλ᾽ εἰς τὸν ὅλον οὐρανὸν ἀποβλέψας τὸ ἓν εἶναί φησι τὸν θεόν.[1] οὗτοι μὲν οὖν, καθάπερ εἴπομεν, ἀφετέοι πρὸς τὴν νῦν ζήτησιν, οἱ μὲν δύο καὶ πάμπαν ὡς ὄντες μικρὸν ἀγροικότεροι, Ξενοφάνης καὶ Μέλισσος [. . . cf. **PARM. R12**].

[1] τὸν θεόν E: om. A[b]

Melissus were the first to say things of this sort [...]. That is why these thought that what exists is one and that what is other does not exist, and that nothing comes about or perishes or moves at all.

R11 (< A36) Theodoret, *Cure of the Greek Maladies*

Xenophanes [...], who was the originator of the Eleatic sect, said that the whole is one, spherical, and limited, not generated, but eternal and entirely motionless. Then, forgetting these statements, he said that all things are generated out of earth; for this verse is his: [... = **D27**].

Peripatetic Criticisms (R12–R14)

R12 (<A30) Aristotle, *Metaphysics*

Parmenides seems to have treated of the one according to definition, and Melissus according to matter; that is why the former says that it is limited, the latter that it is unlimited [cf. **PARM. D8.47; MEL. D3–D5**]. But Xenophanes [...] said nothing that was clear, nor does he seem to have touched upon the nature of either of these [scil. the definition of the form and matter], but with reference to the whole world (*ouranos*) he says that the one is god.[1] So, as we have said, for the purposes of the present investigation [scil. the investigation of the first causes], these men [i.e. Xenophanes, Parmenides, and Melissus] should be disregarded—and two of them, Xenophanes and Melissus, completely, since they are a bit too unsophisticated [...].

[1] Or "god is the one." Cf. **D16.**

R13 (< A47)

a Arist. *Cael.* 2.13 294a21–24

οἱ μὲν γὰρ διὰ ταῦτα ἄπειρον τὸ κάτω τῆς γῆς εἶναί φασιν, ἐπ᾽ ἄπειρον αὐτὴν ἐρριζῶσθαι λέγοντες,[1] ὥσπερ Ξενοφάνης ὁ Κολοφώνιος, ἵνα μὴ πράγματ᾽ ἔχωσι ζητοῦντες τὴν αἰτίαν.

[1] ἐπ᾽ . . . λέγοντες H et recc.: om. EJ

b Simpl. *In Cael.*, p. 522.7–11

ἀγνοῶ δὲ ἐγὼ τοῖς Ξενοφάνους ἔπεσι τοῖς περὶ τούτου μὴ ἐντυχών, πότερον τὸ κάτω μέρος τῆς γῆς ἄπειρον εἶναι λέγων διὰ τοῦτο μένειν αὐτήν φησιν ἢ τὸν ὑποκάτω τῆς γῆς τόπον καὶ αἰθέρα ἄπειρον καὶ διὰ τοῦτο ἐπ᾽ ἄπειρον καταφερομένην τὴν γῆν δοκεῖν ἠρεμεῖν· οὔτε γὰρ ὁ Ἀριστοτέλης διεσάφησεν [. . .].

R14 (< A28) Ps.-Arist. *MXG* 4 977b21–979a9

[. . . = **R6**] [1] πρῶτον μὲν οὖν λαμβάνει τὸ γιγνόμενον καὶ οὗτος ἐξ ὄντος γίγνεσθαι, ὥσπερ ὁ Μέλισσος. καίτοι τί κωλύει μήτ᾽ ἐξ ὁμοίου ⟨μήτ᾽ ἐξ ἀνομοίου⟩[1] τὸ γιγνόμενον γίγνεσθαι ἀλλ᾽ ἐκ μὴ ὄντος; ἔτι οὐδὲν μᾶλλον ὁ θεὸς ἀγένητος ἢ καὶ τἆλλα πάντα, εἴπερ ἅπαντα ἐξ ὁμοίου ἢ ἐξ[2] ἀνομοίου γέγονεν (ὅπερ ἀδύ-

multa menda quae praesertim in ms. R exhibentur omittimus   [1] add. Brandis   [2] ἢ ἐξ Apelt ut vid.: ἢ καὶ ἐξ L: ἢ R

XENOPHANES

R13 (< A47)

a Aristotle, *On the Heavens*

It is for this reason that some people state that the lower part of the earth is unlimited, saying that its roots go to the unlimited, like Xenophanes of Colophon: the reason is so that they don't have the trouble of searching for the cause.

b Simplicius, *Commentary on Aristotle's* On the Heavens

Since I could not find the verses of Xenophanes on this subject, I do not know whether he says that it is because the lower part of the earth is unlimited that the earth is at rest, or because the space below the earth and the aether are unlimited that the earth, which goes down to the unlimited, seems to be at rest. For neither has Aristotle made this clear [. . .].

R14 (< A28) Ps.-Aristotle, *On Melissus, Xenophanes, and Gorgias*

[. . .] [1] First then, he too, like Melissus, assumes that what comes about comes about from what is. And yet what prevents what comes about from coming about neither from the similar ‹nor from the dissimilar›, but from what is not? Furthermore, if indeed all things come about from the similar or from the dissimilar, god would no more be ungenerated than all other things—but this is impossible.

EARLY GREEK PHILOSOPHY III

νατον)· ὥστε ἢ οὐδέν ἐστι παρὰ τὸν θεὸν ἢ καὶ τὰ ἄλλα ἀίδια πάντα.

[2] ἔτι κράτιστον τὸν θεὸν λαμβάνει, τοῦτο δυνατώτατον καὶ βέλτιστον λέγων· οὐ δοκεῖ δὲ τοῦτο κατὰ τὸν νόμον, ἀλλὰ πολλὰ κρείττους εἶναι ἀλλήλων οἱ θεοί. οὐκ οὖν ἐκ τοῦ δοκοῦντος εἴληφε ταύτην κατὰ τοῦ θεοῦ τὴν ὁμολογίαν.

[3] τό τε κράτιστον εἶναι τὸν θεὸν οὐχ οὕτως ὑπολαμβάνειν[3] λέγεται,[4] ὡς πρὸς ἄλλο τι τοιαύτη ἡ τοῦ θεοῦ φύσις, ἀλλὰ πρὸς τὴν αὐτοῦ διάθεσιν, ἐπεί τοί γε πρὸς ἕτερον οὐδὲν ἂν κωλύοι μὴ τῇ αὐτοῦ ἐπικρατείᾳ[5] καὶ ῥώμῃ ὑπερέχειν, ἀλλὰ διὰ τὴν τῶν ἄλλων ἀσθένειαν. θέλοι δ' ἂν οὐδεὶς οὕτω τὸν θεὸν φάναι κράτιστον εἶναι, ἀλλ' ὅτι αὐτὸς ἔχει ὡς οἷόν τε ἄριστα, καὶ οὐδὲν ἐλλείπει καὶ εὖ καὶ καλῶς ἔχειν αὐτῷ· ἅμα[6] γὰρ ἴσως ⟨οὕτως⟩[7] ἔχοντι κἀκεῖνο ἂν συμβαίνοι. [. . .]

[6] ἔτι τοιοῦτος ὢν διὰ τί σφαιροειδὴς ἂν εἴη, ἀλλ' οὐχ[8] ἑτέραν τινὰ μᾶλλον ἔχων ἰδέαν, ὅτι πάντῃ ἀκούει καὶ πάντῃ κρατεῖ; ὥσπερ γὰρ ὅταν λέγωμεν τὸ ψιμύθιον ὅτι πάντῃ ἐστὶ λευκόν, οὐδὲν ἄλλο σημαίνομεν ἢ ὅτι ἐν ἅπασιν αὐτοῦ τοῖς μέρεσιν ἐγκέχρωσται ἡ λευκότης· τί δὴ κωλύει οὕτως κἀκεῖ τὸ πάντῃ ὁρᾶν καὶ ἀκούειν καὶ κρατεῖν λέγεσθαι, ὅτι ἅπαν ὃ ἄν τις

[3] ὑπολαμβάνων mss., corr. Vahlen
[4] ἐνδέχεται Vahlen
[5] ἐπικρατείᾳ Diels: ἐπιεικείᾳ mss. Wendland
[6] ἄλλα Bergk: ἄριστα
[7] ⟨οὕτως⟩ Wilson mss.: del. Karsten
[8] ὅτι post οὐχ habent

So that either there is nothing else besides god, or else all the other things are eternal.

[2] Furthermore, he assumes that god is the most powerful (*kratiston*), meaning by this the one that has the most power (*dunatôtaton*) and is the best. But this does not seem to be in accordance with usage, but rather the gods are thought to be superior (*kreittous*) to one another in many ways. So it is not from customary opinion that he took this point as established.

[3] He is said to assume that god is the most powerful not in the sense that the nature of god would be this with regard to something else, but rather with regard to its own condition, since in that case nothing would prevent his being superior not by his own supremacy and force, but by the weakness of the others. But no one would wish to say that it is in this sense that he has stated that god is most powerful, but because he exists in the best possible condition, and lacks nothing for existing perfectly well; for if he is in a condition ⟨like this one⟩, then doubtless this [i.e. being the most powerful] will accrue to him too. [. . .]

[6] Furthermore, if he is like this, for what reason would he be spherical and not possess instead some other shape, because he hears in every part and dominates in every part? For when we say of white lead that it is white in every part, we only mean that whiteness is its color in all of its parts. If so, then what prevents it from being the case there too that he sees, hears, and dominates in every part in the sense that, whatever part of him one might take, it

αὑτοῦ λαμβάνῃ μέρος, τοῦτ᾽ ἔσται πεπονθός; ὥσπερ δὲ οὐδὲ τὸ ψιμύθιον, οὐδὲ τὸν θεὸν ἀνάγκη εἶναι διὰ τοῦτο σφαιροειδῆ.

[7] ἔτι μήτε ἄπειρον ‹εἶναι›[9] μήτε πεπεράνθαι σῶμά γε ὄν[10] καὶ ἔχον[11] μέγεθος πῶς οἷόν τε, εἴπερ τοῦτ᾽ ἐστὶν ἄπειρον ὃ ἂν μὴ ἔχῃ πέρας δεκτικὸν ὂν πέρατος, πέρας δ᾽ ἐν μεγέθει καὶ πλήθει ἐγγίγνεται καὶ ἐν ἅπαντι τῷ ποσῷ, ὥστε εἰ μὴ ἔχει πέρας μέγεθος ὂν ἄπειρόν ἐστιν;

[8] ἔτι δὲ σφαιροειδῆ ὄντα ἀνάγκη πέρας ἔχειν· ἔσχατα γὰρ ἔχει, εἴπερ μέσον ἔχει αὐτοῦ, οὗ πλεῖστον ἀπέχει. μέσον δὲ ἔχει σφαιροειδὲς ὄν·[12] τοῦτο γάρ ἐστι σφαιροειδὲς ὃ ἐκ τοῦ μέσου ὁμοίως πρὸς τὰ ἔσχατα. σῶμα δ᾽ ἔσχατα ἢ πέρατα ἔχειν, οὐδὲν διαφέρει.[13] [. . .]

[13] ἔτι τί κωλύει πεπεράνθαι καὶ ἔχειν πέρατα ἓν ὄντα τὸν θεόν; ὡς καὶ ὁ Παρμενίδης λέγει ἓν ὂν εἶναι αὐτὸν

πάντοθεν εὐκύκλου σφαίρας ἐναλίγκιον ὄγκῳ,
μεσσόθεν ἰσοπαλές [. . . = **PARM. D8.48–49**].

τὸ γὰρ πέρας τινὸς μὲν ἀνάγκη[14] εἶναι, οὐ μέντοι πρός τί γε, οὐδὲ ἀνάγκη τὸ ἔχον πέρας πρός τι ἔχειν πέρας, ὡς πεπερασμένον πρὸς τὸ ἐφεξῆς[15] ἄπειρον,[16] ἀλλ᾽

---

[9] εἶναι Karsten: εἶ L, μήτε corr. L[1]   [10] ὂν Bekker: ὦν L: om. R   [11] ἔχον R: ἔχων L   [12] σφαιροειδὴς ὢν Diels   [13] οὐδὲν διαφέρει Bergk: οἷον διαφέρει L: οἷος διαφορεῖ R   [14] ἀνάγκῃ ἴσως R: ἀνάγκην L

will have these properties? But just as little as for the white lead, it is not necessary that god have for this reason a spherical shape.

[7] Further, how is it possible that, being a body and having a magnitude, he be neither unlimited nor limited, since that is unlimited which does have a limit but is capable of receiving a limit, and a limit comes about in a magnitude and a plurality and in everything that is quantitative? So that if he does not have a limit, although he is a magnitude, he is unlimited?

[8] Furthermore, if he is spherical, he must necessarily have a limit: for he has extremities, if indeed he has his own center from which they are most distant. But he has a center, since he is spherical: for what has the same distance from its center to its extremities is spherical; and for a body, to have extremities or limits does not differ at all [...].

[13] Furthermore, what prevents god, if he is one, from being limited and having limits, as Parmenides says that, being one, he is

> On every side, similar to the volume of a well-rounded ball,
> Everywhere balanced equally starting from its center
> [... = **PARM. D8.48–49**]?

For it is necessary that the limit be of something, but not necessarily with regard to something, and it is not necessary that what has a limit have a limit with regard to something, like what is limited with regard to the unlimited that is contiguous, but to be limited is to possess extremities,

---

¹⁵ μὴ ante ἐφεξῆς habent mss.: del. Mullach   ¹⁶ ἄπειρον Mullach: ἀπείρου mss.: ὡς ... ἀπείρου del. Wilson

ἔστι τὸ πεπεράνθαι ἔσχατα ἔχειν, ἔσχατα δ' ἔχον οὐκ ἀνάγκη πρός τι ἔχειν. [. . .]

[15] πάλιν περὶ τοῦ ἀκίνητον εἶναι τὸ ὄν [. . .]· ἆρά γε οὐ ταὐτὸ ἄν τις ὑπολάβοι τὸ μὴ κινεῖσθαι καὶ τὸ ἀκίνητον εἶναι, ἀλλὰ τὸ μὲν ἀπόφασιν τοῦ[17] κινεῖσθαι [. . .], τὸ δὲ ἀκίνητον τῷ ἔχειν πως ἤδη λέγεσθαι [. . .]. [18] ἔτι εἰ καὶ διὰ τοῦτο μὴ κινεῖται ὁ θεός τε καὶ τὸ ἕν, ὅτι τὰ πολλὰ κινεῖται τῷ εἰς ἄλληλα ἰέναι, τί κωλύει καὶ τὸν θεὸν κινεῖσθαι εἰς ἄλλο; οὐδα‹μοῦ γὰρ λέγει›[18] ὅτι ‹ἕν ἐστι› μόνον,[19] ἀλλ' ὅτι εἷς μόνος θεός. [19] εἰ δὲ καὶ οὕτως,[20] τί κωλύει εἰς ἄλληλα κινουμένων τῶν μερῶν τοῦ ‹θεοῦ›[21] κύκλῳ φέ‹ρεσθαι τὸν›[22] θεόν; οὐ γὰρ δὴ τὸ τοιοῦτον ἕν, ὥσπερ ὁ Ζήνων, πολλὰ εἶναι φήσει. αὐτὸς γὰρ σῶμα λέγει εἶναι τὸν θεόν, εἴτε τόδε τὸ πᾶν εἴτε ὅ τι δήποτε αὐτὸ λέγων· ἀσώματος γὰρ ὢν πῶς ἂν σφαιροειδὴς εἴη;

[17] τοῦ Bekker: τῷ L: om. R   [18] et [19] suppl. Kern: οὐδα (lac. X litt. L, V litt. R) ὅτι (τι R) (lac. VII litt. L, V litt. R) μόνον (μον R) mss.   [20] οὕτως Apelt: οὗτος L: αὐτὸς R   [21] θεοῦ Bergk post Apelt: lac. V litt. mss.   [22] add. Bergk: φε (lac. VII litt.) L: om. R

The Skeptical Tradition (R15–R23)
Xenophanes' Special Role in Timon of Phlius'
Mockeries (Silloi) *(R15–R16)*

R15 (≠ DK) Diog. Laert. 9.111 (= Timo Frag. 1 Di Marco)

τῶν δὲ Σίλλων τρία ἐστίν, ἐν οἷς ὡς ἂν Σκεπτικὸς ὢν

but what possesses extremities does not necessarily possess them with regard to something. [...]

[15] Once again, on the question of the motionlessness of what is [...]: would one not assume that not to move and to be immobile are not identical, but rather that the one is the negation of moving [...], while one speaks of "being immobile" if the thing possesses this in a certain way [...]?
[...]

[18] Further, even if the reason why god and the one do not move is because it is a plurality of things that move by going toward one another, what prevents god too from moving toward something else? For ⟨he nowhere says⟩ that he ⟨is⟩ only ⟨one⟩, but only that he is the only god.

[19] But even if this is so, what prevents ⟨god's⟩ parts from ⟨moving⟩ toward one another while god moves in a circle? For he certainly will not say, like Zeno, that a one like this is multiple. For he himself says that god is a body, whether he means by that this totality or something else; for if he were bodiless, how could he be spherical?

The Skeptical Tradition (R15–R23)
Xenophanes' Special Role in Timon of Phlius'
Mockeries (Silloi) *(R15–R16)*

R15 (≠ DK) Diogenes Laertius

Of the *Mockeries* [*Silloi*] there are three [scil. books] in which, being a Skeptic, he [i.e. Timon] reviles and mocks

πάντας λοιδορεῖ καὶ σιλλαίνει τοὺς δογματικοὺς ἐν
παρῳδίας εἴδει. ὧν τὸ μὲν πρῶτον αὐτοδιήγητον ἔχει
τὴν ἑρμηνείαν, τὸ δὲ δεύτερον καὶ τρίτον ἐν διαλόγου
σχήματι. φαίνεται γοῦν ἀνακρίνων Ξενοφάνη τὸν
Κολοφώνιον περὶ ἑκάστων, ὁ δ' αὐτῷ διηγούμενός
ἐστι· καὶ ἐν μὲν τῷ δευτέρῳ περὶ τῶν ἀρχαιοτέρων, ἐν
δὲ τῷ τρίτῳ περὶ τῶν ὑστέρων.

R16 (< A35) Sext. Emp. *Pyrrh. Hyp.* 1.224

ἐν πολλοῖς γὰρ αὐτὸν ἐπαινέσας,[1] ὡς καὶ τοὺς Σίλλους αὐτῷ ἀναθεῖναι, ἐποίησεν αὐτὸν ὀδυρόμενον καὶ
λέγοντα [Frag. 59 Di Marco]

> ὡς καὶ ἐγὼν ὄφελον πυκινοῦ νόου ἀντιβολῆσαι
> ἀμφοτερόβλεπτος·[2] δολίῃ δ' ὁδῷ ἐξαπατήθην
> πρεσβυγενὴς ἔτ' ἐὼν καὶ ἀμενθήριστος[3] ἁπάσης
> σκεπτοσύνης. ὅππῃ[4] γὰρ ἐμὸν νόον εἰρύσαιμι,
> εἰς ἓν ταὐτό τε πᾶν ἀνελύετο· πᾶν δ' ἐὸν αἰεί
> πάντῃ ἀνελκόμενον μίαν εἰς φύσιν ἵσταθ' ὁμοίην.

διὰ τοῦτο γοῦν καὶ ὑπάτυφον αὐτὸν λέγει, καὶ οὐ
τέλειον ἄτυφον, δι' ὧν φησι [Frag. 60 Di Marco]

> Ξεινοφάνης ὑπάτυφος, Ὁμηραπάτης ἐπικόπτης,[5]

[1] τὸν Ξενοφάνην post ἐπαινέσας mss., del. Kayser [2] ἀμ-
φοτερόβλεπτος LM: ἀμφοτερόβλεπτα EAB: ἀμφοτεροβλέ-
πτου dubit. Bekker [3] ἀμενθήριστος Bergk: ἀπενθήριστος
mss. [4] ὅππῃ Fabricius (ut vid.): ὅπη ML: ὅπου EAB

XENOPHANES

all the dogmatic philosophers in the form of a parody. In the first one he speaks in the first person, the second and third ones are in the form of dialogue. For he introduces himself questioning Xenophanes of Colophon about each of them, and the latter describes them for him, in the second book the more ancient ones, in the third the more recent ones.

R16 (< A35) Sextus Empiricus, *Outlines of Pyrrhonism*

For after he [i.e. Timon] had praised him [i.e. Xenophanes] in many passages, to the point of dedicating his *Mockeries* [*Silloi*] to him, he represented him lamenting and saying,

> If only I too had gotten a share of a solid intelligence
> And looked at both sides. But I was fooled by a deceitful method,
> Since I was born long ago and did not bother about any kind of
> Examination. For in whatever direction I directed my mind,
> Everything dissolved into one and the same thing: all that exists,
> Drawn in every direction, always became immobile in a single, similar nature.

This is why he calls him "not too arrogant" and not entirely "without arrogance," when he says,

> Xenophanes, not too arrogant, censor of Homer's deceit,

---

⁵ ἐπικόπτης edd.: ἐπικόπτην Diog. Laert. 9.18: ἐπισκώπτην mss.

ἐκτὸς[6] ἀπ' ἀνθρώπων θεὸν ἐπλάσατ' ἶσον ἁπάντῃ,
<ἀτρεμῆ>[7] ἀσκηθῆ νοερώτερον[8] ἠὲ νόημα.

ὑπάτυφον μὲν γὰρ εἶπε τὸν κατά τι ἄτυφον, ὁμηραπάτης δὲ ἐπισκώπτην, ἐπεὶ τὴν παρ' Ὁμήρῳ ἀπάτην διέσυρεν [. . . = **R21a**].

[6] ἐκτὸς Fabricius: ἐκτὸν N: ἔκ τὸν Par. suppl. 133: ἔα τὸν cett.: εἰ τὸν Diels: ὃς τὸν Roeper   [7] <ἀτρεμῆ> Diels

[8] νοερώτερον Diels: νοερωτὸν mss.

Was Xenophanes Skeptical or Dogmatic? (R17–R22)

R17 (< A25) Cic. *Acad.* 2.74

Parmenides Xenophanes [. . . = **R27**] increpant eorum adrogantiam quasi irati, qui cum sciri nihil possit audeant se scire dicere.

R18 (< A49) Aët. 4.9.1 (Stob.) [εἰ ἀληθεῖς αἱ αἰσθήσεις καὶ φαντασίαι]

[. . .] Ξενοφάνης [. . .] ψευδεῖς εἶναι τὰς αἰσθήσεις.

R19 (< A1) Diog. Laert. 9.20

φησὶ δὲ Σωτίων [Frag. 29 Wehrli] πρῶτον αὐτὸν εἰπεῖν ἀκατάληπτα εἶναι τὰ πάντα, πλανώμενος.

Fashioned a god far from humans, everywhere equal,
⟨Untrembling,⟩ unscathed, more thoughtful than
  thought.

For he called him "not too arrogant" inasmuch as he was free of arrogance in a certain regard, and an insulter of Homer's deceit since he despised the deceit found in Homer.

*Was Xenophanes Skeptical or
Dogmatic? (R17–R22)*

R17 (< A25) Cicero, *Prior Academics*

Parmenides and Xenophanes [. . .] attack, almost in anger, the arrogance of those who dare to say that they know, when nothing can be known.

R18 (< A49) Aëtius

[. . .] Xenophanes [. . .]: sense perceptions are deceptive.

R19 (< A1) Diogenes Laertius

Sotion says, mistakenly, that he was the first to say that all things are inapprehensible.

EARLY GREEK PHILOSOPHY III

R20 (< A33) (Ps.-?) Hippol. *Ref.* 1.14.1

[. . . = **P7**] οὗτος ἔφη πρῶτος ἀκαταληψίαν εἶναι πάντων, εἰπὼν οὕτως· [. . . = **D49.3–4** with a textual variant].

R21 Sext. Emp.

a (cf. A35) *Pyrrh. Hyp.* 1.225

[. . . = **R16**] ἐδογμάτιζε δὲ ὁ Ξενοφάνης παρὰ τὰς τῶν ἄλλων ἀνθρώπων προλήψεις ἓν εἶναι τὸ πᾶν, καὶ τὸν θεὸν συμφυῆ τοῖς πᾶσιν, εἶναι δὲ σφαιροειδῆ καὶ ἀπαθῆ καὶ ἀμετάβλητον καὶ λογικόν· ὅθεν καὶ ῥᾴδιον τὴν Ξενοφάνους πρὸς ἡμᾶς διαφορὰν ἐπιδεικνύναι.

b (≠ DK) *Adv. Math.* 7.48–50

Ξενοφάνης μὲν κατά τινας εἰπὼν πάντα ἀκατάληπτα ἐπὶ ταύτης ἔστη τῆς φορᾶς, ἐν οἷς γράφει [. . . = **D49**]. διὰ τούτων γὰρ σαφὲς μὲν ἔοικε λέγειν τἀληθὲς καὶ τὸ γνώριμον [. . .] ἄνδρα δὲ τὸν ἄνθρωπον, τῷ εἰδικῷ καταχρώμενος ἀντὶ τοῦ γένους [. . .].

c (≠ DK) *Adv. Math* 7.110

Ξενοφάνης δὲ κατὰ τοὺς ὡς ἑτέρως αὐτὸν ἐξηγουμένους, ὅταν λέγῃ [. . . = **D49**] φαίνεται μὴ πᾶσαν κατά-

XENOPHANES

R20 (< A33) (Ps.-?) Hippolytus, *Refutation of All Heresies*

[...] He was the first to assert the inapprehensibility of all things, when he said the following: [... = **D49.3–4** with a textual variant].

R21 Sextus Empiricus

a (cf. A35) *Outlines of Pyrrhonism*

[...] Xenophanes affirmed dogmatically, against the conceptions of all other humans, that the whole is one, that god is [scil. consubstantially] mixed with the nature of all things, and that he is spherical, impassive, unchangeable, and rational; from this it follows that it is easy to indicate the difference between Xenophanes and us [i.e. Pyrrhonian Skeptics].

b (≠ DK) *Against the Logicians*

[...] Xenophanes, according to some people, adopts this position [scil. the one that abolishes the criterion] when he says that all things are inapprehensible, in the verses where he writes, [... = **D49**]. For in these verses he seems to mean by "clear" what is true and known [...] and by "man" the human being, using the specific term instead of the general one [...]

c (≠ DK) *Against the Logicians*

According to those who interpret Xenophanes differently [scil. from **R21b**], when he says, [... = **D49**] he does not

103

ληψιν ἀναιρεῖν ἀλλὰ τὴν ἐπιστημονικὴν καὶ ἀδιάπτωτον, ἀπολείπειν δὲ τὴν δοξαστήν· τοῦτο γὰρ ἐμφαίνει τὸ "**δόκος δ' ἐπὶ πᾶσι τέτυκται**" [= **D49.4**] ὥστε κριτήριον γίνεσθαι κατὰ τοῦτον τὸν δοξαστὸν λόγον, τουτέστι τὸν τοῦ εἰκότος ἀλλὰ μὴ τὸν τοῦ παγίου ἐχόμενον.

R22 (A35) Ps.-Gal. *Hist. phil.* 7

[. . .] Ξενοφάνην μὲν περὶ πάντων ἠπορηκότα, δογματίσαντα δὲ μόνον τὸ εἶναι πάντα ἓν καὶ τοῦτο ὑπάρχειν θεὸν πεπερασμένον λογικὸν ἀμετάβλητον [. . .].

An Epicurean Criticism of Xenophanes'
Theology (R23)

R23 (A34) Cic. *Nat. deor.* 1.28

tum Xenophanes, qui mente adiuncta omne praeterea, quod esset infinitum, deum voluit esse, de ipsa mente item reprehenditur[1] ut ceteri, de infinitate autem vehementius, in qua nihil neque sentiens neque coniunctum potest esse.

[1] reprehenditur*NOB²FM*: reprehendetur*dett.*: reprehenderet *B¹*: reprehenderetur *AC*

seem to abolish all apprehension whatsoever but only that which is scientific and infallible, and to accept that which is probable; for this is what is shown by the phrase **"opinion is set upon all things"** [= **D49.4**], so that according to him what the criterion is is reason belonging to opinion, i.e. the reason of what is probable, and not the one that possesses solidity.

R22 (A35) Ps.-Galen, *Philosophical History*

[. . .] Xenophanes was in aporia about all things, and held as his only dogmatic view that all things are one and that this is god, who is limited, rational, and changeless [. . .].

See also **R10**

An Epicurean Criticism of Xenophanes' Theology (R23)

R23 (A34) Cicero, *On the Nature of the Gods*

[Velleius, an Epicurean:] Next, Xenophanes, who claimed that god, once the mind has been added, is everything else, which is unlimited, is refuted in the same way as all the others concerning the mind itself, but more severely concerning the unlimited, for in this there can be nothing that either perceives or is connected.

EARLY GREEK PHILOSOPHY III

A Problem of Interpretation: Does Everything Come from Earth According to Xenophanes? (R24–R26)
Aristotle's Report (R24)

R24 (cf. ad A36) Arist. *Metaph.* A8 989a3–10

τοιοῦτον δὲ καὶ τῶν ἄλλων ἕκαστος ὁμολογεῖ τὸ στοιχεῖον εἶναι τὸ τῶν σωμάτων· οὐθεὶς γοῦν ἠξίωσε τῶν ὕστερον καὶ ἓν λεγόντων γῆν εἶναι στοιχεῖον, δηλονότι διὰ τὴν μεγαλομέρειαν, τῶν δὲ τριῶν ἑκάστου στοιχείων εἴληφέ κριτήν τινα, οἱ μὲν γὰρ πῦρ οἱ δ' ὕδωρ οἱ δ' ἀέρα τοῦτ' εἶναί φασιν· καίτοι διὰ τί ποτ' οὐ καὶ τὴν γῆν λέγουσιν, ὥσπερ οἱ πολλοὶ τῶν ἀνθρώπων [. . .];

The Disagreement of the Traditions (R25–R26)

R25 (< A36)

a Theod. *Cur.* 4.5

[. . . cf. **R11**] ἐκ τῆς γῆς φῦναι ἅπαντα εἴρηκεν. αὐτοῦ γὰρ δὴ τόδε τὸ ἔπος ἐστίν· [. . . = **D27**].

b Ps.-Olymp. *Ars sacra* 24

τὴν [. . .] γῆν οὐδεὶς ἐδόξασεν εἶναι ἀρχήν, εἰ μὴ Ξενοφάνης ὁ Κολοφώνιος.

XENOPHANES

*A Problem of Interpretation: Does Everything
Come from Earth According to
Xenophanes? (R24–R26)
Aristotle's Report (R24)*

R24 (cf. ad A36) Aristotle, *Metaphysics*

Each of the others [scil. besides those who take the fire as the primary material element, i.e. essentially Heraclitus] recognizes that the element of bodies is like this [i.e. very fine]; at least none of those who are later and who say that there is only one[1] has judged that earth is the element, evidently because of the thickness of its texture, while each of the three elements has found a judge in its favor, for some people say that it is fire, others water, and others air. But then why do they not also mention earth, like most people? [. . .].[2]

[1] On the basis of these indications one can maintain that Aristotle is deliberately setting aside Xenophanes. [2] Aristotle goes on to attribute to Hesiod the idea that the Earth is born first of all; this is not strictly true, cf. **COSM. T11.1–2**.

The Disagreement of the Traditions (R25–R26)

R25 (< A36)

a Theodoret, *Cure of the Greek Maladies*

[. . .] he said that all things are born out of earth; for this verse is his: [. . . = **D27**].

b Ps.-Olympiodorus, *On the Sacred Art*

No one has held the view that earth is a principle except Xenophanes of Colophon.

R26 (A36) Gal. *In Hipp. Nat. hom.* 1.2

κακῶς δὲ καὶ τῶν ἐξηγητῶν ἔνιοι κατεψεύσαντο Ξενοφάνους, ὥσπερ καὶ Σαβῖνος, ὡδί πως γράψας αὐτοῖς ὀνόμασιν. "οὔτε γὰρ τὸ πάμπαν ἀέρα λέγω τὸν ἄνθρωπον, ὥσπερ Ἀναξιμένης, οὔτε ὕδωρ ὡς Θαλῆς, οὔτε γῆν ὡς ἔν τινι Ξενοφάνης." οὐδαμόθι γὰρ εὑρίσκεται Ξενοφάνης ἀποφηνάμενος οὕτως. [. . .] καὶ Θεόφραστος δ᾽ ἂν ἐν ταῖς τῶν Φυσικῶν δοξῶν ἐπιτομαῖς τὴν Ξενοφάνους δόξαν, εἴπερ οὕτως εἶχεν, ἐγεγράφει [Frag. 231 FSH&G].

Judgments on Xenophanes' Poetry (R27–R29)

R27 (< A25) Cic. *Acad.* 2.74

Parmenides Xenophanes minus bonis quamquam versibus sed tamen illi versibus [. . . = **R17**].

R28 (cf. A26) Phil. *Prov.*, ed. Aucher

a 2.39, pp. 74.31–44, 75.1–2

Այլ եւ ոչ Քսենոփանէս, եւ կամ Պարմենիդէս, եւ կամ Եմպեդոկլէս, կամ որք միանգամ այլք աստուածաբանք, ըմբռնեցան ի քերթողականութենէ աստուածաբանելը. այլ սակայն տեսութիւն գրնութեանս խնդութեամբ ընկալեալք, եւ առ հասարակ զամենայն իրեանց կեանսն ի բարեպաշտութիւն եւ ի գովութիւն աստուածոցն նուիրեալք՝ բարի արք եղեն, բայց

XENOPHANES

R26 (A36) Galen, *Commentary on Hippocrates' On the Nature of Man*

And some of the interpreters have lied badly about Xenophanes, like Sabinus, who writes in his own words, "For neither do I say that a human being is entirely air, like Anaximenes, or water, like Thales, or earth, like Xenophanes somewhere." For nowhere is Xenophanes found to be asserting this. [. . .] And Theophrastus would have included Xenophanes' opinion in his summaries of physical opinions, if this had been the case.

Judgments on Xenophanes' Poetry (R27–R29)

R27 (< A25) Cicero, *Prior Academics*

Parmenides and Xenophanes, although in less good verses [scil than Empedocles'], but nonetheless in verses [. . .].

R28 (cf. A26) Philo of Alexandria, *On Providence*

a

But neither Xenophanes, nor Parmenides, nor Empedocles, nor any other theologian was possessed by poetry as if he had been divinely inspired; nevertheless, embracing the observation of this nature with joy, and dedicating their whole lives entirely to piety and the glory of the gods, they turned out to be good men, but not gifted poets. They

քերթողք ոչ բախտաւորք: զորս պարտ էր ի վերուստ
շունչ ընկալեալ շնորհի ի յերկնէ, չափս, նուագս,
մատունս երկնաւոր եւ աստուածային, իբր ձշմարիտ
քերթուածս թողուլ՝ իբր սկզբնատիպ զրոյն կատարեալ,
եւ զեղեցիկ ցոյց այլոցն եղեալ:

b 2.42, p. 76.26–29

Արդ ընդէ՞ր Եմպեդոկլէս, եւ Պարմենիդէս, եւ
Քսենոփանէս, եւ հոմանախանձորդք նոցա պարք, ոչ
ընկալան հոգի Երաժշտաց՝ աստուածաբանելով:

R29 (A27) Athen. *Deipn.* 14.32 632C

ὅτι δὲ πρὸς τὴν μουσικὴν οἰκειότατα[1] διέκειντο οἱ ἀρχαῖοι δῆλον καὶ ἐξ Ὁμήρου· ὃς διὰ τὸ μεμελοποιηκέναι πᾶσαν ἑαυτοῦ τὴν ποίησιν ἀφροντιστὶ πολλοὺς[2] ἀκεφάλους ποιεῖ στίχους καὶ λαγαρούς, ἔτι δὲ μειούρους. Ξενοφάνης δὲ καὶ Σόλων καὶ Θέογνις καὶ Φωκυλίδης, ἔτι δὲ Περίανδρος ὁ Κορίνθιος ἐλεγειοποιὸς καὶ τῶν λοιπῶν οἱ μὴ προσάγοντες πρὸς τὰ ποιήματα μελῳδίαν ἐκπονοῦσι τοὺς στίχους τοῖς ἀριθμοῖς καὶ τῇ τάξει τῶν μέτρων[3] καὶ σκοποῦσιν ὅπως αὐτῶν μηθεὶς ⟨μήτε⟩[4] ἀκέφαλος ἔσται μήτε λαγαρὸς μήτε μείουρος.

[1] οἰκεότητα A, corr. Musurus   [2] τοὺς ante πολλοὺς del. Meineke   [3] post μέτρων suppl. e.g. τελείους Kaibel
[4] ⟨μήτε⟩ Meineke

would have had to receive inspiration from above, grace from Heaven, meters, harmonies, divine and heavenly dactyls, if they were to leave behind real poems, as a perfect prototype of writing that would also be a good model for others.

b

So why did Empedocles, Parmenides and Xenophanes and the crowd of their emulators not receive the inspiration of the Muses when discussing theology?[1]

[1] Both texts translated by Irene Tinti.

R29 (A27) Athenaeus, *Deipnosophists*

It is clear from the case of Homer too that the very ancient [scil. poets] were naturally disposed toward music: for since he composed all his poetry to be sung, he thoughtlessly makes many verses that have a short syllable instead of a long one at the beginning of the first foot, or that display the same feature in a middle foot or at the end of the verse. By contrast, Xenophanes, Solon, Theognis, Phocylides, and also Periander of Corinth, the elegiac poet, and all those who do not add a melody to their poems, polish off their verses in conformity with the numbers and order of the metrical feet and take care that none of them is irregularly shortened at either the beginning, the middle, or the end.

Xenophanes in The Assembly of Philosophers *(R30)*

R30 (≠ DK) *Turba Phil.* Sermo IX, p. 82.1–8 Plessner

ait Eximenus: quod Deus suo verbo omnia creavit, quibus dixit: estote, et facta sunt cum aliis quatuor elementis, terra, aqua, aere et igne, quae invicem copulavit, et commixta sunt inimica. videmus enim ignem aquae inimicum esse et aquam igni, et utrumque terrae et aeri. Deus tamen ea pace copulavit, quousque ad invicem dilecta sunt. ex his igitur quatuor elementis omnia creata sunt, coelum, thronus, angeli, sol, luna, stellae, terra et mare ac omnia, quae in mari sunt, quae varia sunt et non similia, quorum naturas Deus diversas fecit, sicut et creationes.

XENOPHANES

Xenophanes in The Assembly of Philosophers *(R30)*

R30 (≠ DK) *The Assembly of Philosophers*

Eximenus [i.e. probably Xenophanes[1]] said: "God created all things through His Word: He said to them, 'Be!' and they came to be, together with the other four elements, earth, water, air, and fire, which He conjoined reciprocally, and the things that were hostile were mixed together. For we see that fire is hostile to water and water to fire, and both of them to earth and air. Nonetheless, God conjoined them together in peace, so that they are reciprocally amicable. Thus out of these four elements all things were created: heaven, the throne, the angels, the sun, the moon, the stars, the earth, and the sea, and everything that is in the sea. All these things are different and not similar, as God made their natures diverse, just like the creatures too."

[1] Identified as Xenophanes by Plessner, as Anaximenes by Ruska.

9. HERACLITUS [HER.]

Heraclitus' activity can be situated toward the end of the sixth century BC. The general form of his book is controversial: was it made up of a series of relatively independent reflections and maxims, as is rather suggested by the sentences or groups of sentences that are transmitted, and as is most often thought, or of a more unified text, indeed of a continuous argument, as is sometimes suggested? In any case, no proposed arrangement can seriously claim to reflect the original sequence of Heraclitus' book—notoriously, Diels, in despair at the many incompatible proposals that had already been put forward at his time, placed the fragments as far as possible in the alphabetical sequence of the authors who cited them. Our own order (like other, different ones before ours) aspires only to suggest possible associations and to gather together, for convenience of consultation, fragments that seem to form thematic groupings.

Heraclitus' work with the Greek language is remarkable and distinctive. Paradox, antithesis, etymology, semantic and syntactic ambiguity—all the features that led antiquity to speak of Heraclitus "the Obscure"—are put into the service of a mode of thought that undoes commonplace identifications and classifications. Whether this approach, which often takes on the appearance of a de-

nunciation, is subordinated to a critique of identity in general or is, on the contrary, in the service of a higher identity—called god or *logos*—is a question that already divided the ancient interpreters (Aristotle vs. the Stoics). In any case, Heraclitus is the early Greek philosopher who in antiquity became the object of the largest number of divergent interpretations—of which the most celebrated one remains that of Plato, who attributes to him a conception of becoming in perpetual "flux"—and even today he continues to fascinate and divide his readers.

BIBLIOGRAPHY

Editions

H. Diels, ed. *Herakleitos von Ephesos* (Berlin, 1901).

M. Marcovich, ed. *Heraclitus. Greek Text with a Short Commentary* (Merida, 1967; repr. Sankt Augustin, 2001).

———. *Eraclito. Frammenti* (Florence, 1978).

S. N. Mouraviev, ed. *Heraclitea. Édition critique complète des témoignages sur la vie et l'œuvre d'Héraclite et des vestiges de son livre* (Sankt Augustin, 1999–): 10 vols. published hitherto, including *Fragmenta: Traditio* in 4 vols. (II.A. 1–4), 1999–2003; *Recensio: Memoria* (III.1), 2003; *Recensio: Placita* (III.2), 2008; *Recensio: Fragmenta* (III.3. B/i), 2006; *Refectio* (IV.A), 2011.

T. M. Robinson, ed. *Heraclitus: Fragments* (Toronto, 1987).

EARLY GREEK PHILOSOPHY III

Studies

C. H. Kahn. *The Art and Thought of Heraclitus* (Cambridge, 1979).

OUTLINE OF THE CHAPTER

P

Father, City, Chronology (P1–P2)
Royal Family (P3)
Teachers (P4–P5)
Political Activity (P6–P8)
Character (P9–P12)
   Arrogance (P9–P10)
   Melancholy (P11–P12)
Book (P13)
Sayings (P14–P15)
Death (P16–P17)
Iconography (P18)

D

From Near the Beginning of Heraclitus' Book (D1–D2)
Axiological Considerations (D3–D28)
   Most People Do Not Understand (D3–D9)
   The Best Are Few (D10–D14)
   Against Accepted Views and Practices (D15–D28)
     Against Conventional Religion (D15–D18)
     Against Various Men (D19–D28)
       Against Men Accepted as Wise (D19–D20)
       On Homer (and Archilochus) (D21–D24)
       On Hesiod (D25)
       On Thales (THAL. R1)

On Pythagoras (D26)
　　　On Someone Else? (D27)
　　　A Global Condemnation (D28)
Epistemological Considerations (D29–D45)
　　All Humans Think (D29–D30)
　　The Senses as Sources of Knowledge (D31–D34)
　　Acquiring Knowledge (D35–D40)
　　The Enigmatic Expression of Knowledge (D41–D42)
　　What Is Wisdom? (D43–D45)
Fundamental Principles (D46–D88)
　　All Things Are One (D46)
　　The Opposites (D47–D81)
　　　The Unity of Opposites (D47–D62)
　　　War (D63–D64)
　　　Flux (D65–D66)
　　　Cyclical Alternation of Opposites (D67–D72)
　　　Divine Perspective, Human Perspective (D73–D77)
　　　Animal Perspectives, Human Perspective (D78–D81)
　　Cosmic Fire (D82–D88)
Parts of the World and Physical Phenomena (D89–D97)
　　The Sun (D89–D91)
　　The Moon (D92)
　　The Stars (D93–D95)
　　Meteorological Phenomena (D96–D97)
　　A Doxographical Presentation of Heraclitus' Physics (cf. R46)
Human Beings (D98–D123)
　　The Soul (D98–D104)
　　Human Laws (D105–D110)
　　Human Behavior (D111–D117)
　　Eschatological Considerations (D118–D123)

R

Heraclitus' Book: Commentaries, Form, Contents (R1–R14)
   Attested Ancient Commentaries (R1–R2)
   Characterizations of the Contents of Heraclitus' Book (R3–R4)
   Heraclitus the Obscure (R5–R14)
      Characterizations of His Style (R5–R11)
      Two Examples of Divergent Interpretations of an Aphorism (R12–R13)
      A Facetious Falsification (R14)

Reception of Heraclitus' Doctrine (R15–R92)
   Parody and Allusion in (Ps.–?) Epicharmus (DRAM. T5–T8)
   A Polemic in Parmenides? (R15)
   Hippocratic Adaptations of Heraclitean Ideas and Language (MED. T9–T12)
   The Heracliteans (R16–R26)
      Heraclitus' Reputation (R16)
      Plato on the Heracliteans (R17–R18)
      A Report by Aristotle on the Heracliteans (R19)
      Reports by a Peripatetic on the Heracliteans (R20–R21)
      Cratylus (R22–R26)
   Heraclitus in the Derveni Papyrus (DERV. Col. 4)
   Plato (R27–R34)
      Plato's Debt to Heraclitus and the Heracliteans (R27–R28)
      Discussions and Utilizations of Heraclitus' Doctrines in Plato (R29–R34)
         On the Doctrine of Flux (R29–R30)
         On Unity and Multiplicity (R31)

HERACLITUS

    A Criticism of the Doctrine of Fitting-Together (R32)
    On the Doctrine of Multiple Perspectives (R33)
    An Application to Old Age (R34)
Summaries and Criticisms in Aristotle (R35–R43)
    On Cosmic Fire (R35)
    On the Doctrine of Flux (R36)
    On the Coexistence of Opposites (R37–R39)
    On the Identity of Opposites (R40–R41)
    On Belief and Knowledge (R42)
    On the Soul (R43)
Doxographies of Platonic-Peripatetic Inspiration (R44–R46)
    A Systematization in Terms of Contraries (R44)
    Two Systematizations in Terms of Physics (R45–R46)
Reports Reflecting a Platonic-Aristotelian Appropriation (R47–R49)
    Motion (R47)
    The Soul (R48)
    The Heavens (D49)
Stoics (R50–R66)
    Stoic Appropriations (R50–R56)
        Zeno (R50–R51)
        Cleanthes (R52)
        Chrysippus (R53)
        Marcus Aurelius (R54–R55)
        An Anonymous Paraphrase (R56)
    Some Characteristic Stoic Doctrines Linked with Heraclitus (R57–R66)
        Various Subjects (R57)
        Human Reason, Divine Reason (R58–R60)
        Cosmic Fire (R61–R63)

The Great Year (R64)
Evaporations (R65)
Human Development (R66)
Epicurean Polemics (R67–R69)
Heraclitus Among the Skeptics (R70–R73)
Aenesidemus: Skepticism Leads to Heraclitus (R70–R71)
Sextus Empiricus: Heraclitus Was Not a Skeptic (R72–R73)
Philo: Heraclitus' Doctrines Derive from the Hebrew Bible (R74–R76)
Christian Appropriations and Polemics (R77–R87)
Justin Martyr (R77)
Tatian (R78)
Clement of Alexandria (R79–R85)
(Ps.–?) Hippolytus (R86)
Theodoret (R87)
Neoplatonic Appropriations (R88–R92)
Plotinus (R88–R89)
Porphyry (R90)
Iamblichus (R91)
Proclus (R92)
Invective, Praise, and Variations on Heraclitean Themes in Greek Poetry and Literature (R93–R99)
Scythinus of Teos (R93)
Timon of Phlius (R94)
Epigrams (R95–R98)
Theodoridas (R95)
Meleager (?) (R96)
Anonymous Epigrams (R97–R98)
A Parody (R99)

HERACLITUS

The Text of Heraclitus: Some Examples of Multiple Versions of the Same Phrase (R100–R102)
  "A Nature Tends to Hide." (= D35) (R100)
  "A Dry Soul: Wisest and Best." (= D103) (R101)
  "It Is Better to Hide One's Ignorance." (= D113) (R102)
Doubtful and Pseudepigraphic Texts (R103–R117)
  Variations of Heraclitean Aphorisms Attributed to Democrates or Democritus (R103–R107)
  Other Doubtful Aphorisms (R108–R116)
  Selections from an Apocryphal Correspondence (R117)

HERACLITUS [22 DK]

P

Father, City, Chronology (P1–P2)

P1 (< A1) Diog. Laert. 9.1, 3

[1] Ἡράκλειτος Βλόσωνος ἤ, ὥς τινες, Ἡράκωντος,[1] Ἐφέσιος. οὗτος ἤκμαζε μὲν κατὰ τὴν ἐνάτην καὶ ἑξηκοστὴν Ὀλυμπιάδα. [. . .] [3] ἐτελεύτα βιοὺς ἔτη ἑξήκοντα.

[1] Ἡρακίωντος vel -ίοντος mss., corr. Keil

P2 (< A1a) *Suda* H.472

Ἡράκλειτος Βλόσωνος ἢ Βαύτωρος, οἱ δὲ Ἡρακῖνος,[1] Ἐφέσιος, [. . .] ἦν δὲ ἐπὶ τῆς ξθ΄ Ὀλυμπιάδος, ἐπὶ Δαρείου τοῦ Ὑστάσπου [. . .].

[1] Ἡρακῖνος mss.: Ἡρακῶντος Keil: Ἡρακίωνος coni. Adler

HERACLITUS

P

Father, City, Chronology (P1–P2)

P1 (< A1) Diogenes Laertius

[1] Heraclitus, son of Bloson or, as some say, of Heracon, from Ephesus. He reached his full maturity during the 69th Olympiad [504/500 BC]. [. . .] [3] he died at the age of sixty [cf. **P16[3]**].

P2 (< A1a) *Suda*

Heraclitus, son of Bloson or of Bautor, others say of Heracis, from Ephesus. [. . .] He lived during the 69th Olympiad [504/500] during the time of Darius, son of Hystaspes [. . .].

EARLY GREEK PHILOSOPHY III

Royal Family (P3)

P3 (< A1) Diog. Laert. 9.6

[... cf. **P9[6]**] ἐκχωρῆσαι [...] τἀδελφῷ τῆς βασιλείας.

Teachers (P4–P5)

P4 (< A1) Diog. Laert. 9.5

ἤκουσέ τε οὐδενός, ἀλλ' αὐτὸν ἔφη διζήσασθαι[1] καὶ μαθεῖν πάντα παρ' ἑαυτοῦ. Σωτίων δέ φησιν [Frag. 30 Wehrli] εἰρηκέναι τινὰς Ξενοφάνους αὐτὸν ἀκηκοέναι [... = **P16[5]**].

[1] διζήσασθαι Casaubon: διζήσεσθαι PF: διαζήσεσθαι B[2] (ια in ras.): διζήσθαι Φh

P5 (< A1a) *Suda* H.472

οὗτος ἐμαθήτευσεν οὐδενὶ τῶν φιλοσόφων, φύσει δὲ καὶ ἐπιμελείᾳ ἠσκήθη. [... = **P17**] τινὲς δὲ αὐτὸν ἔφασαν διακοῦσαι Ξενοφάνους καὶ Ἱππάσου τοῦ Πυθαγορείου.

Political Activity (P6–P8)

P6 (< A1) Diog. Laert. 9.2–3

ἀξιούμενος δὲ καὶ νόμους θεῖναι πρὸς αὐτῶν ὑπερεῖδε διὰ τὸ ἤδη κεκρατῆσθαι τῇ πονηρᾷ πολιτείᾳ τὴν πόλιν. [3] ἀναχωρήσας δὲ εἰς τὸ ἱερὸν τῆς Ἀρτέμιδος

HERACLITUS

Royal Family (P3)[1]

P3 (< A1) Diogenes Laertius

He renounced the title of king in favor of his brother.

[1] According to the historian Pherecydes, cited by Strabo (*Geogr.* 14.3), the descendants of Androclus, the founder of Ephesus, were called by the title of kings and enjoyed certain distinctive honors.

Teachers (P4–P5)

P4 (< A1) Diogenes Laertius

He studied with no one, but he said that he searched for himself [cf. **D36**] and that he learned everything from himself. But Sotion says that some people said that he studied with Xenophanes [. . .].

P5 (< A1a) *Suda*

[. . .] He was not the disciple of any of the philosophers, but was educated by his [or: by] nature and diligence. [. . .] Some people said that he studied with Xenophanes and Hippasus the Pythagorean.

Political Activity (P6–P8)

P6 (< A1) Diogenes Laertius

When he was asked by them [i.e. the Ephesians] to give them laws, he scorned to do so, since the city was already dominated by its bad constitution. [3] And he withdrew

μετὰ τῶν παίδων ἠστραγάλιζε· περιστάντων δ' αὐτὸν τῶν Ἐφεσίων, "τί, ὦ κάκιστοι, θαυμάζετε;" εἶπεν· "ἢ οὐ κρεῖττον τοῦτο ποιεῖν ἢ μεθ' ὑμῶν πολιτεύεσθαι;"

P7 (< A3b) Plut. *Garr.* 17 511B

[. . .] ἀξιούντων αὐτὸν τῶν πολιτῶν γνώμην τιν' εἰπεῖν περὶ ὁμονοίας, ἀναβὰς ἐπὶ τὸ βῆμα καὶ λαβὼν ψυχροῦ κύλικα καὶ τῶν ἀλφίτων ἐπιπάσας καὶ τῷ γλήχωνι κινήσας ἐκπιὼν ἀπῆλθεν, ἐνδειξάμενος αὐτοῖς ὅτι τὸ τοῖς τυχοῦσιν ἀρκεῖσθαι καὶ μὴ δεῖσθαι τῶν πολυτελῶν ἐν εἰρήνῃ καὶ ὁμονοίᾳ διατηρεῖ τὰς πόλεις.

P8 (< A3) Clem. Alex. *Strom.* 1.65.4

Ἡράκλειτος γὰρ ὁ Βλύσωνος Μελαγκόμαν τὸν τύραννον ἔπεισεν ἀποθέσθαι τὴν ἀρχήν. οὗτος βασιλέα Δαρεῖον παρακαλοῦντα ἥκειν εἰς Πέρσας ὑπερεῖδεν.

Character (P9–P12)
Arrogance (P9–P10)

P9 (< A1) Diog. Laert. 9.1, 5, 6, 15

[1] μεγαλόφρων δὲ γέγονε παρ' ὁντιναοῦν καὶ ὑπερόπτης, ὡς καὶ ἐκ τοῦ συγγράμματος αὐτοῦ δῆλον, ἐν ᾧ φησι [. . . = **D20**]. εἶναι γὰρ **"ἓν τὸ σοφόν"** [. . . = **D44**]. [5] γέγονε δὲ θαυμάσιος ἐκ παίδων, ὅτε καὶ νέος ὢν ἔφασκε μηδὲν εἰδέναι, τέλειος μέντοι γενόμενος πάντα

into the temple of Artemis, where he spent his time playing dice with the children [cf. **D76**]; when the Ephesians gathered around him he asked, "Why are you surprised, you wretches? Is it not better to do this than to engage in politics with you?"

P7 (< A3b) Plutarch, *On Garrulity*

[...] when his fellow citizens asked him to give his opinion about concord, he went up to the rostrum, took a goblet of cold water, sprinkled some barley groats into it and stirred it with mint [cf. **D59**]; then he drank it out and went away—he had shown them that to be satisfied with one's circumstances and to feel no need for luxuries preserves cities in peace and concord.

P8 (< A3) Clement of Alexandria, *Stromata*

For Heraclitus, the son of Bloson, persuaded the tyrant Melancomas to relinquish his rule. He looked down upon King Darius, who invited him to come to Persia [cf. **R117**].

Character (P9–P12)
Arrogance (P9–P10)

P9 (< A1) Diogenes Laertius

[1] He was surpassingly haughty and contemptuous, as is clear from his book, in which he says, [... = **D20**]. For **"What is wise is one"** [... = **D44**]. [...] [5] He was astonishing from childhood, for when he was young, he said that he knew nothing, but, when he had grown up, he said

ἐγνωκέναι. [. . .] [6] σημεῖον δ' αὐτοῦ τῆς μεγαλοφροσύνης Ἀντισθένης φησὶν ἐν Διαδοχαῖς [FGrHist 508 F10 = Frag. 10 Giannattasio Andria]· ἐκχωρῆσαι γὰρ τἀδελφῷ τῆς βασιλείας. [. . .]· [15] Δημήτριος δέ φησιν ἐν τοῖς Ὁμωνύμοις [Frag. 27 Mejer] καὶ Ἀθηναίων αὐτὸν ὑπερφρονῆσαι, δόξαν ἔχοντα παμπλείστην, καταφρονούμενόν τε ὑπὸ τῶν Ἐφεσίων ἑλέσθαι μᾶλλον τὰ οἰκεῖα.

P10

a (< T143 Mouraviev) Arist. *EN* 7.5 1146b29–30

ἔνιοι γὰρ πιστεύουσιν οὐδὲν ἧττον οἷς δοξάζουσιν ἢ ἕτεροι οἷς ἐπίστανται· δηλοῖ δ' Ἡράκλειτος.

b (< T144 Mouraviev) Ps.-Arist. *MM* 2.6 1201b5–9

εἰ γὰρ ἔσται ἡ δόξα σφοδρὰ τῷ βέβαιον εἶναι καὶ ἀμετάπειστον, οὐθὲν διοίσει τῆς ἐπιστήμης [. . .], οἷον Ἡράκλειτος ὁ Ἐφέσιος τοιαύτην ἔχει δόξαν ὑπὲρ ὧν αὐτῷ ἐδόκει.

Melancholy (P11–P12)

P11 (< A1) Diog. Laert. 9.6 (= Theophr. Frag. 233 FHS&G)

Θεόφραστος δέ φησιν ὑπὸ μελαγχολίας [. . . cf. **R5c**].

that he knew everything. [. . .] [6] Antisthenes gives evidence in his *Successions* for his haughtiness: for he renounced the title of king in favor of his brother. [. . .] [15] Demetrius says in his *Homonyms* that he also looked down on the Athenians, so great was his renown, and that, being scorned by the Ephesians, he preferred his personal matters.

P10

a (≠ DK) Aristotle, *Nicomachean Ethics*

For certain people are not less convinced about their opinions than others are about their knowledge—[scil. the case of] Heraclitus shows this.

b (≠ DK) Ps.-Aristotle, *Magna Moralia*

For if an opinion is strong because it is firm and unshakeable, it will not at all differ from knowledge [. . .]. For example, Heraclitus of Ephesus has this kind of opinion about the things about which he held an opinion.

Melancholy (P11–P12)

P11 (< A1) Theophrastus in Diogenes Laertius

Theophrastus says that it was because of his melancholy [. . .].

EARLY GREEK PHILOSOPHY III

P12 (68 A21) Sotion Περὶ ὀργῆς in Stob. 3.20.53

τοῖς δὲ σοφοῖς ἀντὶ ὀργῆς Ἡρακλείτῳ μὲν δάκρυα, Δημοκρίτῳ δὲ γέλως ἐπῄει.

Book (P13)

P13 (< A1) Diog. Laert. 9.6

ἀνέθηκε δ' αὐτὸ εἰς τὸ τῆς Ἀρτέμιδος ἱερόν [. . . cf. **R5c**].

Sayings (P14–P15)

P14 (< A1) Diog. Laert. 9.12

φασὶ δὲ αὐτὸν ἐρωτηθέντα διὰ τί σιωπᾷ, φάναι "ἵν' ὑμεῖς λαλῆτε."

P15 (< A9) Arist. PA 1.4 645a17–21

καὶ καθάπερ Ἡράκλειτος λέγεται πρὸς τοὺς ξένους εἰπεῖν τοὺς βουλομένους ἐντυχεῖν αὐτῷ, οἳ ἐπειδὴ προσιόντες εἶδον αὐτὸν θερόμενον πρὸς τῷ ἰπνῷ, ἔστησαν (ἐκέλευε γὰρ αὐτοὺς εἰσιέναι θαρροῦντας· εἶναι γὰρ καὶ ἐνταῦθα θεούς), οὕτω καὶ [. . .].

HERACLITUS

P12 (68 A21) Sotion, *On Anger,* in Stobaeus, *Anthology*

Instead of becoming angry, Heraclitus, among the sages, was overcome by tears, and Democritus by laughter [cf. **ATOM. P46–P48**].

Book (P13)

P13 (< A1) Diogenes Laertius

He deposited it [scil. his book] in the temple of Artemis [. . .].

Sayings (P14–P15)

P14 (< A1) Diogenes Laertius

They say that when he was asked why he kept silent, he said, "So that you can chatter."

P15 (< A9) Aristotle, *Parts of Animals*

Just as what Heraclitus is reported to have said to strangers who wanted to meet him—they were approaching him, but they stopped when they saw that he was warming himself by the oven; but he told them not to hesitate but to enter, saying to them, "For there are gods here too"—so too [. . .].

EARLY GREEK PHILOSOPHY III

Death (P16–P17)

P16 (< A1) Diog. Laert. 9.3, 4, 5

[3] καὶ τέλος μισανθρωπήσας καὶ ἐκπατήσας ἐν τοῖς ὄρεσι διῃτᾶτο, πόας σιτούμενος καὶ βοτάνας. καὶ μέντοι καὶ διὰ τοῦτο περιτραπεὶς εἰς ὕδερον κατῆλθεν εἰς ἄστυ καὶ τῶν ἰατρῶν αἰνιγματωδῶς ἐπυνθάνετο εἰ δύναιντο ἐξ ἐπομβρίας αὐχμὸν ποιῆσαι· τῶν δὲ μὴ συνιέντων, αὐτὸν εἰς βούστασιν κατορύξας τῇ τῶν βολβίτων ἀλέᾳ ἤλπισεν ἐξατμισθήσεσθαι. οὐδὲν δὲ ἀνύων οὐδ' οὕτως, ἐτελεύτα βιοὺς ἔτη ἑξήκοντα. [. . .] [4] Ἕρμιππος δέ φησι [Frag. 29 Wehrli] λέγειν αὐτὸν τοῖς ἰατροῖς εἴ τις δύναται ἔντερα[1] ταπεινώσας[2] ὑγρὸν τ'[3] ἐξεράσαι· ἀπειπόντων δέ, θεῖναι αὐτὸν εἰς τὸν ἥλιον καὶ κελεύειν τοὺς παῖδας βολβίτοις καταπλάττειν· οὕτω δὴ κατατεινόμενον δευτεραῖον τελευτῆσαι καὶ ταφθῆναι ἐν τῇ ἀγορᾷ. Νεάνθης δ' ὁ Κυζικηνός φησι [FGrHist 84 F25] μὴ δυνηθέντα αὐτὸν ἀποσπάσαι τὰ βόλβιτα μεῖναι καὶ διὰ τὴν μεταβολὴν ἀγνοηθέντα κυνόβρωτον γενέσθαι. [. . .] [5] Σωτίων δέ φησιν [Frag. 30 Wehrli] [. . . = **P4**] λέγειν τε Ἀρίστωνα ἐν τῷ Περὶ Ἡρακλείτου καὶ τὸν ὕδερον αὐτὸν θεραπευθῆναι, ἀποθανεῖν δὲ ἄλλῃ νόσῳ. τοῦτο δὲ καὶ Ἱππόβοτός φησι [Frag. 20 Gigante].

[1] <τὰ> ἔντερα Cobet Cobet: κεινώσας Diels
[2] ταπεινώσας mss.: πιέσας
[3] ὑγρόν τ' Φh: ὑγρὸν BPF: <τὸ> ὑγρὸν Cobet

HERACLITUS

Death (P16–P17)

P16 (< A1) Diogenes Laertius

[3] In the end he became a misanthrope and withdrew, passing his time in the mountains and eating herbs and plants. But when he came down with dropsy because of this, he returned to the city and asked the doctors, with a riddle, whether they were capable of changing a rainstorm into a drought; they did not understand, so he buried himself in an ox stall, hoping that he would be dried out by the warmth of the manure. But he did not achieve anything in this way either, and he died at the age of sixty [cf. **P1**]. [...] [4] Hermippus says that he asked the doctors whether it was possible to reduce his intestines and their moisture by drying them out; when they said it was not, he placed himself in the sunlight and told his slaves to smear him with cow dung. Stretched out in this way, he died the next day and was buried in the agora. Neanthes of Cyzicus says that he stayed there because he could not tear off the cow dung himself and that, since he was unrecognizable because of his transformation, he was eaten by dogs. [...] [5] But Sotion says [...] that Ariston says in his *On Heraclitus* that he was cured of his dropsy too but died of a different disease; and Hippobotus says the same thing.

P17 (< A1a) *Suda* H.472

οὗτος ὑδρωπιάσας οὐκ ἐνεδίδου τοῖς ἰατροῖς ᾗπερ ἐβούλοντο θεραπεύειν αὐτόν· ἀλλ' αὐτὸς βολβίτῳ χρίσας ὅλον ἑαυτὸν εἴασε ξηρανθῆναι τοῦτο ὑπὸ τῷ ἡλίῳ, καὶ κείμενον αὐτὸν κύνες προελθοῦσαι διέσπασαν· οἱ δὲ ἄμμῳ χωσθέντα φασὶν ἀποθανεῖν.

HERACLITUS

P17 (< A1a) *Suda*

When he came down with dropsy, he did not allow the doctors to cure him in the way they wished, but he himself smeared his whole body with cow dung and let this be dried out by the sun; as he was lying there, dogs came upon him and tore him to pieces. Others say that he died covered in sand.

See also **R78**

Iconography (P18)

P18 (p. 144.25–30 and II, p. 3 DK) Richter I, pp. 80–81 and Figures 306–13; Richter-Smith pp. 127–29 and Figures 88–90; Koch, "Ikonographie," in Flashar, Bremer, Rechenauer (2013), I.1, pp. 223, 224.

HERACLITUS [22 DK]

D

From Near the Beginning of Heraclitus'
Book (D1–D2)

D1 (B1) Sext. Emp. *Adv. Math.* 7.132 (et al.)

ἐναρχόμενος γοῦν τῶν Περὶ φύσεως ὁ προειρημένος ἀνήρ [. . . cf. **R59[132]**] φησί·

τοῦ δὲ[1] λόγου τοῦδ᾽ ἐόντος ἀεὶ[2] ἀξύνετοι γίνονται ἄνθρωποι, καὶ πρόσθεν ἢ ἀκοῦσαι, καὶ ἀκούσαντες[3] τὸ πρῶτον· γινομένων γὰρ πάντων[4] κατὰ τὸν λόγον τόνδε ἀπείροισιν ἐοίκασι, πειρώμενοι ·καὶ ἐπέων καὶ ἔργων τοιούτων, ὁκοίων ἐγὼ[5] διηγεῦμαι κατὰ φύσιν διαιρέων

---

[1] τοῦ δὲ Ps.-Hippol. *Ref.* 9.9.3: τοῦ Clem. Alex. *Strom.* 5.111.7, Arist. *Rhet.* 1407b16–17: non hab. Sext.

[2] ἀεὶ (αἰεὶ) Clem., Ps.-Hipp.: om. Sext.

[3] ἀκούσαντας Ps.-Hipp.

[4] πάντων non hab. Sext.

[5] ὁποῖα ἐγὼ Ps.-Hipp.

HERACLITUS

D

From Near the Beginning of Heraclitus' Book (D1–D2)[1]

[1] Although Sextus Empiricus and Aristotle (*Rhetoric* 3.5 1407b14) both indicate that **D1** comes from the beginning of Heraclitus' book, it was most likely not the very first sentence but was preceded by something along the lines of "This is the account (*logos*) of Heraclitus of Ephesus."

D1 (B1) Sextus Empiricus, *Against the Logicians*

For this is what the abovementioned man [i.e. Heraclitus] [. . .] says at the beginning of his book *On Nature* [or: of his remarks about nature]:

> **And of this account (***logos***) that is—always—humans are uncomprehending, both before they hear it and once they have first heard it. For, although all things come about according to this account (***logos***), they resemble people without experience of them, when they have experience both of words and of things of the sort that I explain when I analyze each** [scil. of them] **in conformity with its nature and indi-**

ἕκαστον καὶ φράζων ὅκως ἔχει. τοὺς δὲ ἄλλους ἀνθρώπους λανθάνει ὁκόσα ἐγερθέντες
ποιοῦσιν, ὅκωσπερ ὁκόσα εὕδοντες ἐπιλανθάνονται.

D2 (< B2) Sext. Emp. *Adv. Math.* 7.133

[. . . cf. **R59**] ὀλίγα προδιελθὼν ἐπιφέρει· διὸ δεῖ ἕπεσθαι τῷ κοινῷ· ξυνὸς γὰρ ὁ κοινός.

τοῦ λόγου δ' ἐόντος ξυνοῦ ζώουσιν οἱ πολλοὶ
ὡς ἰδίαν ἔχοντες φρόνησιν.

Axiological Considerations (D3–D28)
Most People Do Not Understand (D3–D9)

D3 (B17) Clem. Alex. *Strom.* 2.8

οὐ γὰρ φρονέουσι τοιαῦτα πολλοί, ὁκόσοι ἐγκυρεῦσιν,[1] οὐδὲ μαθόντες γινώσκουσιν, ἑωυτοῖσι δὲ δοκέουσι.

[1] ἐγκυρεῦσιν Diels: ἐγκυρσεύουσιν ms.

D4 (B34) Eus. *PE* 13.42 (et al.)

ἀξύνετοι ἀκούσαντες κωφοῖσιν ἐοίκασι· φάτις αὐτοῖσιν μαρτυρεῖ παρεόντας ἀπεῖναι.

cate how it is. But other men are unaware of all they do when they are awake, just as they forget all they do while they are asleep.

D2 (< B2) Sextus Empiricus, *Against the Logicians*

[...] a little later he adds that therefore we ought to follow what is in common (for *xunos* [i.e. the Ionic term] means "in common"):

But although the account (*logos*) is in common (*xunos*), most people live as though they had their own thought (*phronêsis*).

Axiological Considerations (D3–D28)
Most People Do Not Understand (D3–D9)

D3 (B17) Clement of Alexandria, *Stromata*

Many people, as many as encounter things, do not think (*phronein*) that they are such [scil. as they are], **and even after they have learned about them they do not understand them, but they think** [scil. that they do].

D4 (B34) Eusebius, *Evangelical Preparation*

Being uncomprehending, when they have heard they resemble deaf people—the saying bears witness about them: "being present, they are absent."

D5 (B19) Clem. Alex. *Strom.* 2.24.5

ἀπίστους εἶναί τινας ἐπιστύφων Ἡράκλειτός φησιν·
"ἀκοῦσαι οὐκ ἐπιστάμενοι οὐδ' εἰπεῖν."

D6 (< B70) Iambl. *An.* in Stob. 2.1.16

[. . .] Ἡράκλειτος παίδων ἀθύρματα νενόμικεν εἶναι τὰ ἀνθρώπινα δοξάσματα.

D7 (< B74) M. Aur. 4.46

[. . .] οὐ δεῖ ⟨ὡς⟩[1] παῖδας τοκεώνων[2] [scil. ποιεῖν καὶ λέγειν] [. . . = **R54**].

[1] ⟨ὡς⟩ Koraïs   [2] τοκεώνων Headlam: τοκέων ὢν mss.

D8 (B87) Plut. *Aud.* 7 41A; *Aud. poet.* 28D

βλὰξ ἄνθρωπος ἐπὶ παντὶ λόγῳ ἐπτοῆσθαι φιλεῖ.

D9 (B97) Plut. *An seni res. publ. ger. sit* 7 787C

κύνες γὰρ καταβαΰζουσιν ὧν ἂν μὴ γινώσκωσι.

The Best Are Few (D10–D14)

D10 (B104) Procl. *In Alc. I*, p. 117

ὀρθῶς οὖν καὶ ὁ γενναῖος Ἡράκλειτος ἀποσκορακίζει τὸ πλῆθος ὡς ἄνουν καὶ ἀλόγιστον. "τίς," γὰρ, "αὐτῶν," φησί, "νόος ἢ φρήν; δήμων ἀοιδοῖσι πείθον-

HERACLITUS

D5 (B19) Clement of Alexandria, *Stromata*

Criticizing some people as unbelieving, Heraclitus says: **"not knowing how to hear or speak"** [or: they do not know how to speak either].

D6 (< B70) Iamblichus, *On the Soul*

[. . .] Heraclitus thought that human opinions are **children's toys**.

D7 (< B74) Marcus Aurelius, *Meditations*

[. . .] we should not [scil. act and speak] ⟨like⟩ **the children of our parents** [. . .].

D8 (B87) Plutarch, *How to Listen; How the Young Man Should Read Poetry*

A dull-witted [or: fainthearted] **man tends to be alarmed by every account** (*logos*).

D9 (B97) Plutarch, *Whether the State should be Governed by an Old Man*

Dogs bark at whomever they do not know.

The Best Are Few (D10–D14)

D10 (B104) Proclus, *Commentary on Plato's* First Alcibiades

Rightly then the noble Heraclitus curses the mass of men as being mindless and irrational. For he says, **"What is their intelligence or understanding? They believe**

ται[1] καὶ διδασκάλῳ χρείωνται ὁμίλῳ οὐκ εἰδότες ὅτι
οἱ πολλοὶ κακοί, ὀλίγοι δὲ ἀγαθοί."

[1] δήμων ἀοιδοῖσι πείθονται Diels: δήμων αἰδοῦς ἠπιῶν τε ms.

D11 (B39) Diog. Laert. 1.88

ἐν Πριήνῃ Βίας ἐγένετο ὁ Τευτάμεω, οὗ πλείων λόγος ἢ τῶν ἄλλων.

D12 (B49) Theod. Prodr. *Epist.* 1, p. 1239 (et al.)

εἷς ἐμοὶ[1] μύριοι, ἐὰν ἄριστος ᾖ.[2]

[1] ἐμοὶ Gal. *De dignosc. puls.*, 8, p. 773 Kühn: om. Theod.
[2] ἐὰν ἄριστος ᾖ om. Gal.

D13 (B29) Clem. Alex. *Strom.* 5.59.5, cf. 4.50.2

αἱρεῦνται ἓν ἀντὶ ἁπάντων οἱ ἄριστοι, κλέος ἀέναον θνητῶν· οἱ δὲ πολλοὶ κεκόρηνται ὅκωσπερ[1] κτήνεα.

[1] ὅκωσπερ Bernays: οὐχ ὥσπερ Clem. 4: ὅπως Clem. 5

D14 (B121) Strab. 14.2 (et al.)

ἄξιον Ἐφεσίοις ἡβηδὸν ἀπάγξασθαι πᾶσι καὶ τοῖς ἀνήβοις τὴν πόλιν καταλιπεῖν,[1] οἵτινες Ἑρμόδωρον ἄνδρα ἑωυτῶν ὀνήιστον ἐξέβαλον φάντες· "ἡμέων μηδὲ εἷς[2] ὀνήιστος ἔστω, εἰ δὲ μή,[3] ἄλλῃ τε καὶ μετ' ἄλλων."

HERACLITUS

the people's bards and take the crowd as their teacher, for they do not know that 'most men are bad' [cf. Bias, **MOR. T35.6.1**] and that the good are few."

D11 (B39) Diogenes Laertius

In Priene was born Bias, the son of Teutames, who is held in greater account (*logos*) than the others.

D12 (B49) Theodore Prodromus, *Letters*

One man, for me, is ten thousand, if he is the best.

D13 (B29) Clement of Alexandria, *Stromata*

The best men choose one thing instead of all others, the ever-flowing fame of mortals; but most men are sated like cattle.

D14 (B121) Strabo, *Geography*

All the adult Ephesians ought to hang themselves and to leave the city to beardless boys: for they exiled Hermodorus, the one man of them who was most beneficial, saying, "Let there not be one man among us who is the most beneficial—otherwise, may he be elsewhere and among others."

---

¹ πᾶσι . . . καταλιπεῖν Diog. Laert. 9.2: non hab. Strab.

² μηδὲ εἷς Diog. Laert: μηδεὶς Strab.

³ εἰ δὲ μή Strab.: εἰ δέ τις τοιοῦτος Diog. Laert.

EARLY GREEK PHILOSOPHY III

Against Accepted Views and Practices (D15–D28)
Against Conventional Religion (D15–D18)

D15 (B5) Aristocr. *Theos.* 2.68 (et al.)

καθαίρονται δ' ἄλλως[1] αἵματι μιαινόμενοι οἷον εἴ τις εἰς πηλὸν ἐμβὰς πηλῷ ἀπονίζοιτο. μαίνεσθαι δ' ἂν δοκοίη εἴ τις αὐτὸν ἀνθρώπων ἐπιφράσαιτο οὕτω ποιέοντα. καὶ τοῖς ἀγάλμασι δὲ τουτέοισιν εὔχονται,[2] ὁκοῖον εἴ τις δόμοισι λεσχηνεύοιτο,[3] οὔ τι γινώσκων θεοὺς οὐδ' ἥρωας οἵτινές εἰσι.

[1] ἄλλῳ H. Fränkel [2] εὔχονται Buresch: ἔχονται ms.
[3] post λεσχηνεύοιτο hab. θύειν ms., secl. Neumann

D16 (B15) Clem. Alex. *Protr.* 2.34.5

εἰ μὴ γὰρ Διονύσῳ πομπὴν ἐποιοῦντο καὶ ὕμνεον ᾆσμα αἰδοίοισιν, ἀναιδέστατα εἴργαστ' ἄν·[1] ὡυτὸς δὲ Ἅιδης καὶ Διόνυσος, ὅτεῳ μαίνονται καὶ ληναΐζουσιν.

[1] εἴργαστ' ἄν Schleiermacher: εἴργασται ms.

D17 (< B68) Iambl. *Myst.* 1.11

[. . .] ἄκεα Ἡράκλειτος προσεῖπεν [. . .].

D18 (B14) Clem. Alex. *Protr.* 2.22.2 (cf. Eus. *PE* 2.3.37)

τίσι δὴ μαντεύεται Ἡράκλειτος ὁ Ἐφέσιος; νυκτι-

HERACLITUS

Against Accepted Views and Practices (D15–D28)
Against Conventional Religion (D15–D18)

D15 (B5) Aristocritus, *Theosophy*

They are purified in vain, because they are polluted (*miainomenoi*) **by blood, just as if someone who had stepped into mud cleaned himself with mud; if any** [scil. other] **human noticed him doing this, he would think that he was mad** (*mainesthai*). **And they pray to these statues, just as if someone were to converse with houses, not knowing who the gods and heroes are.**

D16 (B15) Clement of Alexandria, *Protreptic*

If it were not for Dionysus that they performed the procession and sang the hymn to the shameful parts (*aidoia*), **most shamefully** (*anaidestata*) **would they be acting; but Hades is the same as Dionysus, for whom they go mad** (*mainesthai*) **and celebrate maenadic rites.**

D17 (< B68) Iamblichus, *On the Mysteries*

Heraclitus calls them [i.e. obscene rituals and hymns] **cures.**

D18 (B14) Clement of Alexandria, *Protreptic*

To whom does Heraclitus of Ephesus address his proph-

πόλοις, μάγοις, βάκχοις, λήναις, μύσταις· τούτοις ἀπειλεῖ τὰ μετὰ θάνατον, τούτοις μαντεύεται τὸ πῦρ· τὰ γὰρ νομιζόμενα κατὰ ἀνθρώπους μυστήρια ἀνιερωστὶ μνεῦνται.

Against Various Men (D19–D28)
Against Men Accepted as Wise (D19–D20)

D19 (< B28) Clem. Alex. *Strom.* 5.9.3

δοκεόντων γὰρ ὁ δοκιμώτατος γινώσκει.

app. vid. ad **R83**

D20 (B40) Diog. Laert. 9.1 (et al.)

πολυμαθίη νόον[1] οὐ διδάσκει· Ἡσίοδον γὰρ ἂν ἐδίδαξε καὶ Πυθαγόρην αὖτίς τε Ξενοφάνεά τε καὶ Ἑκαταῖον.

[1] ἔχειν post νόον hab. Clem. Alex. *Strom.* 1.93.2; Athen. *Deipn.* 13.91

On Homer (and Archilochus) (D21–D24)

D21 (B42) Diog. Laert. 9.1

τόν τε Ὅμηρον ἔφασκεν ἄξιον ἐκ τῶν ἀγώνων ἐκβάλλεσθαι καὶ ῥαπίζεσθαι καὶ Ἀρχίλοχον ὁμοίως.

HERACLITUS

esies? To **night-wanderers, Magi, Bacchants, Maenads, and initiates** (*mustai*). It is to these that he threatens what comes after death, to these that he prophesies **the fire** [cf. **D84**]. For **they are initiated** (*mueisthai*) **impiously into the mysteries** (*mustêria*) **that are recognized among men.**

Against Various Men (D19–D28)
Against Men Accepted as Wise (D19–D20)

D19 (< B28) Clement of Alexandria, *Stromata*

Of those who have opinions (*dokeontes*), **it is the man who enjoys the highest opinion** (*dokimôtatos*) **who knows.**[1]

[1] Text uncertain; we suppose that the word that follows in Clement's text ("maintains") is a gloss by him, but it is sometimes corrected to "to preserve" and attributed to Heraclitus (cf. **R83**).

D20 (B40) Diogenes Laertius

Much learning does not teach intelligence: for otherwise it would have taught it to Hesiod and Pythagoras, and again to Xenophanes and Hecataeus.

On Homer (and Archilochus) (D21–D24)

D21 (B42) Diogenes Laertius

He said that Homer deserved to be driven out of the competitions and thrashed,[1] and Archilochus likewise.

[1] *Rapizesthai* may be intended to recall *rapsôidesthai* ("to be recited by a rhapsode").

D22 (B56) (Ps.-?) Hippol. *Ref.* 9.9.6

ἐξηπάτηνται, φησίν, οἱ ἄνθρωποι πρὸς τὴν γνῶσιν τῶν φανερῶν παραπλησίως Ὁμήρῳ, ὃς ἐγένετο τῶν Ἑλλήνων σοφώτερος πάντων· ἐκεῖνόν τε γὰρ παῖδες φθεῖρας κατακτείνοντες ἐξηπάτησαν εἰπόντες· ὅσα εἴδομεν καὶ ἐλάβομεν,[1] ταῦτα ἀπολείπομεν, ὅσα δὲ οὔτε εἴδομεν οὔτ' ἐλάβομεν, ταῦτα φέρομεν.

[1] ἐλάβομεν Bernays: κατελάβομεν ms.

D23 (A22) Arist. *EE* 7.1 1235a25–28

καὶ Ἡράκλειτος ἐπιτιμᾷ τῷ ποιήσαντι "ὡς ἔρις ἔκ τε θεῶν καὶ ἀνθρώπων ἀπόλοιτο"· οὐ γὰρ ἂν εἶναι ἁρμονίαν μὴ ὄντος ὀξέος καὶ βαρέος οὐδὲ τὰ ζῷα ἄνευ θήλεος καὶ ἄρρενος ἐναντίων ὄντων.

D24 (B105) Schol. AT in *Il.* 18.251

Ἕκτορι δ' ἦεν ἑταῖρος, ἰῇ δ' ἐν νυκτὶ γένοντο] Ἡράκλειτος ἐντεῦθεν ἀστρολόγον φησὶ τὸν Ὅμηρον καὶ ἐν οἷς φησι "μοῖραν δ' οὔ τινά φημι πεφυγμένον ἔμμεναι ἀνδρῶν."

HERACLITUS

D22 (B56) (Ps.-?) Hippolytus, *Refutation of All Heresies*

Regarding the knowledge of things that are evident, humans are fooled in the same way as Homer, who was wiser than all the other Greeks. For boys who were killing lice fooled him by saying, "The ones we see and grasp, we leave behind; the ones we do not see or grasp, we take away."

D23 (A22) Aristotle, *Eudemian Ethics*

Heraclitus criticizes the poet [i.e. Homer] who wrote, "If only strife would vanish from gods and men!" (*Il.* 18.107): for there would not be any harmony (*harmonia*) if there were not high-pitched and low-pitched, nor would there be any animals without female and male, which are opposites.

D24 (B105) Scholia on Homer's *Iliad*

"He [i.e. Polydamas] was Hector's comrade, and they were born the same night" [*Il.* 18.107]: It is on the basis of this verse that Heraclitus calls Homer an astronomer, and also of the one in which he says, "I say that there exists no man who has ever escaped his fate" [*Il.* 6.488].

On Hesiod (D25)

D25

a (B57) (Ps.-?)-Hippol. *Ref.* 9.10

διδάσκαλος δὲ πλείστων Ἡσίοδος· τοῦτον ἐπίστανται πλεῖστα εἰδέναι, ὅστις ἡμέρην καὶ εὐφρόνην[1] οὐκ ἐγίνωσκεν· ἔστι γὰρ ἕν.

[1] εὐφρόνην Miller: εὐφροσύνην ms.

b (< B106) Plut. *Cam.* 19

[. . .] Ἡράκλειτος ἐπέπληξεν Ἡσιόδῳ τὰς μὲν ἀγαθὰς ποιουμένῳ, τὰς δὲ φαύλας, ὡς ἀγνοοῦντι φύσιν ἡμέρας ἁπάσης μίαν οὖσαν [. . .]

On Thales

See **THAL. R1**

On Pythagoras (D26)

D26 (B129) Diog. Laert. 8.6

Πυθαγόρης Μνησάρχου ἱστορίην ἤσκησεν ἀνθρώπων μάλιστα πάντων, καὶ ἐκλεξάμενος ταύτας τὰς συγγραφὰς ἐποιήσατο ἑαυτοῦ σοφίην, πολυμαθίην, κακοτεχνίην.

HERACLITUS

On Hesiod (D25)

D25

a (B57) (Ps.-?) Hippolytus, *Refutation of All Heresies*

The teacher of the most people is Hesiod; they are certain (*epistasthai*) **that it is he who knows** (*eidenai*) **the most things—he who did not understand** (*gignôskein*) **day and night, for they are one.**

b (< B106) Plutarch, *Camillus*

[...] Heraclitus disparaged Hesiod for thinking that some [i.e. days] are good, others bad, saying that he did not know that the nature of every day is one [...]

See also **R12**

On Thales

See **THAL. R1**

On Pythagoras (D26)

D26 (B129) Diogenes Laertius

Pythagoras, son of Mnesarchus, devoted himself to investigation more than all other men, and after he had made a selection of these writings [scil. probably: the writings of other people] **he devised his own wisdom: much learning, evil artifice.**

On Someone Else? (D27)

D27 (< B81) Philod. *Rhet.* 1, Col. 57.12–13; cf. Col. 62.8–9, p. 351 (cf. p. 354 Sudhaus)

[. . .] κοπίδων ἐστὶν[1] ἀρχη|[γός] [. . .].

[1] ἐστὶν om. Col. 62.8

A Global Condemnation (D28)

D28 (< B28) Clem. Alex. *Strom.* 5.9.3

Δίκη καταλήψεται ψευδῶν τέκτονας καὶ μάρτυρας.

Epistemological Considerations (D29–D45)
All Humans Think (D29–D30)

D29 (B113) Stob. 3.1.179

ξυνόν ἐστι πᾶσι τὸ φρονέειν.

D30 (B116) Stob. 3.5.6

ἀνθρώποισι πᾶσι μέτεστι γινώσκειν ἑωυτοὺς καὶ σωφρονεῖν.

HERACLITUS

On Someone Else? (D27)

D27 (< B81) Philodemus, *Rhetoric*

[...] he is **the chief of glib speakers** [...].[1]

[1] This phrase is sometimes referred to Pythagoras, to whom Diogenes Laertius 8.8 attributes a text entitled *Kopides* (according to a plausible emendation of Diels).

A Global Condemnation (D28)

D28 (< B28) Clement of Alexandria, *Stromata*

Justice will seize hold of those who fabricate lies and of those who bear witness to them.

Epistemological Considerations (D29–D45)
All Humans Think (D29–D30)

D29 (B113) Stobaeus, *Anthology*

Thinking (*phroneein*) is in common for all.

D30 (B116) Stobaeus, *Anthology*

All humans have a share in knowing themselves and in thinking with moderation (*sôphronein*).

EARLY GREEK PHILOSOPHY III

The Senses as Sources of Knowledge (D31–D34)

D31 (B55) (Ps.-?) Hippol. *Ref.* 9.9.5

ὅσων[1] ὄψις ἀκοὴ μάθησις, ταῦτα ἐγὼ προτιμέω.

[1] ὅσων Miller: ὅσον ms.

D32 (< B101a) Polyb. 12.27

ὀφθαλμοὶ τῶν ὤτων ἀκριβέστεροι μάρτυρες.

D33 (B107) Sext. Emp. *Adv. Math.* 7.126

κακοὶ μάρτυρες ἀνθρώποισιν ὀφθαλμοὶ καὶ ὦτα βαρβάρους ψυχὰς ἐχόντων.

D34 (B7) Arist. *Sens.* 5 443a23

εἰ πάντα τὰ ὄντα καπνὸς γένοιτο, ῥῖνες ἂν διαγνοῖεν.

Acquiring Knowledge (D35–D40)

D35 (B123) Them. *Orat.* 5, p. 69b; cf. 12, p. 159b

φύσις κρύπτεσθαι φιλεῖ.

Cf. app. ad **R100**

D36 (B101) Plut. *Adv. Col.* 20 1118C

ἐδιζησάμην ἐμεωυτόν.

HERACLITUS

The Senses as Sources of Knowledge (D31–D34)

D31 (B55) (Ps.-?) Hippolytus, *Refutation of All Heresies*

All the things of which sight and hearing are knowledge (*mathêsis*)[1] **I honor most.**

[1] Many interpreters understand: "all the things of which there is sight, hearing, knowledge . . . "

D32 (< B101a) Polybius, *Histories*

The eyes are more accurate witnesses than the ears.

D33 (B107) Sextus Empiricus, *Against the Logicians*

Bad witnesses for humans are the eyes and ears of those who possess barbarian souls.

D34 (B7) Aristotle, *On Sensation*

If all the things that exist became smoke, the nostrils would be able to identify them.

Acquiring Knowledge (D35–D40)

D35 (B123) Themistius, *Oration*

A nature tends to hide.[1]

[1] The phrase is transmitted in different forms by numerous authors (cf. **R100**).

D36 (B101) Plutarch, *Against Colotes*

I searched for myself.

D37 (B18) Clem. Alex. *Strom.* 2.17.4

ἐὰν μὴ ἔλπηται ἀνέλπιστον οὐκ ἐξευρήσει, ἀνεξερεύνητον ἐὸν καὶ ἄπορον.

D38 (B86) Plut. *Cor.* 38 (et al.)

ἀπιστίη[1] διαφυγγάνει μὴ γιγνώσκεσθαι.

[1] ἀπιστίη Clem. Alex. *Strom.* 5.88.5

D39 (B22) Clem. Alex. *Strom.* 4.4.2

χρυσὸν γὰρ οἱ διζήμενοι γῆν πολλὴν ὀρύσσουσι καὶ εὑρίσκουσιν ὀλίγον.

D40 (B35) Clem. Alex. *Strom.* 5.140.6

χρὴ γὰρ εὖ μάλα πολλῶν ἵστορας φιλοσόφους ἄνδρας εἶναι καθ' Ἡράκλειτον.

*The Enigmatic Expression of
Knowledge (D41–D42)*

D41 (B93) Plut. *Pyth. orac.* 21 404D

ὁ ἄναξ οὗ τὸ μαντεῖόν ἐστι τὸ ἐν Δελφοῖς οὔτε λέγει οὔτε κρύπτει ἀλλὰ σημαίνει.

HERACLITUS

D37 (B18) Clement of Alexandria, *Stromata*

If one does not expect the unexpected one will not find it (*exeurein*), **for it cannot be searched out** (*anexereunêton*) **nor arrived at** (*aporon*).

D38 (B86) Plutarch, *Coriolanus*

Because of disbelief, it escapes being known.

D39 (B22) Clement of Alexandria, *Stromata*

Those who search for gold dig up much earth and find little.

D40 (B35) Clement of Alexandria, *Stromata*

For according to Heraclitus, men who love wisdom must be **investigators** into very many things.[1]

[1] It is uncertain whether the whole sentence is to be attributed to Heraclitus or only some parts of it, and whether in particular the term *philosophoi* ("men who love wisdom") belongs to him and what exactly it means here.

The Enigmatic Expression of
Knowledge (D41–D42)

D41 (B93) Plutarch, *On the Pythian Oracles*

The lord whose oracle is the one in Delphi neither speaks nor hides, but gives signs.

D42 (< B92) Plut. *Pyth. orac.* 6 397A

Σίβυλλα δὲ μαινομένῳ στόματι, καθ' Ἡράκλειτον [. . .].

What Is Wisdom? (D43–D45)

D43 (B108) Stob. 3.1.174

ὁκόσων λόγους ἤκουσα, οὐδεὶς ἀφικνεῖται ἐς τοῦτο ὥστε γινώσκειν ὅτι σοφόν ἐστι πάντων κεχωρισμένον.

D44 (B41) Diog. Laert. 9.1

ἓν τὸ σοφόν, ἐπίστασθαι γνώμην, ὁτέη ἐκυβέρνησε[1] πάντα διὰ πάντων.

[1] ὁτέη ἐκυβέρνησε Diels: ὅτε ἡ κυβερνῆσαι B[1] (ἦ B[2]): ὁτέη κ- P[1] (Q)

D45 (B32) Clem. Alex. *Strom.* 5.115.1

ἓν τὸ σοφόν, μοῦνον λέγεσθαι οὐκ ἐθέλει καὶ ἐθέλει Ζηνὸς ὄνομα.

Fundamental Principles (D46–D88)
All Things Are One (D46)

D46 (< B50) (Ps.-?) Hippol. *Ref.* 9.9.1

οὐκ ἐμοῦ ἀλλὰ τοῦ λόγου[1] ἀκούσαντας ὁμολογεῖν σοφόν ἐστιν ἓν πάντα εἶναι.[2]

HERACLITUS

D42 (< B92) Plutarch, *On the Pythian Oracles*

The Sibyl with her raving mouth, according to Heraclitus [. . .].

What Is Wisdom? (D43–D45)

D43 (B108) Stobaeus, *Anthology*

Of all those whose accounts (*logoi*) I have heard, no one has arrived at the point of knowing that what is wise is separated from all.

D44 (B41) Diogenes Laertius

One thing, what is wise: to know the thought (*gnômê*) that steers all things through all things.

D45 (B32) Clement of Alexandria, *Stromata*

One thing, what is wise: it does not want and does want to be called only by the name of Zeus.

Fundamental Principles (D46–D88)
All Things Are One (D46)

D46 (< B50) (Ps.-?) Hippolytus, *Refutation of All Heresies*

After you have listened not to me (*emos*) but to the account (*logos*), it is wise to recognize (*homologein*) that all things are one.

---

¹ λόγου Bernays: δόγματος ms.   ² εἶναι Miller: εἰδέναι ms.

EARLY GREEK PHILOSOPHY III

The Opposites (D47–D81)
The Unity of Opposites (D47–D62)

D47 (< B10) Ps.-Arist. *Mund.* 5 396b20–22 (et al.)

συνάψιες[1] ὅλα καὶ οὐχ ὅλα, συμφερόμενον καὶ[2] διαφερόμενον, συνᾷδον διᾷδον, καὶ[3] ἐκ πάντων ἓν καὶ ἐξ ἑνὸς πάντα.

[1] συνάψιες A²CEGT: συλλάψιες (superscriptum ν) Lp: συλλήψιες P: συλλάψει ἐς Stob. 1.40.5   [2] καὶ del. Zeller   [3] καὶ om. F Fl 2

D48 (B67) (Ps.-?) Hippol. *Ref.* 9.10.8

ὁ θεὸς ἡμέρη εὐφρόνη,[1] χειμὼν θέρος, πόλεμος εἰρήνη, κόρος λιμός· ἀλλοιοῦται δὲ ὅκωσπερ ⟨πῦρ⟩,[2] ὁκόταν[3] συμμιγῇ θυώμασιν, ὀνομάζεται καθ' ἡδονὴν ἑκάστου.

[1] εὐφρόνη Miller: εὐφράνθη ms.   [2] ⟨πῦρ⟩ Diels   [3] ⟨ὃ⟩ ὁκόταν Marcovich

D49 (< B51) (Ps.-?) Hippol. *Ref.* 9.9.2 (et al.)

οὐ ξυνιᾶσιν ὅκως διαφερόμενον ἑωυτῷ ὁμολογέει·[1] παλίντροπος[2] ἁρμονίη ὅκωσπερ τόξου καὶ λύρης.

[1] ὁμολογέειν ms., corr. Miller   [2] παλίντονος Plut. *Is. et Os.* 369B, *Tranquil. an.* ms. D, Porph. *Antr.* 29

HERACLITUS

The Opposites (D47–D81)
The Unity of Opposites (D47–D62)

D47 (< B10) Ps.-Aristotle, *On the World*

Conjoinings: wholes and not wholes, converging and diverging, harmonious dissonant; and out of all things one, and out of one all things.

D48 (B67) (Ps.-?) Hippolytus, *Refutation of All Heresies*

God: day night, winter summer, war peace, satiety hunger. He changes just as ‹fire›, when it is mixed together with incense, is named according to the scent of each one.

D49 (< B51) (Ps.-?) Hippolytus, *Refutation of All Heresies*

They do not comprehend how, diverging, it accords with itself:[1] a backward-turning fitting-together (*harmoniê*), as of a bow and a lyre.[2]

[1] Or, following Plato's paraphrase (*Symposium* 187A, cf. **R32**), "it converges with itself."   [2] The bow and the lyre are the two fundamental attributes of Apollo.

D50 (B54) Plut. *An. proc.* 27 1026C

ἁρμονίη ἀφανὴς φανερῆς κρείττων.

D51 (B60) (Ps.-?) Hippol. *Ref.* 9.10.4

ὁδὸς ἄνω κάτω μία καὶ ὠυτή.

D52 (< B59) (Ps.-?) Hippol. *Ref.* 9.10.4

γνάφων[1] ὁδὸς εὐθεῖα καὶ σκολιή.

[1] γνάφων Marcovich: γραφέων ms.: γναφείῳ Bernays

D53 (B48) *Etym. Mag.* s.v. βίος, p. 198.26

τῷ οὖν τόξῳ ὄνομα βίος, ἔργον δὲ θάνατος.

D54 (B103) Porph. *Quaest. Hom.* ad *Il.* 14.200

ξυνὸν γὰρ ἀρχὴ καὶ πέρας ἐπὶ κύκλου περιφερείας, κατὰ τὸν Ἡράκλειτον.

D55 (B23) Clem. Alex. *Strom.* 4.10.1

Δίκης ὄνομα οὐκ ἂν ᾔδεσαν,[1] εἰ ταῦτα μὴ ἦν.

[1] ᾔδεσαν Sylburg: ἔδησαν ms.: ἔδεισαν Höschel

D50 (B54) Plutarch, *On the Generation of the Soul in Plato's* Timaeus

Invisible fitting-together (*harmoniê*), **stronger than a visible one.**

D51 (B60) (Ps.-?) Hippolytus, *Refutation of All Heresies*

The way upward and downward: one and the same.

D52 (< B59) (Ps.-?) Hippolytus, *Refutation of All Heresies*

The way of carding-combs: straight and crooked.[1]

[1] (Ps.-?) Hippolytus' paraphrase (**R86[4]**) helps explain this difficult and corrupt sentence.

D53 (B48) Etymologicum Magnum

The name of the bow (cf. *biós*) **is life** (*bíos*), **but its work is death**.

D54 (B103) Porphyry, *Homeric Questions on the* Iliad

For on the circumference of a circle, the beginning and the end are **in common,** according to Heraclitus.[1]

[1] It is uncertain how much of this sentence is to be attributed to Heraclitus besides the Ionic term "in common."

D55 (B23) Clement of Alexandria, *Stromata*

They would not know the name of Justice if these things [i.e. unjust actions?] **did not exist.**

D56 (B111) Stob. 3.1.177

νοῦσος ὑγιείην ἐποίησεν ἡδὺ καὶ ἀγαθόν, λιμὸς κόρον, κάματος ἀνάπαυσιν.

D57 (< B58) (Ps.-?) Hippol. *Ref.* 9.10.3

οἱ γοῦν ἰατροί, φησὶν ὁ Ἡράκλειτος, τέμνοντες, καίοντες, πάντῃ βασανίζοντες κακῶς τοὺς ἀρρωστοῦντας, ἐπαιτιῶνται μηδέν' ἄξιον μισθὸν[1] λαμβάνειν παρὰ τῶν ἀρρωστούντων, ταὐτὰ ἐργαζόμενοι, †τὰ ἀγαθὰ καὶ τὰς νόσους†.[2]

[1] μισθῶν ms., corr. Wordsworth [2] τὰ ἀγαθὰ καὶ τὰς νόσους ms.: τὰ καὶ αἱ νοῦσοι Wilamowitz, alii alia

D58 (B84a) Plot. 4.8.1

μεταβάλλον ἀναπαύεται.

D59 (B125) Theoph. *Vert.* 9 (et al.)

[. . .] καὶ ὁ κυκεὼν διίσταται[1] κινούμενος.

[1] διίσταται ⟨μὴ⟩ Bernays, cf. Ps.-Alex. *Probl.* 3.42 (p. 11.16–17 Usener) ὁ δὲ κυκεών [. . .] ἐὰν μή τις ταράττῃ, διίσταται.

HERACLITUS

D56 (B111) Stobaeus, *Anthology*

Illness makes health sweet and good, hunger does so for satiety, toil for repose.

D57 (< B58) (Ps.-?) Hippolytus, *Refutation of All Heresies*

Doctors, Heraclitus says, **cutting, cauterizing,** badly mistreating their patients in every way, **complain that they do not receive an adequate payment from their patients—and are producing the same effects,** †benefits and diseases†.[1]

[1] The passage is very uncertain, regarding not only its text but also what is to be assigned to Heraclitus and what to (Ps.-?) Hippolytus. It seems to illustrate the unity of opposites, good and bad, by the example of doctors.

D58 (B84a) Plotinus, *Enneads*

Changing, it remains at rest.

D59 (B125) Theophrastus, *On Dizziness*

A *kukeôn* too separates out if it is stirred.[1]

[1] Or, with a different text, "A *kukeôn* too separates out if it is not stirred." *Kukeôn* is a drink made out of a suspended mixture of barley, cheese, and water or wine.

EARLY GREEK PHILOSOPHY III

D60 (< B124) Theophr. *Metaph.* 7a14

ὥσπερ †σὰρξ†¹ εἰκῆ κεχυμένων² ὁ³ κάλλιστος ὁ⁴ κόσμος.

¹ σὰρξ mss.: σάρον Bernays: σωρὸς Usener, alii alia: an σωρῶν? ² κεχυμένων mss.: -η Bergk: -ον Usener ³ ὁ del. Bergk ⁴ ὁ del. Usener

D61 (B122) *Suda* A.398 et A.1762 (ad ἀμφισβατεῖν)

[. . .] ἀγχιβασίην Ἡράκλειτος.

D62 (B8) Arist. *EN* 9.2 1155b4–6

[. . .] Ἡράκλειτος τὸ ἀντίξουν συμφέρον καὶ ἐκ τῶν διαφερόντων καλλίστην ἁρμονίαν καὶ πάντα κατ' ἔριν γίνεσθαι.

War (D63–D64)

D63 (B80) Orig. *Cels.* 6.42

εἰδέναι¹ χρὴ τὸν πόλεμον ἐόντα ξυνόν, καὶ δίκην ἔριν,² καὶ γινόμενα πάντα κατ' ἔριν καὶ χρεών.³

¹ εἰδέναι Schleiermacher: εἰ δὲ mss. ² ἔριν Schleiermacher: ἐρεῖν mss. ³ χρεών Diels: χρεώμενα mss.

HERACLITUS

D60 (< B124) Theophrastus, *Metaphysics*

Like †flesh† of things spread out at random, the most beautiful order (*kosmos*).

D61 (B122) *Suda*

an approach: Heraclitus.[1]

[1] This isolated word may belong to the theme of the fitting-together of opposites.

D62 (B8) Aristotle, *Nicomachean Ethics*

[...] Heraclitus [scil. says] that what is opposed converges [cf. **D47**], and that the most beautiful harmony (*harmonia*) comes out of what diverges [cf. **D49**], and that all things come about by strife [cf. **D63**].

War (D63–D64)

D63 (B80) Origen, *Against Celsus*

One must know that war is in common, that justice is strife, and that all things come about by strife and constraint.

D64 (B53) (Ps.-?) Hippol. *Ref.* 9.9.4

πόλεμος πάντων μὲν πατήρ ἐστι, πάντων δὲ βασιλεύς, καὶ τοὺς μὲν θεοὺς ἔδειξε τοὺς δὲ ἀνθρώπους, τοὺς μὲν δούλους ἐποίησε τοὺς δὲ ἐλευθέρους.

Flux (D65–D66)

D65

a (B49a) Heracl. *Alleg.* 24.4

ποταμοῖς τοῖς αὐτοῖς ἐμβαίνομέν τε καὶ οὐκ ἐμβαίνομεν, εἶμέν τε καὶ οὐκ εἶμεν [cf. **R9**].

b (< B12) Cleanthes apud Ar. Did. in Eus. *PE* 15.20.2

ποταμοῖσι τοῖσιν αὐτοῖσιν ἐμβαίνουσιν ἕτερα καὶ ἕτερα ὕδατα ἐπιρρεῖ.

c (< A6) Plat. *Crat.* 402a

[ΣΩ.] λέγει που Ἡράκλειτος ὅτι πάντα χωρεῖ καὶ οὐδὲν μένει καὶ ποταμοῦ ῥοῇ ἀπεικάζων τὰ ὄντα λέγει ὡς δὶς ἐς τὸν αὐτὸν ποταμὸν οὐκ ἂν ἐμβαίης.

d (< T353 Mouraviev) Sen. *Epist.* 58.23

hoc est, quod ait Heraclitus: "in idem flumen bis descendimus et non discendimus." manet enim idem fluminis nomen, aqua transmissa est.

HERACLITUS

D64 (B53) (Ps.-?) Hippolytus, *Refutation of All Heresies*

War is the father of all and the king of all, and has revealed that the ones are gods and the others humans, and has made the ones slaves and the others free.

Flux (D65–D66)

D65

a (B49a) Heraclitus, *Homeric Allegories*

We step and we do not step into the same rivers, we are and we are not [cf. **R9**].

b (< B12) Cleanthes in Arius Didymus in Eusebius, *Evangelical Preparation*

It is always different waters that flow toward those who step into the same rivers.

c (< A6) Plato, *Cratylus*

[Socrates:] Heraclitus says something like this: that all things flow and nothing remains; and comparing the things that are to the flowing of a river, he says that you could not step twice into the same river.

d (≠ DK) Seneca, *Letters to Lucilius*

This is what Heraclitus says: "Into the same river we do and do not step twice." For the name 'river' remains the same, but the water passes by.

D66 (< T156 Mouraviev) Arist. *Metaph.* A6 987a32

[. . .] ταῖς Ἡρακλειτείοις δόξαις, ὡς ἁπάντων τῶν αἰσθητῶν ἀεὶ ῥεόντων καὶ ἐπιστήμης περὶ αὐτῶν οὐκ οὔσης [. . .].

Cyclical Alternation of Opposites (D67–D72)

D67 (B126) Schol. in Tzetz. *In Il.*, p. 126

τὰ ψυχρὰ θέρεται, θερμὸν ψύχεται, ὑγρὸν αὐαίνεται, καρφαλέον νοτίζεται.

D68 (B88) Ps.-Plut. *Cons. Ap.* 10 106E

ταὐτό γ' ἔνι ζῶν καὶ τεθνηκὸς καὶ τὸ[1] ἐγρηγορὸς καὶ καθεῦδον καὶ νέον καὶ γηραιόν· τάδε γὰρ μεταπεσόντα ἐκεῖνά ἐστι, κἀκεῖνα πάλιν μεταπεσόντα ταῦτα.

[1] τὸ del. Reiske

D69 (A19) Plut. *Def. orac.* 11 415E

οἱ μὲν 'ἡβώντων' [Hes. Frag. 304.2 Merkelbach-West] ἀναγιγνώσκοντες ἔτη τριάκοντα ποιοῦσι τὴν γενεὰν καθ' Ἡράκλειτον, ἐν ᾧ χρόνῳ γεννῶντα παρέχει τὸν ἐξ αὐτοῦ γεγεννημένον ὁ γεννήσας.

HERACLITUS

D66 (≠ DK) Aristotle, *Metaphysics*

[. . .] the Heraclitean doctrines according to which all perceptible things are constantly flowing and there is no knowledge about them [. . .].

Cyclical Alternation of Opposites (D67–D72)

D67 (B126) Tzetzes, Scholia on *Commentary on Homer's Iliad*

Cold things become warm, warm becomes cold, wet becomes dry, parched becomes moist.

D68 (B88) Ps.-Plutarch, *Consolation to Apollonius*

There is the same within, what is living and what is dead, what is awake and what is sleeping, and what is young and what is old; for these, changing, are those, and those, changing in turn, are these.[1]

[1] The last phrase probably belongs not to Heraclitus but to Ps.-Plutarch.

D69 (A19) Plutarch, *The Obsolescence of Oracles*

Those who read "of men who have reached puberty" [i.e. in a fragment of Hesiod] define a generation as lasting thirty years, according to Heraclitus, for it is in this period of time that a parent produces an offspring from himself that produces offspring.

D70 (B62) (Ps.-?) Hippol. *Ref.* 9.10.6

ἀθάνατοι θνητοί, θνητοὶ ἀθάνατοι, ζῶντες τὸν ἐκείνων θάνατον, τὸν δὲ ἐκείνων βίον τεθνεῶτες.

D71 (B26) Clem. Alex. *Strom.* 4.143

ἄνθρωπος ἐν εὐφρόνῃ[1] φάος ἅπτεται ἑαυτῷ ἀποθανών,[2] ἀποσβεσθεὶς ὄψεις·[3] ζῶν δὲ ἅπτεται τεθνεῶτος εὕδων·[4] ἐγρηγορὼς ἅπτεται εὕδοντος.

[1] εὐφρόνῃ Sylburg: εὐφροσύνηι ms. [2] ἀποθανών secl. Wilamowitz [3] ἀποσβεσθεὶς ὄψεις secl. Stählin [4] post εὕδων hab. ms. ἀποσβεσθεὶς ὄψεις, del. Wilamowitz

D72 (< B21) Clem. Alex. *Strom.* 3.21.1 (cf. 5.105.2)

θάνατός ἐστιν ὁκόσα ἐγερθέντες ὁρέομεν, ὁκόσα δὲ εὕδοντες ὕπνος.

Divine Perspective, Human
Perspective (D73–D77)

D73 (B102) Porph. *Quaest Hom.* ad *Il.* 4.4

τῷ μὲν θεῷ καλὰ πάντα καὶ ἀγαθὰ καὶ δίκαια, ἄνθρωποι δὲ ἃ μὲν ἄδικα ὑπειλήφασιν ἃ δὲ δίκαια.

D70 (B62) (Ps.-?) Hippolytus, *Refutation of All Heresies*

Immortals mortals, mortals immortals, living the death of these, dying the life of those.

D71 (B26) Clement of Alexandria, *Stromata*

A human being, in the night, lights [*haptesthai*] **a lamp for himself,** dead,[1] **his eyes extinguished; living, he touches on** [*haptesthai*] **a dead man when sleeping; when awake, he touches on** [*haptesthai*] **a sleeping man.**

[1] This word seems to be a gloss by Clement.

D72 (< B21) Clement of Alexandria, *Stromata*

Death is whatever we see when awakened; whatever we see when sleeping is slumber.

*Divine Perspective, Human
Perspective (D73–D77)*

D73 (B102) Porphyry, *Homeric Questions on the* Iliad

For god, all things are beautiful, good, and just, but humans have assumed that some things are unjust, others just.

D74 (B78) Orig. *Cels.* 6.12

ἦθος γὰρ ἀνθρώπειον μὲν οὐκ ἔχει γνώμας, θεῖον δὲ ἔχει.

D75 (B79) Orig. *Cels.* 6.12

ἀνὴρ νήπιος ἤκουσε πρὸς δαίμονος ὅκωσπερ παῖς πρὸς ἀνδρός.

D76 (B52) (Ps.-?) Hippol. *Ref.* 9.9.4

αἰὼν παῖς ἐστι παίζων, πεσσεύων· παιδὸς ἡ βασιληίη.

D77 (B83) Plat. *Hipp. mai.* 289b

ἀνθρώπων ὁ σοφώτατος πρὸς θεὸν πίθηκος φανεῖται καὶ σοφίᾳ καὶ κάλλει καὶ τοῖς ἄλλοις πᾶσιν.

Animal Perspectives, Human Perspective (D78–D81)

D78 (B61) (Ps.-?) Hippol. *Ref.* 9.10.5

θάλασσα, ὕδωρ καθαρώτατον καὶ μιαρώτατον, ἰχθύσι μὲν πότιμον καὶ σωτήριον, ἀνθρώποις δὲ ἄποτον καὶ ὀλέθριον.

HERACLITUS

D74 (B78) Origen, *Against Celsus*

The human character does not possess judgments (*gnômai*), but the divine one possesses them.

D75 (B79) Origen, *Against Celsus*

A grown man is called puerile by a divinity, just as a child is by a grown man.

D76 (B52) (Ps.-?) Hippolytus, *Refutation of All Heresies*

A lifetime (*aiôn*)[1] is a child playing, playing checkers: the kingship belongs to a child.

[1] *aiôn* designates the vital force or the duration of a life.

D77 (B83) Plato, *Greater Hippias*

The wisest human being will seem to be a monkey compared to a god in wisdom, beauty, and everything else.

*Animal Perspectives, Human
Perspective (D78–D81)*

D78 (B61) (Ps.-?) Hippolytus, *Refutation of All Heresies*

The sea, the purest water and the foulest: for fish it is drinkable and life-giving, but for humans undrinkable and deadly.

D79 (< B9) Arist. *EN* 10.5 1176a7

[. . .] ὄνους σύρματ' ἂν ἑλέσθαι μᾶλλον ἢ χρυσόν.

D80

a (B13) Clem. Alex. *Strom.* 1.2.2

ὕες βορβόρῳ ἥδονται μᾶλλον ἢ καθαρῷ ὕδατι.

b (B37) Colum. *Agric.* 8.4

[. . .] si modo credimus Ephesio Heracleto qui ait sues caeno, cohortales aves pulvere vel cinere lavari.

D81 (B82) Plat. *Hipp. mai.* 289a

πιθήκων ὁ κάλλιστος αἰσχρὸς ἀνθρώπων[1] γένει συμβάλλειν.

[1] ἀνθρώπων Bekker: ἄλλῳ mss.

Cosmic Fire (D82–D88)

D82 (< B64) (Ps.-?) Hippol. *Ref.* 9.10.7

τάδε[1] πάντα οἰακίζει κεραυνός.

[1] τὰ δὲ ms., corr. Sauppe

D83 (< B16) Clem. Alex. *Paed.* 2.99.5

τὸ μὴ δῦνόν ποτε πῶς ἄν τις λάθοι;

HERACLITUS

D79 (< B9) Aristotle, *Nicomachean Ethics*

Asses would choose sweepings rather than gold.

D80

a (B13) Clement of Alexandria, *Stromata*

Pigs take greater pleasure in mire than in pure water.

b (B37) Columella, *On Agriculture*

[...] at least if we believe Heraclitus of Ephesus, who says that pigs bathe in filth, barnyard poultry in dust or ashes.

D81 (B82) Plato, *Greater Hippias*

The most beautiful monkey is ugly compared with the human race.

Cosmic Fire (D82–D88)

D82 (< B64) (Ps.-?) Hippolytus, *Refutation of All Heresies*

All these things the thunderbolt steers.

D83 (< B16) Clement of Alexandria, *Pedagogue*

How could one possibly escape the notice of what never sets?

D84 (B66) (Ps.-?) Hippol. *Ref.* 9.10.6

πάντα τὸ πῦρ ἐπελθὸν κρινεῖ καὶ καταλήψεται.

D85 (B30) Clem. Alex. *Strom.* 5.105.2 (et al.)

κόσμον τόνδε,[1] τὸν αὐτὸν ἁπάντων,[2] οὔτε τις θεῶν οὔτε ἀνθρώπων ἐποίησεν, ἀλλ' ἦν ἀεὶ καὶ ἔστιν καὶ ἔσται, πῦρ ἀείζωον, ἁπτόμενον μέτρα καὶ ἀποσβεννύμενον μέτρα.

[1] τόνδε Plut. *An. proc.* 1014a; Simpl. *In Cael.* 294.15–16 (et 294.6): om. Clem. [2] τὸν αὐτὸν ἁπάντων om. Plut. Simpl.

D86 (< B31) Clem. Alex. *Strom.* 5.105.3, 5 (et al.)

πυρὸς τροπαί, πρῶτον θάλασσα, θαλάσσης δὲ τὸ μὲν ἥμισυ γῆ, τὸ δὲ ἥμισυ πρηστήρ. [. . .] θάλασσα διαχέεται, καὶ μετρέεται εἰς τὸν αὐτὸν λόγον, ὁκοῖος πρόσθεν[1] ἦν ἢ γενέσθαι γῆ.

[1] πρόσθεν Eus. *PE* 13.13.31: πρῶτον Clem.

D87 (B90) Plut. *E ap. Delph.* 8 388E

πυρός τε[1] ἀνταμοιβὴ τὰ[2] πάντα [. . .] καὶ πῦρ ἁπάντων ὅκωσπερ[3] χρυσοῦ χρήματα καὶ χρημάτων χρυσός.

[1] τε X³gB: om. cett. [2] ἀνταμοιβὴ τὰ Diels: ἀνταμοίβηται X¹F¹D: ἀνταμείβεται cett.: ἀνταμοιβὴν τὰ Bernardakis [3] ὅκωσπερ Bernardakis: ἐκ ὥσπερ Γ: ὥσπερ cett.

D84 (B66) (Ps.-?) Hippolytus, *Refutation of All Heresies*

When the fire has come upon all things, it will judge them and seize hold of them.

D85 (B30) Clement of Alexandria, *Stromata*

This world order (*kosmos*), the same for all, none of the gods or humans made it, but it always was and is and will be: fire ever-living, kindled in measures and extinguished in measures.

D86 (< B31) Clement of Alexandria, *Stromata*

Turnings of fire: first sea; then half of the sea, earth; and the other half, lightning storm (*prêstêr*).[1] [. . .] It spreads out as sea and its measure reaches the same account (*logos*) as it was before it became earth.

[1] There is no exact equivalent for this term in English. Cf. **D96**.

D87 (B90) Plutarch, *On the Letter E in Delphi*

All things are in exchange for fire, and fire for all things, just like goods for gold and gold for goods.

EARLY GREEK PHILOSOPHY III

D88 (< B65) (Ps.-?) Hippol. *Ref.* 9.10.7

[. . .] χρησμοσύνην καὶ κόρον.

*Parts of the World and Physical
Phenomena (D89–D97)
The Sun (D89–D91)*

D89

a (F 3–94 Mouraviev) P. Derv. Col. IV.5–9 [= **DERV. Col. IV.5–9**].

[. . .] Ἡράκλειτος [. . .] [ἔφη·] "ἥλιο[ς" . . .]μου κατὰ φύσιν "ἀνθρω[πηΐου] εὖρος ποδός [ἐστι,"] τὸ μ[έγεθο]ς οὐχ ὑπερβάλλων. εἰ γά[ρ τι οὔ]ρους ἑ[ωυτοῦ ὑπερβαλε]ῖ, "Ἐρινύε[ς] νιν ἐξευρήσου[σι]."

b (B3) Aët. 2.21.4 (Ps.-Plut.) [περὶ μεγέθους ἡλίου]

Ἡράκλειτος εὖρος ποδὸς ἀνθρωπείου.

c (B94) Plut. *Exil.* 11 604A

ἥλιος γὰρ οὐχ ὑπερβήσεται μέτρα, φησὶν ὁ Ἡράκλειτος· εἰ δὲ μή, Ἐρινύες μιν Δίκης ἐπίκουροι ἐξευρήσουσιν.

180

HERACLITUS

D88 (< B65) (Ps.-?) Hippolytus, *Refutation of All Heresies*

[Scil. fire is] **shortage and satiety.**

*Parts of the World and Physical
Phenomena (D89–D97)
The Sun (D89–D91)*

D89

a (≠ DK) Derveni Papyrus

[. . .] Heraclitus [. . .] said, **"The sun"** in accordance with the nature of the world (?) **"is of the breadth of a human foot,"** not exceeding that size. For if it exceeds at all its own limits, **"the Erinyes will find it out."**

b (B3) Aëtius

Heraclitus: [scil. the size of the sun is] **the breadth of a human foot.**

c (B94) Plutarch, *On Exile*

"The sun will not overstep measures," says Heraclitus; **"otherwise, the Erinyes, Justice's helpers, will find it out."**

D90 (< B100) Plut. *Quaest. Plat.* 8.4 1007D–E

[. . .] ὧν ὁ ἥλιος ἐπιστάτης ὢν καὶ σκοπὸς[1] ὁρίζειν καὶ βραβεύειν καὶ ἀναδεικνύναι καὶ ἀναφαίνειν μεταβολὰς καὶ ὥρας αἳ πάντα φέρουσι καθ' Ἡράκλειτον τῷ ἡγεμόνι καὶ πρώτῳ θεῷ γίγνεται συνεργός.

[1] ‹ἐπιταχθεὶς ἐπί›σκοπος Reinhardt

D91

a (< B6) Arist. *Meteor.* 2.2 355a13–14

ὁ ἥλιος [. . .] *νέος ἐφ' ἡμέρῃ ἐστίν.*

b (< T 135 Mouraviev) Schol. in Plat. *Rep.* 498a

Ἡράκλειτος ὁ Ἐφέσιος, φυσικὸς ὤν, ἔλεγεν ὅτι ὁ ἥλιος ἐν τῇ δυτικῇ θαλάσσῃ ἐλθὼν καὶ καταδὺς ἐν αὐτῇ σβέννυται, εἶτα διελθὼν τὸ ὑπὸ γῆν καὶ εἰς ἀνατολὴν φθάσας ἐξάπτεται[1] πάλιν, καὶ τοῦτο ἀεὶ γίγνεται.

[1] ἐξάπτεται edd.: ἐξάπτει mss.

HERACLITUS

D90 (< B100) Plutarch, *Platonic Questions*

[. . .] the sun, which is the overseer and observer of these things [i.e. limits and periods], becomes the collaborator of the god who leads and is first, by limiting, judging, revealing, and illuminating the changes and seasons that bring all things, according to Heraclitus.[1]

[1] It is uncertain how much of this sentence belongs to Heraclitus.

D91

a (< B6) Aristotle, *Meteorology*

The sun [. . .] is **new every day.**

b (≠ DK) Scholia on Plato's *Republic*

Heraclitus of Ephesus, a natural philosopher, said that when the sun arrives at the western sea, it sets in it and is extinguished; then, passing under the earth and arriving in the east, it is kindled once again; and this is repeated incessantly.

See also **R46 [7, 10, 11]**

EARLY GREEK PHILOSOPHY III

The Moon (D92)

D92 (< T 212 Mouraviev) Aristarch. Samius in Comm. in *Od.* 20.156 (P.Oxy. 3710; vol. 53 [1986] 96–99, ed. Haslam)

a (> F 80A^a Mouraviev) Col. 2.36–37, 43–47

ὅτι ἐν νουμηνίᾳ αἱ ἐκλείψεις δηλο[ῖ] | Ἀρίσταρχος ὁ Σάμ[ι]ος γράφων· [. . .] Ἡράκλειτος· συνιόντων | τῶν μηνῶν ἡμέρας ἐξ [ὅ]του φαί|νεται προτέρην νουμην[ί]ην δευ|τέρην ἄλλοτ' ἐλάσσονας μεταβάλλε|ται ἄλλοτε πλεῦνας.

b (F 80A^c Mouraviev) Col. 3.7–11

μεὶς τρ[ιταῖος]¹ φαινόμενος ἑκκαιδ[ε]κάτηι πασσέλη|νος φαίνεται ἐν ἡμέραις τεσσαρεσκαί|δεκα· ἀπολιμπάνει τὸ[ν]² ὑπομετρον | ἐν ἡμέρηισι ιγ′.

¹ τρ[ιταῖος] Haslam   ² τὸ[ν] Haslam

The Stars (D93–D95)

D93 (< B120) Strab. 1.6

a

ἠοῦς καὶ ἑσπέρας τέρματα ἡ ἄρκτος.

HERACLITUS

The Moon (D92)

D92 (≠ DK) Aristarchus of Samos in an anonymous commentary on Homer's *Odyssey*[1]

a

The fact that eclipses [scil. occur] on the day of the new moon is made clear by Aristarchus of Samos, who writes, "[. . .] Heraclitus [scil. says]: 'When the months meet, it [i.e. the moon] changes during the days following its appearance—the first day on the new moon, the second—sometimes during fewer ones [scil. days], sometimes during more.'"

b

The moon that appears on the third day appears on the sixteenth day as a full moon, fourteen days later; it decreases with regard to what remains during thirteen days.

[1] Although both of these texts, whose expression and meaning are obscure, are doubtless based upon some statement made by Heraclitus, it is difficult to derive from them anything more than an indication that Heraclitus must have spoken about the phases of the moon. For another text mentioning the moon in relation to Heraclitus, see also **R49.**

The Stars (D93–D95)

D93 (< B120) Strabo, *Geography*

a

The limits of East and West: the Bear.

b

ἀντίον τῆς ἄρκτου οὖρος αἰθρίου Διός.

D94 (B99) Ps.-Plut. *Aqu. et ign. comp.* 7.957A (et al.)

[. . .] εἰ μὴ ἥλιος ἦν, ἕνεκα τῶν ἄλλων ἄστρων[1] εὐφρόνη ἂν ἦν.

[1] ἕνεκα τῶν ἄλλων ἄστρων add. Diels ex Plut. *Fort.* 98D et Clem. Alex. *Protr.* 1.113.3

D95 (< T 564 Mouraviev) Theon Al. *In Ptol. Almag.* 1.3, p. 340.5

τὸ ἀνάπτεσθαι καὶ σβέννυσθαι τὰ ἄστρα καθ' Ἡράκλειτον [. . .].

Meteorological Phenomena (D96–D97)

D96 (A14) Aët. 3.3.9 (Stob.) [περὶ βροντῶν ἀστραπῶν κεραυνῶν πρηστήρων τυφώνων]

Ἡράκλειτος βροντὴν μὲν κατὰ συστροφὰς ἀνέμων καὶ νεφῶν καὶ ἐμπτώσεις πνευμάτων εἰς τὰ νέφη, ἀστραπὰς δὲ κατὰ τὰς τῶν ἀναθυμιωμένων[1] ἐξάψεις, πρηστῆρας δὲ κατὰ νεφῶν ἐμπρήσεις καὶ σβέσεις.

[1] θυμιωμένων mss., corr. Schuster

b

Opposite to the Bear [*Arktou*]: **the watcher** [*ouros*] **of bright Zeus** [i.e. Arcturus].[1]

[1] Strabo seems to be citing two brief sentences from Heraclitus in order to illustrate the meaning of the term *arktos* and is connecting them himself with his own conjunction 'and'; other scholars have taken the quotation to involve one single, longer sentence. The translation 'watcher' is uncertain (other possible renderings are 'wind' or 'boundary'), and the interpretation of the passage is controversial.

D94 (B99) Ps.-Plutarch, *Whether Water or Fire is More Useful*

If there were no sun, on account of the other stars it would be night.

D95 (≠ DK) Theon of Alexandria, *Commentary on Ptolemy's* Almagest

The fact that the stars are kindled and extinguished, according to Heraclitus [. . .].

Meteorological Phenomena (D96–D97)

D96 (A14) Aëtius

Heraclitus: thunder [scil. is caused] by the gathering of winds and clouds and the crashing of winds into the clouds, lightning by the kindling of evaporations, lightning storms (*prêstêres*)[1] by the burning and extinguishing of the clouds.

[1] See note on **D86.**

EARLY GREEK PHILOSOPHY III

D97 (ad A14, Nachtrag I, p. 492.6) Sen. *Quaest. nat.* 2.56

Heraclitus existimat fulgurationem esse velut apud nos incipientium ignium conatum et primam flammam incertam, modo intereuntem, modo resurgentem.

*A Doxographical Presentation of
Heraclitus' Physics*

See **R46**

*Human Beings (D98–D123)
The Soul (D98–D104)*

D98 (B45) Diog. Laert. 9.7

ψυχῆς πείρατα ἰὼν[1] οὐκ ἂν ἐξεύροι ὁ[2] πᾶσαν ἐπιπορευόμενος ὁδόν· οὕτω βαθὺν[3] λόγον ἔχει.

[1] πείρατα (iam Hermann) ἰὼν Diels: πειρατέ*ον Β[2] (έ* in ras.): πειρατέ ον P[1](Q): πειραταιον B[1]: πειρᾶται ὂν FP[4] [2] ἐξεύροι ὁ B[2]P[x]: εὕροι ὁ F: ἐξεύροιο B[1]P[1]   [3] βαθὺν F: βαθὺς BP[1](Q)

D99 (B115) Stob. 3.1.180a (Σωκράτους[1])

ψυχῆς[2] ἐστι λόγος ἑαυτὸν αὔξων.

[1] Heraclito trib. Schenkl   [2] an ψυχὴ?

D97 (ad A14 = Nachtrag I, p. 492.6) Seneca, *Natural Questions*

Heraclitus thinks that sheet lightning is like, among us, the attempt and the first uncertain flame of beginning fires, which die down at one moment and come to life again at another.

*A Doxographical Presentation of
Heraclitus' Physics*

See **R46**[1]

[1] We consider that the doxography transmitted by Diogenes Laertius belongs more to the reception of Heraclitus, in the sense of providing a cosmological interpretation of various statements by him, than to simple doctrinal information.

*Human Beings (D98–D123)
The Soul (D98–D104)*

D98 (B45) Diogenes Laertius

He who travels on every road would not find out the limits of the soul in the course of walking: so deep is its account (*logos*).

D99 (B115) Stobaeus, *Anthology*

An account (*logos*) **that increases itself is that of the soul.**[1]

[1] Perhaps: "Soul is an account that increases itself." Stobaeus cites this sentence under the name of Socrates, but comparison with **D98** makes its attribution to Heraclitus plausible.

D100 (B36) Clem. Alex. *Strom.* 6.17.2 (et al.)

ψυχῆσι[1] θάνατος ὕδωρ γενέσθαι, ὕδατι[2] δὲ θάνατος γῆν γενέσθαι, ἐκ γῆς δὲ ὕδωρ γίνεται, ἐξ ὕδατος δὲ ψυχή.

[1] ψυχῆσι Clem., Phil. *Aeter. mund.* 108 UHP: ψυχῆς εἰ Ps.-Hippol. *Ref.* 5.16.4: ψυχῆς Phil. M   [2] ὕδατος Phil.

D101 (B77) Porph. *Antr.* 10

[. . .] ὅθεν καὶ Ἡράκλειτον ψυχῆσι φάναι τέρψιν μὴ[1] θάνατον ὑγρῆσι γενέσθαι [cf. **R90a**].

[1] ἢ Diels, καὶ Kranz

D102 (< B12) Cleanth. apud Ar. Did. in Eus. *PE* 15.20.2

ψυχαὶ ἀπὸ τῶν ὑγρῶν ἀναθυμιῶνται.

D103 (B118) Mus. Ruf. in Stob. 3.5.8 (et al.)

αὔη ψυχή, σοφωτάτη καὶ ἀρίστη.

app. cf. ad **R101**

D104 (B117) Stob. 3.5.7

ἀνὴρ ὁκόταν μεθυσθῇ, ἄγεται ὑπὸ παιδὸς ἀνήβου σφαλλόμενος, οὐκ ἐπαΐων ὅκη βαίνει, ὑγρὴν τὴν ψυχὴν ἔχων.

HERACLITUS

D100 (B36) Clement of Alexandria, *Stromata*

For souls it is death to become water, for water it is death to become earth; but out of earth, water comes to be, and out of water, soul.

D101 (B77) Porphyry, *The Cave of the Nymphs in the Odyssey*

[. . .] that is why [scil. probably according to Numenius] Heraclitus also says that for souls it is a pleasure, and not death, to become moist.

D102 (< B12) Cleanthes in Arius Didymus in Eusebius, *Evangelical Preparation*

Souls evaporate from moist things.

D103 (B118) Musonius Rufus in Stobaeus, *Anthology*

A dry soul: wisest and best.[1]

[1] The phrase is transmitted in different forms by numerous authors (cf. **R101**), and the exact text is uncertain.

D104 (B117) Stobaeus, *Anthology*

When a man has become drunk, he is led stumbling by a slave, a mere boy; he does not know where he is going, his soul is wet.

EARLY GREEK PHILOSOPHY III

Human Laws (D105–D110)

D105 (B114) Stob. 3.1.179

ξὺν νόῳ λέγοντας ἰσχυρίζεσθαι χρὴ τῷ ξυνῷ πάντων, ὅκωσπερ νόμῳ πόλις καὶ πολὺ[1] ἰσχυροτέρως. τρέφονται γὰρ πάντες οἱ ἀνθρώπειοι νόμοι ὑπὸ ἑνὸς τοῦ θείου· κρατεῖ γὰρ τοσοῦτον ὁκόσον ἐθέλει καὶ ἐξαρκεῖ πᾶσι καὶ περιγίνεται.

[1] πολὺ Schleiermacher: πόλις ed. Trincavelliana: πόλιος Preller

D106 (B44) Diog. Laert. 9.2

μάχεσθαι χρὴ τὸν δῆμον ὑπὲρ τοῦ νόμου[1] ὅκωσπερ[2] τείχεος.

[1] post νόμου hab. ὑπὲρ τοῦ γινομένου BP[1], del. P[x] (om. Q)
[2] ὅκωσπερ rec. (et coni. Meineke): ὅκως ὑπὲρ BPF

D107 (B47) Diog. Laert. 9.73

μὴ εἰκῇ περὶ τῶν μεγίστων συμβαλλώμεθα.

D108 (B33) Clem. Alex. *Strom.* 5.115.2 (et al.)

νόμος καὶ βουλῇ[1] πείθεσθαι ἑνός.

[1] βουλῆι (= βουλῇ) Eus. *PE* 13.13.42 I[2]: βουλὴ Clem., Eus. cett.

HERACLITUS

Human Laws (D105–D110)

D105 (B114) Stobaeus, *Anthology*

Those who speak with their mind (*xun noôi*) **must rely** (*iskhurizesthai*) **on what is in common** (*xunôi*) **for all, just as a city does on its law, and much more strongly** (*iskhuroterôs*) [scil. than a city]. **For all human laws are nourished by one law, the divine one: for it dominates as much as it wants to, and it suffices for all, and there is some left over.**

D106 (B44) Diogenes Laertius

The people must fight for their law just as for their city wall.

D107 (B47) Diogenes Laertius

Let us not agree in a haphazard way about the most important things.[1]

[1] We presume that "the most important things" refers to politics.

D108 (B33) Clement of Alexandria, *Stromata*

It is also a law to obey the plan of just one man.

D109 (B84b) Plot. 4.8.1

κάματός ἐστι τοῖς αὐτοῖς μοχθεῖν καὶ ἄρχεσθαι.

D110 (< B11) Ps.-Arist. Mund. 6 401a10 (et al.)

πᾶν γὰρ ἑρπετὸν πληγῇ[1] νέμεται.

[1] πληγῇ Stob. 1.1.36: τὴν γῆν Ps.-Arist.

Human Behavior (D111–D117)

D111 (B119) Stob. 4.40.23 (et al.)

ἦθος ἀνθρώπῳ[1] δαίμων.

[1] ἀνθρώπῳ Stob.: -ου Plut. Quaest. Plat. 999E: -ων Alex. Fat. p. 170.16

D112 (B43) Diog. Laert. 9.2

ὕβριν χρὴ σβεννύναι μᾶλλον ἢ πυρκαϊήν.

D113 (< B95) Plut. Quaest. conv. 3.1 644F

ἀμαθίην γὰρ ἄμεινον, ὥς φησιν Ἡράκλειτος, κρύπτειν [. . .].

D114 (B112) Stob. 3.1.178

a

σωφρονεῖν ἀρετὴ μεγίστη.

HERACLITUS

D109 (B84b) Plotinus, *Enneads*

It is wearisome to work hard for the same ones and to be ruled by them.[1]

[1] The words "and to be ruled by them" may be a gloss by Plotinus.

D110 (< B11) Ps.-Aristotle, *On the World*

Every beast is driven to pasture by blows.

Human Behavior (D111–D117)

D111 (B119) Stobaeus, *Anthology*

Character, for a human, is his personal deity.

D112 (B43) Diogenes Laertius

One must extinguish arrogant violence (*hubris*) more than a conflagration.

D113 (< B95) Plutarch, *Table Talk*

It is better to hide one's ignorance, as Heraclitus says [. . .].[1]

[1] The phrase is transmitted in different forms by numerous authors (cf. **R102**).

D114 (B112) Stobaeus, *Anthology*

a

To be moderate: the greatest virtue.

b

σοφίη ἀληθέα λέγειν καὶ ποιεῖν κατὰ[1] φύσιν ἐπαΐοντας.

[1] καλὰ Valckenaer

D115 (< A21) Clem. Alex. *Strom.* 2.130. 2

[. . . = **ANAXAG. P36**] Ἡράκλειτον [. . .] τὸν Ἐφέσιον τὴν εὐαρέστησιν.

D116 (B85) Plut. *Cor.* 22 (et al.)

θυμῷ μάχεσθαι χαλεπόν· ὃ γὰρ ἂν θέλῃ, ψυχῆς ὠνεῖται.

D117 (B110) Stob. 3.1.176

ἀνθρώποις γίνεσθαι ὁκόσα θέλουσιν οὐκ ἄμεινον.

Eschatological Considerations (D118–D123)

D118 (< B20) Clem. Alex. *Strom.* 3.14.1

γενόμενοι ζώειν ἐθέλουσι μόρους τ' ἔχειν, μᾶλλον δὲ ἀναπαύεσθαι, καὶ παῖδας καταλείπουσι μόρους γενέσθαι.

---

[1] This is probably Clement's paraphrase.   [2] Or perhaps: "to be born as allotted deaths for those who leave children behind."

HERACLITUS

b

Wisdom: to speak the truth and to act in conformity with the nature [scil. of each thing], **understanding it.**[1]

[1] These two quotations are linked in Stobaeus by an "and" that seems to derive from Stobaeus, not Heraclitus. The grammar and meaning of the second sentence are uncertain.

D115 (< A21) Clement of Alexandria, *Stromata*

[. . .] Heraclitus of Ephesus [scil. said that the goal of life is] contentment.

D116 (B85) Plutarch, *Coriolanus*

To fight against an ardor (*thumos*) **is hard: for whatever it wants, it purchases it at the price of the soul** [i.e. of life].[1]

[1] Aristotle quotes this aphorism with approval several times (*EN* 2.2 1105a7–8; *EE* 2.7 1223b22–24) but interprets *thumos* (ardor, passion) restrictively as referring only to anger.

D117 (B110) Stobaeus, *Anthology*

For humans, that whatever they wish happens is not better.

Eschatological Considerations (D118–D123)

D118 (< B20) Clement of Alexandria, *Stromata*

When they have been born they want to live and to have their allotted deaths (*moroi*), or rather to have their repose,[1] **and they leave children behind to be born as allotted deaths.**[2]

D119 (B96) Strab. 16.4.26

νέκυες κοπρίων ἐκβλητότεροι.

D120 (B27) Clem. Alex. *Strom.* 4.146

ἀνθρώπους μένει ἀποθανόντας ἄσσα οὐκ ἔλπονται οὐδὲ δοκέουσιν.

D121 (B98) Plut. *Fac. orb. lun.* 28 943E

αἱ ψυχαὶ ὀσμῶνται καθ' Ἅιδην.

D122 Theod. *Cur.* 8.39 (cf. Clem. Alex. *Strom.* 4.16.1, 4.49.3)

a (B24)

ἀρηιφάτους θεοὶ τιμῶσι καὶ ἄνθρωποι.

b (B25)

μόροι γὰρ μέζονες μέζονας μοίρας λαγχάνουσι.

D123 (< B63) (Ps.-?) Hippol. *Ref.* 9.10

ἔνθα δ' ἐόντι ἐπανίστασθαι καὶ φύλακας γίνεσθαι ἐγερτὶ ζώντων[1] καὶ νεκρῶν.

[1] ἐγερτιζόντων ms., corr. Bernays

HERACLITUS

D119 (B96) Strabo, *Geography*

Corpses are more to be thrown out than manure.

D120 (B27) Clement of Alexandria, *Stromata*

What awaits humans after they have died is everything that they do not expect nor suppose.

D121 (B98) Plutarch, *On the Face in the Moon*

Souls perceive smells in Hades.

D122 Theodoret, *Cure of the Greek Maladies*

a (B24)

Gods and humans honor those men whom Ares has slain.

b (B25)

Greater deaths (*moroi*) obtain greater portions (*moirai*).

D123 (< B63) (Ps.-?) Hippolytus, *Refutation of All Heresies*

For the one who is there they rise up and become wakeful guardians of the living and of the dead.

HERACLITUS [22 DK]

R

Heraclitus' Book: Commentaries, Form, Contents
(R1–R14)
Attested Ancient Commentaries (R1–R2)

R1 Diog. Laert.

a (< A1) 9.15

πλεῖστοί τέ εἰσιν ὅσοι ἐξήγηνται αὐτοῦ τὸ σύγγραμμα· καὶ γὰρ Ἀντισθένης [cf. 66 DK] καὶ Ἡρακλείδης ὁ Ποντικὸς [Frag. 39 Wehrli, cf. **R1b**] Κλεάνθης [cf. **R1d**] τε[1] καὶ Σφαῖρος ὁ Στωικός [cf. **R1e**], πρὸς δὲ Παυσανίας ὁ κληθεὶς Ἡρακλειτιστής, Νικομήδης τε καὶ Διονύσιος· τῶν δὲ γραμματικῶν Διόδοτος [. . . = **R3b**].

[1] ὁ ποντικὸς post τε hab. mss., del. Bake

b (≠ DK) 5.86, 88

[. . . = **R1a**] φέρεται δ' αὐτοῦ [scil. Heraclides] συγγράμματα [. . .] Ἡρακλείτου ἐξηγήσεις δ' [. . .] [Frag. 22 Wehrli].

HERACLITUS

R

Heraclitus' Book: Commentaries, Form, Contents
(R1–R14)
Attested Ancient Commentaries (R1–R2)

R1 Diogenes Laertius

a (< A1)

There are many people who have explained his treatise: among them, Antisthenes, Heraclides of Pontus, Cleanthes, Sphaerus the Stoic, and also Pausanias called 'the Heraclitist,' Nicomedes, and Dionysius;[1] and among grammarians, Diodotus [. . .].

[1] None of these authors is known or datable; the Antisthenes mentioned is certainly identical with the 'Heraclitist' mentioned at 6.19.

b (≠ DK)

Treatises by him [i.e. Heraclides of Pontus] are in circulation: [. . .] *Interpretations of Heraclitus,* in four books [. . .].

c (< A1) 9.5

λέγειν τε Ἀρίστωνα [Frag. 28 Wehrli] ἐν τῷ Περὶ Ἡρακλείτου [. . .].

d (≠ DK) 7.174

βιβλία δὲ κάλλιστα καταλέλοιπεν, ἅ ἐστι τάδε· [. . .] Τῶν Ἡρακλείτου ἐξηγήσεις τέσσαρα [. . .] [SVF 1.481].

e (≠ DK) 7.178

βιβλία δὲ γέγραφε τάδε· [. . .] Περὶ Ἡρακλείτου πέντε [. . .] [SVF 1.620].

R2 (T 469 Mouraviev) Lampr. *Libr. Plut.* n. 205 Treu

περὶ τοῦ τί ἔδοξεν Ἡρακλείτῳ.

*Characterizations of the Contents of
Heraclitus' Book (R3–R4)*

R3 (< A1) Diog. Laert.

a 9.5

τὸ δὲ φερόμενον αὐτοῦ βιβλίον ἐστὶ μὲν ἀπὸ τοῦ συνέχοντος Περὶ φύσεως, διῄρηται δ' εἰς τρεῖς λόγους, εἴς τε τὸν περὶ τοῦ παντὸς καὶ πολιτικὸν καὶ θεολογικόν.

HERACLITUS

c (< A1)

Ariston says in his book *On Heraclitus* [. . .].

d (≠ DK)

He [i.e. Cleanthes] has left behind the following books: [. . .] *Interpretations of the Doctrines of Heraclitus,* in four books [. . .].

e (≠ DK)

He [i.e. Sphaerus] wrote the following books: [. . .] *On Heraclitus,* in five books [. . .].

R2 (≠ DK) Lamprias, *Index of Plutarch's Works*

On Heraclitus' Opinions.

Characterizations of the Contents of Heraclitus' Book (R3–R4)

R3 (< A1) Diogenes Laertius

a

The book of his that is in circulation is entitled *On Nature* [or: is about nature] as a whole, but it is divided into three accounts (*logoi*), about the universe, on politics, and on theology.

b 9.15

[... = **R1a**] Διόδοτος, ὃς οὔ φησι περὶ φύσεως εἶναι τὸ σύγγραμμα, ἀλλὰ περὶ πολιτείας, τὰ δὲ περὶ φύσεως ἐν παραδείγματος εἴδει κεῖσθαι.

c 9.12

ἐπιγράφουσι δ᾽ αὐτῷ οἱ μὲν "Μούσας," οἱ δὲ "Περὶ φύσεως," Διόδοτος δὲ "ἀκριβὲς οἰάκισμα πρὸς στάθμην βίου," ἄλλοι †γνώμην ἠθῶν τρόπου κόσμον ἑνὸς τῶν ξυμπάντων†.[1]

[1] τρόπου κόσμον mss.: κόσμον τρόπων Suda locus desperatus, alii alia tempt.: γνώμης Patillon, γνώμην ἤτοι Bernays, γνώμον᾽ ... ἕνα Kuster, τροπὰς κόσμου Deichgräber

R4 (< T 687 Mouraviev) Sext. *Adv. Math.* 7.7

ἐζητεῖτο δὲ καὶ περὶ Ἡρακλείτου, εἰ μὴ μόνον φυσικός ἐστιν ἀλλὰ καὶ ἠθικὸς φιλόσοφος.

Heraclitus the Obscure (R5–R14)
Characterizations of His Style (R5–R11)

R5 Diog. Laert.

a (A4) 2.22 (cf. 9.11)

φασὶ δ᾽ [Ariston Frag. 29 Wehrli] Εὐριπίδην αὐτῷ δόντα τὸ Ἡρακλείτου σύγγραμμα ἐρέσθαι, "τί δοκεῖ;" τὸν

HERACLITUS

b

[. . .] Diodotus, who says that the treatise is not about nature but about the constitution, and that the remarks about nature serve as examples.

c

Some people entitle it [i.e. his book] *The Muses*, others *On Nature;* Diodotus calls it "an accurate rudder for setting life straight," others †"thought of characters way world one of all things."†[1]

[1] The text is hopelessly corrupt; we translate its words without reproducing fully its syntax.

R4 (≠ DK) Sextus Empiricus, *Against the Logicians*

The question has also been studied regarding Heraclitus whether he is not only a natural philosopher but also a moral philosopher.

Heraclitus the Obscure (R5–R14)
Characterizations of His Style (R5–R11)

R5 Diogenes Laertius

a (A4)

They say that Euripides, after he had given Heraclitus' treatise to him [i.e. Socrates], asked, "What do you think

δὲ φάναι, "ἃ μὲν συνῆκα, γενναῖα· οἶμαι δὲ καὶ ἃ μὴ συνῆκα· πλὴν Δηλίου γέ τινος δεῖται κολυμβητοῦ."

b (< A1) 9.12

Σέλευκος μέντοι φησὶν ὁ γραμματικὸς Κρότωνά τινα ἱστορεῖν ἐν τῷ Κατακολυμβητῇ Κράτητά[1] τινα πρῶτον εἰς τὴν Ἑλλάδα κομίσαι τὸ βιβλίον· ὃν[2] καὶ εἰπεῖν Δηλίου τινὸς δεῖσθαι κολυμβητοῦ, ὃς οὐκ ἀποπνιγήσεται ἐν αὐτῷ.

[1] κράτητα F: κράτη BP[1]   [2] ὃν P: om. BF

c (< A1) 9. 6–7

[. . . = **P13**] ὡς μέν τινες, ἐπιτηδεύσας ἀσαφέστερον γράψαι, ὅπως οἱ δυνάμενοι ⟨μόνοι⟩[1] προσίοιεν αὐτῷ καὶ μὴ ἐκ τοῦ δημώδους εὐκαταφρόνητον ᾖ. [. . .] Θεόφραστος δέ φησιν [Frag. 233 FHS&G] ὑπὸ μελαγχολίας τὰ μὲν ἡμιτελῆ, τὰ δὲ ἄλλοτε ἄλλως ἔχοντα γράψαι. [. . .] [7] [. . .] λαμπρῶς τε ἐνίοτε ἐν τῷ συγγράμματι καὶ σαφῶς ἐκβάλλει, ὥστε[2] καὶ τὸν νωθέστατον ῥᾳδίως γνῶναι καὶ διάρμα ψυχῆς λαβεῖν· ἥ τε βραχύτης καὶ τὸ βάρος τῆς ἑρμηνείας ἀσύγκριτον.

[1] ⟨μόνοι⟩ Rohde   [2] ἐκβάλλει, ὥστε rec.: ἐκβόλως τε BPF: ἐκβοᾷ ὥστε Bywater

of it?" The other answered, "What I understand is splendid; I think that what I did not understand, is too; but it needs a Delian diver [i.e. a real expert]."

b (< A1)

The grammarian Seleucus says that a certain Croton reports in his *Diver* that it was a certain Crates who was the first person to bring the book to Greece and that it was he who said that it needed a Delian diver who would not drown in it.

c (< A1)

[...] Some people say that he took care to write it [i.e. his book] quite obscurely, in order that ⟨only⟩ those would have access to it who were capable of doing so and that it not be despised because of its having a popular character. [...] Theophrastus says that it was because of his melancholy [cf. **P11**] that he left some things unfinished and rewrote others in different ways. [...] [7] [...] Sometimes he lets fall a brilliant and clear utterance in his treatise, so that even the dullest man can easily understand it and acquire elevation of the soul; the brevity and the gravity of his style are incomparable.

R6 (< A4) Arist. *Rhet.* 3.5 1407b11–18

ὅλως δὲ δεῖ εὐανάγνωστον εἶναι τὸ γεγραμμένον καὶ εὔφραστον· [. . .] ὅπερ [. . .] οὐκ ἔχουσιν [. . .] ἃ μὴ ῥᾴδιον διαστίξαι, ὥσπερ τὰ Ἡρακλείτου. τὰ γὰρ Ἡρακλείτου διαστίξαι ἔργον διὰ τὸ ἄδηλον εἶναι ποτέρῳ πρόσκειται, τῷ ὕστερον ἢ τῷ πρότερον, οἷον ἐν τῇ ἀρχῇ αὐτοῦ τοῦ συγγράμματος· φησὶ γὰρ "τοῦ λόγου τοῦδ' ἐόντος[1] αἰεὶ ἀξύνετοι ἄνθρωποι γίγνονται" [cf. **D1**]· ἄδηλον γὰρ τὸ αἰεί, πρὸς ποτέρῳ[2] διαστίξαι.[3]

[1] τοῦδ' ἐόντος Victorius: τοῦ δέοντος A: τοῦ ὄντος β
[2] ποτέρῳ Susemihl: προτέρῳ A: ὁποτέρω β   [3] διαστίξαι secl. Kassel

R7 (< A4) Demetr. *Eloc.* 191–92

τὸ δὲ σαφὲς [. . .] ἐν τοῖς συνδεδεμένοις· τὸ δὲ ἀσύνδετον καὶ διαλελυμένον ὅλον ἀσαφὲς πᾶν· ἄδηλος γὰρ ἡ ἑκάστου κώλου ἀρχὴ διὰ τὴν λύσιν, ὥσπερ τὰ Ἡρακλείτου· καὶ γὰρ ταῦτα σκοτεινὰ ποιεῖ τὸ πλεῖστον ἡ λύσις.

R8 (< T 301 Mouraviev) Cic. *Fin.* 2.5.15

[. . .] quod duobus modis sine reprehensione fit: si aut de industria facias ut Heraclitus, "cognomento qui Σκοτεινός perhibetur, quia de natura nimis obscure memoravit," aut cum rerum obscuritas, non verborum, facit [. . .].

HERACLITUS

R6 (< A4) Aristotle, *Rhetoric*

In general, what is written should be easy to read and easy to pronounce [...]. This is a feature lacking in [...] writings that are difficult to punctuate, like Heraclitus'. For it is hard work to punctuate Heraclitus' statements because it is unclear with what [scil. a given term] is connected, with what follows or what precedes, as in the beginning of his book: for he says, **"And of this account that is always humans are uncomprehending"** [cf. **D1**], and it is unclear if "always" is to be punctuated so as to go with the one or the other.

R7 (< A4) Demetrius, *On Style*

Clarity depends [...] on connecting particles. For a whole that is asyndetic and unconnected is completely devoid of clarity, for in the absence of connection it is unclear where each phrase begins, as in Heraclitus' writings; and in fact it is usually the absence of connection that makes these obscure.

R8 (≠ DK) Cicero, *On Ends*

[...] which [i.e. not being understood] can come about in two ways without being blameworthy: either if you produce this intentionally, like Heraclitus, "who is called 'Obscure' because he wrote very obscurely on nature";[1] or when it is caused by the obscurity of the subject matter, not of the language [...].

---

[1] This phrase is generally considered to be a quotation from an unknown poet.

R9 (> B49a, cf. B62) Heracl. *Alleg.* 24.3–5

ὁ γοῦν σκοτεινὸς Ἡράκλειτος ἀσαφῆ καὶ διὰ συμβόλων εἰκάζεσθαι δυνάμενα θεολογεῖ τὰ φυσικὰ δι' ὧν φησί· [. . . = **D70** with textual variants]· καὶ πάλιν [. . . = **D65a**]· ὅλον τε τὸ περὶ φύσεως αἰνιγματῶδες ἀλληγορεῖ.

R10 (< T 609 Mouraviev) Clem. Alex. *Strom.* 5.8.50.2

καὶ μυρία ἐπὶ μυρίοις εὕροιμεν ἂν ὑπό τε φιλοσόφων ὑπό τε ποιητῶν αἰνιγματωδῶς εἰρημένα, ὅπου γε καὶ ὅλα βιβλία ἐπικεκρυμμένην τὴν τοῦ συγγραφέως βούλησιν ἐπιδείκνυται, ὡς καὶ τὸ Ἡρακλείτου Περὶ φύσεως, ὃς καὶ δι' αὐτὸ τοῦτο Σκοτεινὸς προσηγόρευται.

R11 (< A1a) *Suda* H.472

[. . .] καὶ ἔγραψε πολλὰ ποιητικῶς.

Two Examples of Divergent Interpretations of an Aphorism (R12–R13)

R12 (> B106) Sen. *Epist.* 12.7

ideo Heraclitus, cui cognomen fecit orationis obscuritas "unus," inquit, "dies par omni est" [cf. **D25**]. hoc alius aliter excepit. dixit enim parem esse horis, nec mentitur. nam si dies est tempus viginti et quattuor horarum,

HERACLITUS

R9 (> B49a, cf. B62) Heraclitus, *Homeric Allegories*

Surely it is theologically that the obscure Heraclitus speaks of natural phenomena as being subjects that are unclear but that can be represented figuratively by means of symbols, when he says, [... = **D70**], and again, [... = **D65a**]. And he allegorizes enigmatically everything that concerns nature.[1]

[1] Or: in his work *On Nature*.

R10 (≠ DK) Clement of Alexandria, *Stromata*

And we would find thousands upon thousands of things expressed enigmatically by philosophers and poets, and sometimes whole books show us their author's meaning in a concealed way, like the *On Nature* of Heraclitus, who is called 'the Obscure' for this very reason.

R11 (< A1a) *Suda*

[...] and he wrote many things poetically.

Two Examples of Divergent Interpretations of an Aphorism (R12–R13)

R12 (> B106) Seneca, *Letters to Lucilius*

Heraclitus, who owes his epithet [i.e. 'the Obscure'] to the obscurity of his style, said, "One day is the same as every day" [cf. **D25**]. Different people have interpreted this in different ways. For one said that it is equal in the number of hours, and he spoke truly: for if "day" means twenty-

necesse est omnes inter se dies pares esse, quia nox habet quod dies perdidit. alius ait parem esse unum diem omnibus similitudine: nihil enim habet longissimi temporis spatium, quod non et in uno die invenias, lucem et noctem [. . .].

R13 (cf. B30) Simpl. *In Cael.*, p. 294.4–23

καὶ Ἡράκλειτος δὲ ποτὲ μὲν ἐκπυροῦσθαι λέγει τὸν κόσμον, ποτὲ δὲ ἐκ τοῦ πυρὸς συνίστασθαι πάλιν αὐτὸν κατά τινας χρόνων περιόδους, ἐν οἷς φησι· "μέτρα ἁπτόμενος καὶ μέτρα σβεννύμενος" [cf. **D85**]. [. . .] καὶ Ἡράκλειτος δὲ δι' αἰνιγμῶν τὴν ἑαυτοῦ σοφίαν ἐκφέρων οὐ ταῦτα, ἅπερ δοκεῖ τοῖς πολλοῖς, σημαίνει· ὁ γοῦν ἐκεῖνα εἰπὼν περὶ γενέσεως, ὡς δοκεῖ, τοῦ κόσμου καὶ τάδε γέγραφε· "κόσμον τόνδε οὔτε τις θεῶν οὔτε ἀνθρώπων ἐποίησεν, ἀλλ' ἦν ἀεί" [cf. **D85**]. πλὴν ὅτι ὁ Ἀλέξανδρος βουλόμενος τὸν Ἡράκλειτον γενητὸν καὶ φθαρτὸν λέγειν τὸν κόσμον ἄλλως ἀκούει τοῦ κόσμου νῦν. "οὐ γὰρ μαχόμενα," φησί, "λέγει ὡς ἄν τῳ δόξαι· κόσμον γάρ," φησίν, "ἐνταῦθα οὐ τήνδε λέγει τὴν διακόσμησιν, ἀλλὰ καθόλου τὰ ὄντα καὶ τὴν τούτων διάταξιν, καθ' ἣν εἰς ἑκάτερον ἐν μέρει ἡ μεταβολὴ τοῦ παντός, ποτὲ μὲν εἰς πῦρ, ποτὲ δὲ εἰς τὸν τοιόνδε κόσμον· ἡ γὰρ τοιαύτη τούτων ἐν μέρει μεταβολὴ καὶ ὁ τοιοῦτος κόσμος οὐκ ἤρξατό ποτε, ἀλλ' ἦν ἀεί."

four hours, then all days must necessarily be equal, inasmuch as the night contains what the day loses. But another one said that one day is equal to all the others from the point of view of resemblance, because the extent of the very longest time contains nothing which you could not find in a single day—that is, light and night [. . .].

R13 (cf. B30) Simplicius, *Commentary on Aristotle's* On the Heavens

Heraclitus says that the world sometimes undergoes a conflagration and sometimes is reconstituted again out of the fire, following certain periods of time, when he says, **"kindled in measures and extinguished in measures"** [cf. **D85**]. [. . .] And Heraclitus, who expresses his wisdom by means of enigmas, is not signifying either [i.e. besides Empedocles] what most people think he means. For in any case having said this about the generation of the world, as it seems, he has also written the following: **"this world order, none of the gods or humans made it, but it always was"** [cf. **D85**]. Except that Alexander, who wants Heraclitus to say that the world is generated and perishable, now understands "world" differently. He says, "He does not say anything contradictory, as someone might suppose; for he does not mean by 'world' here the organization of this world, but in general the things that exist and their arrangement, in virtue of which the change of the whole takes place alternately in both directions, sometimes into fire, sometimes into this world. For this sort of alternation in the changes of these things and this sort of world did not ever begin, but always existed."

EARLY GREEK PHILOSOPHY III

A Facetious Falsification (R14)

R14 (T 574A, T 565 Mouraviev) Gal. *In Hipp. Epid.* 2 (*CMG* 5/10/1, p. 402.27)

[1] والأمر فيها عندي أنّه إنّما ألحق تلك الأقاويل في كتب أبقراط بعض أهل الخبث، وهو يريد أن يفضح بها أولائك السوفسطائيين الأشقياء1 ويهتكهم ويتبيّن جهلهم، كما فعل رجل من أهل دهرنا يقال له لوقيانوس. [2] فإنّه افتعل كتاباً ألّف فيه كلاماً غامضاً ليس تحته2 معنىً أصلاً، ونسبه إلى إراقليطوس3. ودفعه إلى قوم وأتوا به رجلاً فيلسوفاً مقبول القول مصدقاً موثوقاً به عند الناس. فسألوه تفسيره وشرحه لهم. فلم يفطن ذلك البائس أنهم إنما قصدوا السخرية به. فجعل يأتي بتأويلات في ذلك الكلام، وهو عند نفسه في غاية الحذق4 فافتضح بذلك.

mss. A1 = Istanbul, Aya Sofia MS 3592, fol. 146b, line 16–fol. 147a, line 10; E1 = Madrid, Escorial MS Árabe 804, fol. 122a, lines 3–10; M = Milan, Biblioteca Ambrosiana, MS B 135 Sup., fol. 82a

1 الاشقياء E1, A1: والأشقياء M   يوجبه M: تحته2 E1, A1: *fort.* بوجيه   3 إراقليطوس M: ارافلنطس E1: اراقليطنو A1   4 الحذق A1 الجد E1, M: *leg.*

Reception of Heraclitus' Doctrine (R15–R92)
Parody and Allusion in (Ps.-?) Epicharmus

See **DRAM. T5–T8**

HERACLITUS

A Facetious Falsification (R14)

R14 (≠ DK) Galen, *Commentary on Hippocrates'* Epidemics II

[1] My view about them [scil. interpolated texts in works by Hippocrates] is that an ill-intentioned person appended these texts to the writings of Hippocrates, seeking to shame and disgrace those miserable sophists, so that their ignorance would be revealed, just as one of our contemporaries named Lucian[1] has done. [2] For he forged a book in which he collected obscure words that have no meaning at all, and then attributed it to Heraclitus. He then gave it to some people who presented it to a philosopher whose utterances were well regarded and whom people found to be truthful and trustworthy. They asked him to explain it and comment on it for them. But this poor man did not realize that they only wanted to mock him. So, thinking himself to be extremely clever, he began to deliver expositions on the book, but brought disgrace upon himself as a result.[2]

[1] This Lucian may or may not be identical with Galen's celebrated contemporary, Lucian of Samosata.   [2] Translated by Peter E. Pormann, based on an earlier version produced by Bink Hallum, and revised by Kamran Karimullah and Peter E. Pormann.

Reception of Heraclitus' Doctrine (R15–R92)
Parody and Allusion in (Ps.-?) Epicharmus

See **DRAM. T5–T8**

EARLY GREEK PHILOSOPHY III

A Polemic in Parmenides? (R15)

R15 (28 B6.4–9) Simpl. *In Phys.*, p. 117.8–13, 78.3–4 (v. 8–9)

[. . . = **PARM. D7.1–4**] ἣν δὴ βροτοὶ εἰδότες οὐδέν
πλάττονται δίκρανοι· ἀμηχανίη γὰρ ἐν αὐτῶν
στήθεσιν ἰθύνει πλαγκτὸν νόον. οἱ δὲ φοροῦνται
κωφοὶ ὁμῶς τυφλοί τε, τεθηπότες, ἄκριτα φῦλα,
οἷς τὸ πέλειν τε καὶ οὐκ εἶναι ταὐτὸν νενόμισται
κοὐ ταὐτόν, πάντων δὲ παλίντροπός ἐστι
κέλευθος.

app. cf. **PARM. D7**

Hippocratic Adaptations of Heraclitean
Ideas and Language

See **MED. T9, T12**

The Heracliteans (R16–R26)
Heraclitus' Reputation (R16)

R16 (< A1) Diog. Laert. 9.6

τοσαύτην δὲ δόξαν ἔσχε τὸ σύγγραμμα, ὡς καὶ αἱρετιστὰς ἀπ' αὐτοῦ γενέσθαι τοὺς κληθέντας Ἡρακλειτείους.

HERACLITUS

A Polemic in Parmenides? (R15)

R15 (28 B6.4–9) Parmenides **D7**

[. . . scil that road], which mortals who know nothing
Invent, two-headed [scil. creatures]! For the helplessness in their
Breast directs their wandering mind; and they are borne along,
Deaf and likewise blind, stupefied, tribes undecided [or: without judgment],
Who suppose that "this is and is not" [or: that to be and not to be] is the same
And not the same, and that of all things [or: for all] the path is backward-turning.

Hippocratic Adaptations of Heraclitean Ideas and Language

See **MED. T9, T12**

The Heracliteans (R16–R26)
Heraclitus' Reputation (R16)

R16 (< A1) Diogenes Laertius

His treatise acquired such fame that followers of his even arose because of it, the people who are called the Heracliteans.

EARLY GREEK PHILOSOPHY III

Plato on the Heracliteans (R17–R18)

R17 (> 66.3) Plat. *Theaet.* 179d–180c

[ΣΩ.] [. . .] προσιτέον οὖν ἐγγυτέρω [. . .], καὶ σκεπτέον τὴν φερομένην ταύτην οὐσίαν διακρούοντα εἴτε ὑγιὲς εἴτε σαθρὸν φθέγγεται· μάχη δ᾽ οὖν περὶ αὐτῆς οὐ φαύλη οὐδ᾽ ὀλίγοις γέγονεν.

[ΘΕ.] πολλοῦ καὶ δεῖ φαύλη εἶναι, ἀλλὰ περὶ μὲν τὴν Ἰωνίαν καὶ ἐπιδίδωσι πάμπολυ. οἱ γὰρ τοῦ Ἡρακλείτου ἑταῖροι χορηγοῦσι τούτου τοῦ λόγου μάλα ἐρρωμένως.

[ΣΩ.] τῷ τοι, ὦ φίλε Θεόδωρε, μᾶλλον σκεπτέον καὶ ἐξ [179e] ἀρχῆς, ὥσπερ αὐτοὶ ὑποτείνονται.

[ΘΕ.] παντάπασι μὲν οὖν. καὶ γάρ, ὦ Σώκρατες, περὶ τούτων τῶν Ἡρακλειτείων ἤ, ὥσπερ σὺ λέγεις, Ὁμηρείων καὶ ἔτι παλαιοτέρων, αὐτοῖς μὲν τοῖς περὶ τὴν Ἔφεσον, ὅσοι προσποιοῦνται ἔμπειροι, οὐδὲν μᾶλλον οἷόν τε διαλεχθῆναι ἢ τοῖς οἰστρῶσιν. ἀτεχνῶς γὰρ κατὰ τὰ συγγράμματα φέρονται, τὸ δ᾽ ἐπιμεῖναι ἐπὶ λόγῳ καὶ ἐρωτήματι καὶ ἡσυχίως ἐν μέρει ἀποκρίνασθαι καὶ ἐρέσθαι ἧττον [180a] αὐτοῖς ἔνι ἢ τὸ μηδέν· μᾶλλον δὲ ὑπερβάλλει τὸ οὐδ᾽ οὐδὲν πρὸς τὸ μηδὲ σμικρὸν ἐνεῖναι τοῖς ἀνδράσιν ἡσυχίας. ἀλλ᾽ ἄν τινά τι ἔρῃ, ὥσπερ ἐκ φαρέτρας ῥηματίσκια αἰνιγματώδη ἀνασπῶντες ἀποτοξεύουσι, κἂν τούτου ζητῇς λόγον λαβεῖν τί εἴρηκεν, ἑτέρῳ πεπλήξῃ καινῶς μετωνομασμένῳ. περανεῖς δὲ οὐδέποτε οὐδὲν πρὸς οὐδένα αὐτῶν· οὐδέ γε ἐκεῖνοι αὐτοὶ πρὸς ἀλλήλους, ἀλλ᾽ εὖ

HERACLITUS

Plato on the Heracliteans (R17–R18)

R17 (> 66.3) Plato, *Theaetetus*

[Socrates:] [. . .] So we must go closer [. . .] to examine this being in motion and give it a tap to find out whether it rings true or is defective. For the battle that has taken place concerning this is no minor one and has not involved only a few people.

[Theodorus:] Indeed, it is far from minor, and it is even spreading very much across Ionia. For it is with great vigor that Heraclitus' companions lead the chorus that proclaims this account.

[Socrates:] That, my dear Theodorus, is just why we must examine it all the more, and from [179e] the beginning, just as they themselves present it.

[Theodorus:] Absolutely. For, about these Heraclitisms or, as you say, these Homerisms and other ideas that are even more ancient [cf. **DOX. T2**], it is just as impossible to converse with those Ephesians who profess to be experts in them, as it is with lunatics. For, honestly, their behavior is entirely in accordance with their writings, and they are not at all capable of sticking with the argument and the question, or of calmly answering and asking in turn; [180a] indeed, the absence of even the smallest bit of calmness in them exceeds this 'not at all.' But if you ask one of them something, they draw enigmatic little phrases as though from a quiver and shoot them; and if you try to get an explanation of what he has said, you will be hit by another unheard-of phrase. You will never get anywhere with any of them—nor, for that matter, do they with one another,

πάνυ φυλάττουσι τὸ [b] μηδὲν βέβαιον ἐᾶν εἶναι μήτ᾽ ἐν λόγῳ μήτ᾽ ἐν ταῖς αὑτῶν ψυχαῖς, ἡγούμενοι, ὡς ἐμοὶ δοκεῖ, αὐτὸ στάσιμον εἶναι· τούτῳ δὲ πάνυ πολεμοῦσιν, καὶ καθ᾽ ὅσον δύνανται πανταχόθεν ἐκβάλλουσιν.

[ΣΩ.] ἴσως, ὦ Θεόδωρε, τοὺς ἄνδρας μαχομένους ἑώρακας, εἰρηνεύουσιν δὲ οὐ συγγέγονας· οὐ γὰρ σοὶ ἑταῖροί εἰσιν. ἀλλ᾽ οἶμαι τὰ τοιαῦτα τοῖς μαθηταῖς ἐπὶ σχολῆς φράζουσιν, οὓς ἂν βούλωνται ὁμοίους αὑτοῖς ποιῆσαι.

[ΘΕ.] ποίοις μαθηταῖς, ὦ δαιμόνιε; οὐδὲ γίγνεται τῶν [c] τοιούτων ἕτερος ἑτέρου μαθητής, ἀλλ᾽ αὐτόματοι ἀναφύονται ὁπόθεν ἂν τύχῃ ἕκαστος αὐτῶν ἐνθουσιάσας, καὶ τὸν ἕτερον ὁ ἕτερος οὐδὲν ἡγεῖται εἰδέναι.

R18 (< T 112 Mouraviev) Plat. *Crat.* 411b–c

[ΣΩ.] καὶ μήν, νὴ τὸν κύνα, δοκῶ γέ μοι οὐ κακῶς μαντεύεσθαι, ὃ καὶ νυνδὴ ἐνενόησα, ὅτι οἱ πάνυ παλαιοὶ ἄνθρωποι οἱ τιθέμενοι τὰ ὀνόματα παντὸς μᾶλλον, ὥσπερ καὶ τῶν νῦν οἱ πολλοὶ τῶν σοφῶν, ὑπὸ τοῦ πυκνὰ περιστρέφεσθαι ζητοῦντες ὅπῃ ἔχει τὰ ὄντα εἰλιγγιῶσιν, κἄπειτα αὐτοῖς φαίνεται περιφέρεσθαι τὰ πράγματα καὶ πάντως φέρεσθαι. αἰτιῶνται δὴ οὐ τὸ ἔνδον τὸ παρὰ σφίσιν πάθος αἴτιον εἶναι ταύτης τῆς δόξης, ἀλλὰ αὐτὰ τὰ πράγματα οὕτω πεφυκέναι, οὐδὲν αὐτῶν μόνιμον εἶναι οὐδὲ βέβαιον, ἀλλὰ ῥεῖν καὶ φέρεσθαι καὶ μεστὰ εἶναι πάσης φορᾶς καὶ γενέσεως ἀεί.

but they take great care to [b] allow nothing firm to be established, either in argument or in their souls, supposing, I guess, that this would be something stable. And it is this that they wage total war against and that they banish everywhere as far as they can.

[Socrates:] But maybe, Theodorus, you have only seen those men when they were battling and have not been present when they are at peace: for they are not your comrades. But I suppose they say these kinds of things at school [or: at leisure] to their disciples, whom they wish to make similar to themselves.

[Theodorus:] What disciples, my good man? None of these [c] people ever becomes the disciple of another, but they grow up on their own, from whatever place each of them happens to have been inspired, and one man thinks that the other knows nothing at all [. . .].

R18 (≠ DK) Plato, *Cratylus*

[Socrates:] By the dog, I think that it was a pretty good inspiration that occurred to me just now: that the very ancient men who established names, like many of the present-day philosophers, more than anything got dizzy because of the intense whirling they were subjected to when they attempted to investigate the condition of the things that are, and that because of this they suppose that things are whirling around and moving in all ways possible. But they say that the cause for this opinion is not the internal affection that they feel but the fact that the nature of things is such that none of them is at rest or stable, but that they are flowing, are being borne along, and are always full of every kind of motion and generation.

EARLY GREEK PHILOSOPHY III

A Report by Aristotle on the Heracliteans (R19)

R19 (< 65.4) Arist. *Metaph.* Γ5 1010a7–12

ἔτι δὲ πᾶσαν ὁρῶντες ταύτην κινουμένην τὴν φύσιν, κατὰ δὲ τοῦ μεταβάλλοντος οὐθὲν ἀληθευόμενον, περί γε τὸ πάντῃ πάντως μεταβάλλον οὐκ ἐνδέχεσθαι ἀληθεύειν. ἐκ γὰρ ταύτης τῆς ὑπολήψεως ἐξήνθησεν ἡ ἀκροτάτη δόξα τῶν εἰρημένων, ἡ τῶν φασκόντων ἡρακλειτίζειν καὶ οἵαν Κρατύλος εἶχεν [. . . = **R23**].

Reports by a Peripatetic on the Heracliteans (R20–R21)

R20 (< Nachtrag II, pp. 421–22) Ps.-Arist. *Probl.* 13.6 908a28–34

διὰ τί, ἐάν τις σκόροδα φάγῃ, τὸ οὖρον ὄζει, ἄλλων δὲ ἐχόντων ἰσχυρὰν ὀσμὴν οὐκ ὄζει ἐδεσθέντων; πότερον, ὥσπερ τινὲς τῶν ἡρακλειτιζόντων φασίν, ὅτι ἀναθυμιᾶται, ὥσπερ ἐν τῷ ὅλῳ, καὶ ἐν τῷ σώματι, εἶτα πάλιν ψυχθὲν συνίσταται ἐκεῖ μὲν ὑγρόν, ἐνταῦθα δὲ οὖρον; [. . .]

R21 (> 66.2) Ps.-Arist. *Probl.* 23.30 934b23–24, 32–36

[. . .] διὰ τοῦτο δὲ καὶ θερμότερα τὰ ἄνω· τὸ γὰρ ἁλμυρὸν θερμότερον τοῦ ποτίμου. διὸ καὶ φασί τινες τῶν ἡρακλειτιζόντων ἐκ μὲν τοῦ ποτίμου ξηραινομένου καὶ πηγνυμένου λίθους γίνεσθαι καὶ γῆν, ἐκ δὲ τῆς θαλάττης τὸν ἥλιον ἀναθυμιᾶσθαι.

HERACLITUS

A Report by Aristotle on the Heracliteans (R19)

R19 (< 65.4) Aristotle, *Metaphysics*

Furthermore, observing that all this [i.e. perceptible and indeterminate] nature is in motion, and that "true" cannot be said about anything that is changing, [scil. they thought] that it is evidently not possible to say something true about what is changing completely in every way. It was on the basis of this idea that the most extreme doctrine blossomed forth among those we have mentioned, that of those who claim that they are Heraclitizing and the one held by Cratylus [. . .].

Reports by a Peripatetic on the Heracliteans (R20–R21)

R20 (< Nachtrag II, pp. 421–22) Ps.-Aristotle, *Problems*

Why, if one eats garlic, does the urine smell, whereas when other things that have a strong odor are eaten, it does not smell? Is it, as some of the Heraclitizers say, that an evaporation takes place, just as in the universe, so too in the body, and that, when it has cooled off again, moisture forms there and urine here? [. . .]

R21 (> 66.2) Ps.-Aristotle, *Problems*

This [scil. because the sun attracts the lighter elements of a liquid] is why the upper parts [scil. of the sea] are also warmer [scil. besides being salty]; for salty [scil. water] is warmer than potable. And that is why some of the Heraclitizers say that stones and earth are produced from the drying out and solidifying of potable water and that the sun is an evaporation coming from the sea.

EARLY GREEK PHILOSOPHY III

Cratylus (R22–R26)

R22 (< T 78 Mouraviev) Plat. *Crat.* 436e–437a

[ΣΩ.] [. . .] ὡς τοῦ παντὸς ἰόντος τε καὶ φερομένου καὶ ῥέοντός φαμεν σημαίνειν ἡμῖν τὴν οὐσίαν τὰ ὀνόματα. ἄλλο τι οὕτω σοι δοκεῖ δηλοῦν;
[ΚΡ.] πάνυ σφόδρα, καὶ ὀρθῶς γε σημαίνει.

R23 (< 65. 4) Arist. *Metaph.* Γ5 1010a12–15

Κρατύλος [. . .] ὃς τὸ τελευταῖον οὐθὲν ᾤετο δεῖν λέγειν ἀλλὰ τὸν δάκτυλον ἐκίνει μόνον, καὶ Ἡρακλείτῳ ἐπετίμα εἰπόντι ὅτι δὶς τῷ αὐτῷ ποταμῷ οὐκ ἔστιν ἐμβῆναι· αὐτὸς γὰρ ᾤετο οὐδ' ἅπαξ.

R24 Plat. *Crat.*

a (65.5) 383a–b

[ΕΡ.] Κρατύλος φησὶν ὅδε, ὦ Σώκρατες, ὀνόματος ὀρθότητα εἶναι ἑκάστῳ τῶν ὄντων φύσει πεφυκυῖαν, καὶ οὐ τοῦτο εἶναι ὄνομα ὃ ἄν τινες συνθέμενοι καλεῖν καλῶσι, τῆς αὑτῶν φωνῆς μόριον ἐπιφθεγγόμενοι, ἀλλὰ ὀρθότητά τινα τῶν ὀνομάτων πεφυκέναι καὶ Ἕλλησι καὶ βαρβάροις τὴν αὐτὴν ἅπασιν.

b (T 57 Mouraviev) 390d–e

[ΣΩ.] [. . .] καὶ Κρατύλος ἀληθῆ λέγει λέγων φύσει τὰ ὀνόματα εἶναι τοῖς πράγμασι, καὶ οὐ πάντα δημι-

HERACLITUS

Cratylus (R22–R26)

R22 (≠ DK) Plato, *Cratylus*

[Socrates:] [...] we say that names signify being for us, on the idea that everything is going, moving, and flowing. Do you think that they indicate something else?
[Cratylus:] This is absolutely how it is, and they signify correctly.

R23 (< 65.4) Aristotle, *Metaphysics*

[...] Cratylus, who in the end thought that it was necessary not to say anything but merely moved his finger, and who reproached Heraclitus for saying that it is not possible to step twice into the same river [cf. **D65**]—for he himself thought that this was not possible even once.

R24 Plato, *Cratylus*

a (65.5)

[Hermogenes:] Cratylus here says, Socrates, that there exists by nature a correct name for each of the things that are, and that a name is not whatever some people say who have agreed to use it, uttering some part of their own language, but that there exists naturally a certainly correctness of names that is identical for all, both Greeks and non-Greeks (*barbaroi*).

b (≠ DK)

[Socrates:] And Cratylus says the truth when he says that names belong by nature to things, and that not just anyone

ουργὸν ὀνομάτων εἶναι, ἀλλὰ μόνον ἐκεῖνον τὸν ἀποβλέποντα εἰς τὸ τῇ φύσει ὄνομα ὂν ἑκάστῳ καὶ δυνάμενον αὐτοῦ τὸ εἶδος τιθέναι εἴς τε τὰ γράμματα καὶ τὰς συλλαβάς.

R25 (< 65.1) Plat. *Crat.* 429d–e

[ΣΩ.] [. . .] ὅμως μέντοι εἰπέ μοι τοσόνδε· πότερον λέγειν μὲν οὐ δοκεῖ σοι εἶναι ψευδῆ, φάναι δέ;
[ΚΡ.] οὔ μοι δοκεῖ οὐδὲ φάναι.

R26 (< 65.2) Aeschin. Socr. in Arist. *Rhet.* 3.16 1417b1–2

καὶ ὡς περὶ Κρατύλου Αἰσχίνης [VI A92 G²], ὅτι διασίζων, τοῖν χεροῖν διασείων.

Heraclitus in the Derveni Papyrus

See **DERV. Col. IV** (cf. **D89a**)

Plato (R27–R34)
Plato's Debt to Heraclitus and the
Heracliteans (R27–R28)

R27 Arist. *Metaph.*

a (< 65.3) A6 987a32–b1

ἐκ νέου τε γὰρ συγγενόμενος[1] πρῶτον Κρατύλῳ καὶ ταῖς Ἡρακλειτείοις δόξαις, ὡς ἁπάντων τῶν αἰσθη-

is a craftsman of names, but only that man who looks to the name that exists by nature for each thing and is capable of putting its form into letters and syllables.

R25 (< 65.1) Plato, *Cratylus*

[Socrates:] But all the same, tell me this much: do you think that it is not possible to speak anything false, but that it is possible to say it?
[Cratylus:] On my view it is not possible to say it either.

R26 (< 65.2) Aeschines the Socratic in Aristotle, *Rhetoric*

And as Aeschines [scil. said] about Cratylus, he was hissing violently, shaking his fists.

Heraclitus in the Derveni Papyrus

See **DERV. Col. IV** (cf. **D89a**)

Plato (R27–R34)
Plato's Debt to Heraclitus and the
Heracliteans (R27–R28)

R27 Aristotle, *Metaphysics*

a (< 65.3)

In his youth, he [i.e. Plato] first became familiar with Cratylus and the Heraclitean doctrines, according to which all

---

¹ συγγενόμενος E: συνήθης γενόμενος A^b

τῶν ἀεὶ ῥεόντων καὶ ἐπιστήμης περὶ αὐτῶν οὐκ οὔσης, ταῦτα μὲν καὶ ὕστερον οὕτως[2] ὑπέλαβεν [. . .].

[2] οὕτως A[b]: οὗτος E

b (T 99 Mouraviev) M4 1078b12–17

συνέβη δ' ἡ περὶ τῶν εἰδῶν δόξα τοῖς εἰποῦσι διὰ τὸ πεισθῆναι περὶ τῆς ἀληθείας τοῖς Ἡρακλειτείοις λόγοις ὡς πάντων τῶν αἰσθητῶν ἀεὶ ῥεόντων, ὥστ' εἴπερ ἐπιστήμη τινὸς ἔσται καὶ φρόνησις, ἑτέρας δεῖν τινὰς φύσεις εἶναι παρὰ τὰς αἰσθητὰς μενούσας· οὐ γὰρ εἶναι τῶν ῥεόντων ἐπιστήμην.

R28 Diog. Laert.

a (65.3) 3.6

τοὐντεῦθεν δὴ γεγονώς, φασίν, εἴκοσιν ἔτη διήκουσε Σωκράτους· ἐκείνου δ' ἀπελθόντος προσεῖχε Κρατύλῳ τε τῷ Ἡρακλειτείῳ καὶ Ἑρμογένει τῷ τὰ Παρμενίδου φιλοσοφοῦντι.

b (T 712 Mouraviev) 3.8

μίξιν τε ἐποιήσατο τῶν τε Ἡρακλειτείων λόγων καὶ Πυθαγορικῶν καὶ Σωκρατικῶν· τὰ μὲν γὰρ αἰσθητὰ καθ' Ἡράκλειτον, τὰ δὲ νοητὰ κατὰ Πυθαγόραν, τὰ δὲ πολιτικὰ κατὰ Σωκράτην ἐφιλοσόφει.

perceptible things are constantly flowing and there is no knowledge about them, and he maintained these views later as well [...].

b (≠ DK)

The theory of Forms occurred to its partisans because they had been convinced, concerning the truth, by the Heraclitean statements according to which all perceptible things are constantly flowing, so that if there is going to be knowledge about something and thought, there must be certain other natures that remain, besides the perceptible ones: for there is no knowledge about what flows.

R28 Diogenes Laertius

a (65.3)

And, they say, afterward [i.e. after he had burned the tragedies he had written], having reached the age of twenty, he [scil. Plato] studied with Socrates. Once that man had died, he attached himself to Cratylus the Heraclitean and to Hermogenes, whose philosophy followed Parmenides' doctrines.[1]

[1] This is an inference based on the position defended by Hermogenes in Plato's *Cratylus* on the arbitrary nature of language.

b (≠ DK)

He [scil. Plato] made a mixture of the Heraclitean, Pythagorean, and Socratic doctrines: for his philosophy followed Heraclitus regarding the perceptibles, Pythagoras regarding the intelligibles, and Socrates regarding politics.

EARLY GREEK PHILOSOPHY III

Discussions and Utilizations of Heraclitus'
Doctrines in Plato (R29–R34)
On the Doctrine of Flux (R29–R30)

R29 (> A6) Plat. *Crat.* 401d–402c

[ΣΩ.] [. . .] ὅσοι δ᾽ αὖ "ὠσίαν," σχεδόν τι αὖ οὗτοι καθ᾽ Ἡράκλειτον ἂν ἡγοῖντο τὰ ὄντα ἰέναι τε πάντα καὶ μένειν οὐδέν· τὸ οὖν αἴτιον καὶ τὸ ἀρχηγὸν αὐτῶν εἶναι τὸ ὠθοῦν, ὅθεν δὴ καλῶς ἔχειν αὐτὸ "ὠσίαν" ὠνομάσθαι. [. . .] μετὰ δ᾽ Ἑστίαν δίκαιον Ῥέαν καὶ Κρόνον ἐπισκέψασθαι. [. . .] ὠγαθέ, ἐννενόηκά τι σμῆνος σοφίας.

[ΕΡ.] ποῖον δὴ τοῦτο;

[ΣΩ.] γελοῖον μὲν πάνυ εἰπεῖν, οἶμαι μέντοι τινὰ πιθανότητα ἔχον.

[ΕΡ.] τίνα ταύτην;

[ΣΩ.] τὸν Ἡράκλειτόν μοι δοκῶ καθορᾶν παλαί᾽ ἄττα σοφὰ λέγοντα, ἀτεχνῶς τὰ ἐπὶ Κρόνου καὶ Ῥέας, ἃ καὶ Ὅμηρος ἔλεγεν.

[ΕΡ.] πῶς τοῦτο λέγεις;

[ΣΩ.] λέγει που Ἡράκλειτος ὅτι "πάντα χωρεῖ καὶ οὐδὲν μένει," καὶ ποταμοῦ ῥοῇ ἀπεικάζων τὰ ὄντα λέγει ὡς "δὶς ἐς τὸν αὐτὸν ποταμὸν οὐκ ἂν ἐμβαίης" [= **D65c**].

[ΕΡ.] ἔστι ταῦτα.

[ΣΩ.] τί οὖν; δοκεῖ σοι ἀλλοιότερον Ἡρακλείτου νοεῖν ὁ τιθέμενος τοῖς τῶν ἄλλων θεῶν προγόνοις ῾Ρέαν᾽ τε

HERACLITUS

*Discussions and Utilizations of Heraclitus'
Doctrines in Plato (R29–R34)
On the Doctrine of Flux (R29–R30)*

R29 (> A6) Plato, *Cratylus*

[Socrates:] [. . .] As for those people who [i.e. explaining the name of Hestia, call the essence of things] "Ôsia,"[1] they seem to think, like Heraclitus, that all of the things that exist are in motion and that none rests in its place: for according to them the cause and originator is what "pushes" (*ôthoun*), and that is why it is quite appropriate that it is called "Ôsia." [. . .] After Hestia it is right to consider Rhea and Cronus [. . .] Dear friend, a swarm of wisdom has just come to my mind.
[Hermogenes:] What kind?
[Socrates:] It is quite ludicrous to say it, but I think there is something plausible about it.
[Hermogenes:] How so?
[Socrates:] I seem to see Heraclitus proclaiming some ancient wise sayings, ones really dating from the time of Cronus and Rhea, and ones that Homer too uttered.
[Hermogenes:] What do you mean?
[Socrates:] Heraclitus says something like this: that all things flow and nothing remains; and comparing the things that are to the flowing (*rhoê*) of a river, he says that you could not step twice into the same river [cf. **D65c**].
[Hermogenes:] That is true.
[Socrates:] Well then, do you think that the man who gave the names 'Rhea' and 'Cronus' to the ancestors of the

---

[1] The term is phonetically very close to *ousia* (being, essence).

καὶ 'Κρόνον'; ἆρα οἴει ἀπὸ τοῦ αὐτομάτου αὐτὸν ἀμφοτέροις ῥευμάτων ὀνόματα θέσθαι; ὥσπερ αὖ Ὅμηρος

> Ὠκεανόν τε θεῶν γένεσίν," φησιν, "καὶ μητέρα
> Τηθύν [**COSM. T10a**]·

οἶμαι δὲ καὶ Ἡσίοδος [cf. *Th.* 776–77 and **COSM. T7**, v. 789, 905–6]. λέγει δέ που καὶ Ὀρφεὺς ὅτι

> Ὠκεανὸς πρῶτος καλλίρροος ἦρξε γάμοιο,
> ὅς ῥα κασιγνήτην ὁμομήτορα Τηθὺν ὄπυιεν.
> [**COSM. T15**]

ταῦτ' οὖν σκόπει ὅτι καὶ ἀλλήλοις συμφωνεῖ καὶ πρὸς τὰ τοῦ Ἡρακλείτου πάντα τείνει.

R30 (> 23 A6) Plat. *Theaet.* 152d–e

[ΣΩ.] [. . .] ἐκ δὲ δὴ φορᾶς τε καὶ κινήσεως καὶ κράσεως πρὸς ἄλληλα γίγνεται πάντα ἃ δή φαμεν εἶναι, οὐκ ὀρθῶς προσαγορεύοντες· [e] ἔστι μὲν γὰρ οὐδέποτ' οὐδέν, ἀεὶ δὲ γίγνεται. καὶ περὶ τούτου πάντες ἑξῆς οἱ σοφοὶ πλὴν Παρμενίδου συμφερέσθων, Πρωταγόρας τε καὶ Ἡράκλειτος καὶ Ἐμπεδοκλῆς [. . .].

HERACLITUS

other gods had something different in mind from Heraclitus? Do you suppose that it is by chance that he gave to both of them the names of flowing things (*rheumata*)?[2] So too, Homer says,

> Ocean, the origin of the gods, and their mother Tethys (*Il.* 14.201, 302);

and, I think, Hesiod too. And Orpheus too says somewhere,

> Fair-flowing Ocean was the first to make a beginning of marriage,
> He who wedded his sister Tethys, his mother's daughter.

Just look how all these statements agree with one another and tend toward Heraclitus' doctrines [cf. **DOX. T3**].

[2] The sound of the Greek term can allude to both *Rhea* and *Kronos* (cf. *krênê, krounos*).

R30 (> 23 A6) Plato, *Theaetetus*

[Socrates:] [. . .] It is from motion, change, and mixture with each other that all the things come about that we say exist, speaking incorrectly: for nothing ever exists, but it is always becoming. And on this point let us admit that all the sages except Parmenides in sequence were in agreement—Protagoras, Heraclitus, and Empedocles [. . .] [cf. **DOX. T2**].

EARLY GREEK PHILOSOPHY III

On Unity and Multiplicity (R31)

R31 (< A10, cf. B10) Plat. *Soph.* 242d–e

[ΣΩ.] Ἰάδες δὲ [. . .] Μοῦσαι συνενόησαν ὅτι συμπλέκειν ἀσφαλέστατον ἀμφότερα καὶ λέγειν ὡς τὸ ὂν πολλά τε καὶ ἕν ἐστιν, ἔχθρα δὲ καὶ φιλίᾳ συνέχεται· "διαφερόμενον" γὰρ "ἀεὶ συμφέρεται" [cf. **D47**], φασὶν αἱ συντονώτεραι τῶν Μουσῶν [. . .].

*A Criticism of the Doctrine of
Fitting-Together (R32)*

R32 (cf. ad B51) Plat. *Symp.* 186e–187b

[ΕΡ.] ἥ τε οὖν ἰατρική, ὥσπερ λέγω, πᾶσα διὰ τοῦ θεοῦ [187a] τούτου κυβερνᾶται, ὡσαύτως δὲ καὶ γυμναστικὴ καὶ γεωργία· μουσικὴ δὲ καὶ παντὶ κατάδηλος τῷ καὶ σμικρὸν προσέχοντι τὸν νοῦν ὅτι κατὰ ταὐτὰ ἔχει τούτοις, ὥσπερ ἴσως καὶ Ἡράκλειτος βούλεται λέγειν, ἐπεὶ τοῖς γε ῥήμασιν οὐ καλῶς λέγει. "τὸ ἓν" γάρ φησι "διαφερόμενον αὐτὸ αὑτῷ συμφέρεσθαι, ὥσπερ ἁρμονίαν τόξου τε καὶ λύρας" [cf. **D49**]. ἔστι δὲ πολλὴ ἀλογία ἁρμονίαν φάναι διαφέρεσθαι ἢ ἐκ διαφερομένων ἔτι εἶναι. ἀλλὰ ἴσως τόδε ἐβούλετο λέγειν, ὅτι ἐκ διαφερομένων πρότερον τοῦ [b] ὀξέος καὶ βαρέος, ἔπειτα ὕστερον ὁμολογησάντων γέγονεν ὑπὸ τῆς μουσικῆς τέχνης. οὐ γὰρ δήπου ἐκ διαφερομένων γε ἔτι τοῦ ὀξέος καὶ βαρέος ἁρμονία ἂν εἴη. ἡ

234

HERACLITUS

On Unity and Multiplicity (R31)

R31 (< A10, cf. B10) Plato, *Sophist*

[The stranger from Elea:] Ionian Muses [i.e. Heraclitus] [. . .] recognized that it would be safest to weave together both positions [i.e. monist and pluralist] and to say that being is at the same time many and one, and that it is held together by discord and friendship. For what is separated always comes together [cf. **D47**], as the more tense of these Muses say [. . .] [cf . **DOX. T4**].

A Criticism of the Doctrine of Fitting-Together (R32)

R32 (cf. ad B51) Plato, *Symposium*

[Eryximachus:] All of medicine, I claim, is governed by this god [i.e. Eros], [187a] and the same applies to gymnastics and agriculture. As for music, it is obvious to anyone who pays even a little bit of attention that the same is true for it as for these others—as it is possible that Heraclitus too means to say, since he does not express it clearly with his words. For he says, "the one, diverging, converges with itself, like the fitting-together (*harmoniê*) of a bow and lyre" [cf. **D49**]. It is quite absurd to say that a harmony (*harmonia*) "diverges," or is made up of elements that still diverge. But perhaps what he meant was that it comes about out of [b] a sharp and a flat that at first diverge but then are accorded by the art of music. For obviously a harmony (*harmonia*) cannot be made up out of sharp and

235

γὰρ ἁρμονία συμφωνία ἐστίν, συμφωνία δὲ ὁμολογία τις· ὁμολογίαν δὲ ἐκ διαφερομένων, ἕως ἂν διαφέρωνται, ἀδύνατον εἶναι· διαφερόμενον δὲ αὖ καὶ μὴ ὁμολογοῦν ἀδύνατον ἁρμόσαι [. . .].

On the Doctrine of Multiple Perspectives (R33)

R33 (> B82, B83) Plat. *Hipp. mai.* 289a–b

[ΣΩ.] [. . .] μανθάνω, ὦ Ἱππία, ὡς ἄρα χρὴ ἀντιλέγειν πρὸς τὸν ταῦτα ἐρωτῶντα τάδε· ὦ ἄνθρωπε, ἀγνοεῖς ὅτι τὸ τοῦ Ἡρακλείτου εὖ ἔχει, ὡς ἄρα **"πιθήκων ὁ κάλλιστος αἰσχρὸς ἀνθρώπων γένει συμβάλλειν"** [= **D81**], καὶ χυτρῶν ἡ καλλίστη αἰσχρὰ παρθένων γένει συμβάλλειν, ὥς φησιν Ἱππίας ὁ σοφός; οὐχ οὕτως, ὦ Ἱππία;

[ΙΠ.] πάνυ μὲν οὖν, ὦ Σώκρατες, ὀρθῶς ἀπεκρίνω.

[ΣΩ.] ἄκουε δή. μετὰ τοῦτο γὰρ εὖ οἶδ᾽ ὅτι φήσει· τί δέ, ὦ Σώκρατες; τὸ τῶν παρθένων γένος θεῶν γένει ἄν τις [b] συμβάλλῃ, οὐ ταὐτὸν πείσεται ὅπερ τὸ τῶν χυτρῶν τῷ τῶν παρθένων συμβαλλόμενον; οὐχ ἡ καλλίστη παρθένος αἰσχρὰ φανεῖται; ἢ οὐ καὶ Ἡράκλειτος αὐτὸ τοῦτο λέγει, ὃν σὺ ἐπάγῃ, ὅτι **"ἀνθρώπων ὁ σοφώτατος πρὸς θεὸν πίθηκος φανεῖται καὶ σοφίᾳ καὶ κάλλει καὶ τοῖς ἄλλοις πᾶσιν"** [**D77**];

flat that still diverge. For a harmony (*harmonia*) is an accord, and an accord is a kind of agreement. And it is impossible for an agreement to result from things that diverge, as long as they are diverging. And inversely, what diverges and does not agree cannot fit together (*harmosai*) [...]."

On the Doctrine of Multiple Perspectives (R33)

R33 (> B82, B83) Plato, *Greater Hippias*

[Socrates:] [...] I know, Hippias, how we ought to respond to the man who asks us this question [scil. whether a beautiful pot is beautiful]: "My man, don't you know that Heraclitus is right to say, **'the most beautiful monkey is ugly compared with the human race'** [= **D81**], and the most beautiful pot is ugly compared with the race of girls, as Hippias the wise says?" Is that not right, Hippias?
[Hippias:] Absolutely, Socrates, you have answered perfectly.
[Socrates:] Then listen. For I know what he will say after this: "What, Socrates? If someone compares the race of girls to that of gods [b], will he not find the same thing as when comparing the race of pots to that of girls? Will not the most beautiful girl seem ugly? And does not Heraclitus, whom you adduce, say the same thing, that **'the wisest human will seem to be a monkey compared to a god in wisdom, beauty, and everything else?'**" [**D77**].

EARLY GREEK PHILOSOPHY III

An Application to Old Age (R34)

R34 (< T 134 Mouraviev) Plat. *Rep.* 6 498a–b

πρὸς δὲ τὸ γῆρας ἐκτὸς δή τινων ὀλίγων ἀποσβέννυνται πολὺ μᾶλλον τοῦ Ἡρακλειτείου ἡλίου, ὅσον αὖθις οὐκ ἐξάπτονται.

Summaries and Criticisms in Aristotle (R35–R43)
On Cosmic Fire (R35)

R35 (> A10) Arist. *Phys.* 3.5 205a1–7

ὅλως γὰρ καὶ χωρὶς τοῦ ἄπειρον εἶναί τι αὐτῶν, ἀδύνατον τὸ πᾶν, κἂν ᾖ πεπερασμένον, ἢ εἶναι ἢ γίγνεσθαι ἕν τι αὐτῶν, ὥσπερ Ἡράκλειτός φησιν ἅπαντα γίγνεσθαί ποτε πῦρ [. . .]· πάντα γὰρ μεταβάλλει ἐξ ἐναντίου εἰς ἐναντίον, οἷον ἐκ θερμοῦ εἰς ψυχρόν.

On the Doctrine of Flux (R36)

R36 (T172 Mouraviev) Arist. *Cael.* 3.1 298b29–33

οἱ δὲ τὰ μὲν ἄλλα πάντα γίνεσθαί φασι καὶ ῥεῖν, εἶναι δὲ παγίως οὐθέν, ἓν δέ τι μόνον ὑπομένειν, ἐξ οὗ ταῦτα πάντα μετασχηματίζεσθαι πέφυκεν· ὅπερ ἐοίκασι βούλεσθαι λέγειν ἄλλοι τε πολλοὶ καὶ Ἡράκλειτος ὁ Ἐφέσιος.

HERACLITUS

An Application to Old Age (R34)

R34 (≠ DK) Plato, *Republic*

When they [i.e. those who have studied dialectic] reach old age, except for a few of them they are extinguished, much more than the Heraclitean sun, insofar as they are not rekindled [cf. **D91**].

Summaries and Criticisms in Aristotle (R35–R43)
On Cosmic Fire (R35)

R35 (> A10) Aristotle, *Physics*

In general, independently of the question of knowing whether one of them [i.e. the elements] is unlimited, it is impossible that the whole, even if it is limited, either be or become one of them, as Heraclitus says that all things become fire at one time [. . .]; for all things are transformed from one contrary into the other, as for example from warm into cold.

See also **EMP. D79a**

On the Doctrine of Flux (R36)

R36 (≠ DK) Aristotle, *On the Heavens*

Others say that all things come about and flow, and that nothing exists stably, except for one thing alone that subsists, out of which all these other things are produced naturally by changing their form. This is what many people seem to have meant, and especially Heraclitus of Ephesus.

EARLY GREEK PHILOSOPHY III

On the Coexistence of Opposites (R37–R39)

R37 (> A7) Arist. *Metaph.* Γ3 1005b23–26

ἀδύνατον γὰρ ὁντινοῦν ταὐτὸν ὑπολαμβάνειν εἶναι καὶ μὴ εἶναι, καθάπερ τινὲς οἴονται λέγειν Ἡράκλειτον. οὐκ ἔστι γὰρ ἀναγκαῖον, ἅ τις λέγει, ταῦτα καὶ ὑπολαμβάνειν.

R38 (< T 148 Mouraviev) Arist. *Metaph.*Γ

a 7 1012a24–26

ἔοικε δ' ὁ μὲν Ἡρακλείτου λόγος, λέγων πάντα εἶναι καὶ μὴ εἶναι, ἅπαντα ἀληθῆ ποιεῖν [. . .].

b 8 1012a33–b2

σχεδὸν γὰρ οὗτοι οἱ λόγοι οἱ αὐτοὶ τῷ Ἡρακλείτου· ὁ γὰρ λέγων ὅτι πάντ' ἀληθῆ καὶ πάντα ψευδῆ, καὶ χωρὶς λέγει τῶν λόγων ἑκάτερον τούτων, ὥστ' εἴπερ ἀδύνατα ἐκεῖνα, καὶ ταῦτα ἀδύνατον εἶναι.

R39 (< T 149 Mouraviev) Arist. *Metaph.* K5 1062a30–b11

ἀπόδειξις μὲν οὖν οὐδεμία τούτων ἐστὶν ἁπλῶς, πρὸς μέντοι τὸν ταῦτα τιθέμενον ἀπόδειξις. ταχέως δ' ἄν τις καὶ αὐτὸν τὸν Ἡράκλειτον τοῦτον ἐρωτῶν[1] τὸν τρόπον ἠνάγκασεν ὁμολογεῖν μηδέποτε τὰς ἀντικειμένας φάσεις δυνατὸν εἶναι κατὰ τῶν αὐτῶν ἀληθεύε-

HERACLITUS

On the Coexistence of Opposites (R37–R39)

R37 (> A7) Aristotle, *Metaphysics*

It is impossible for anyone to think that the same thing both is and is not, as some people believe that Heraclitus said—for it is not necessary that what one says one also think.

R38 (≠ DK) Aristotle, *Metaphysics*

a

The doctrine of Heraclitus, who says that all things are and are not [cf. **D65, R9, R15**], seems to make everything true [. . .].

b

These theses [scil. that nothing is true and that everything is true] are virtually identical with those of Heraclitus: for he who affirms that everything is true and everything is false also affirms each of these propositions separately, so that if they are impossible, it is also impossible that the first one [scil. be true].

R39 (≠ DK) Aristotle, *Metaphysics*

There is no simple demonstration regarding this question [i.e. whether something can be and not be at the same time], but there is a demonstration against the person who poses it. And perhaps if someone asked Heraclitus himself in this way, he would oblige him to recognize that it is

---

[1] ἐρωτῶν A[b]: ἐρωτήσας EJ

σθαι· νῦν δ' οὐ συνιεὶς² ἑαυτοῦ τί ποτε λέγει, ταύτην ἔλαβε τὴν δόξαν. ὅλως δ' εἰ τὸ λεγόμενον ὑπ' αὐτοῦ ἐστὶν ἀληθές, οὐδ' ἂν αὐτὸ τοῦτο εἴη ἀληθές, λέγω δὲ τὸ ἐνδέχεσθαι τὸ αὐτὸ καθ' ἕνα καὶ τὸν αὐτὸν χρόνον εἶναί τε καὶ μὴ εἶναι· καθάπερ γὰρ καὶ διῃρημένων αὐτῶν οὐδὲν μᾶλλον ἡ κατάφασις ἢ ἡ ἀπόφασις ἀληθεύεται, τὸν αὐτὸν τρόπον καὶ τοῦ συναμφοτέρου καὶ τοῦ συμπεπλεγμένου καθάπερ μιᾶς τινὸς καταφάσεως οὔσης οὐθὲν μᾶλλον ἢ³ ἡ ἀπόφασις τὸ ὅλον ὡς ἐν καταφάσει τιθέμενον ἀληθεύσεται.⁴ ἔτι δ' εἰ μηθὲν ἔστιν ἀληθῶς καταφῆσαι, κἂν αὐτὸ τοῦτο ψεῦδος εἴη τὸ φάναι μηδεμίαν ἀληθῆ κατάφασιν ὑπάρχειν. εἰ δ' ἔστι τι, λύοιτ' ἂν τὸ λεγόμενον ὑπὸ τῶν τὰ τοιαῦτα ἐνισταμένων καὶ παντελῶς ἀναιρούντων τὸ διαλέγεσθαι.

² συνιεὶς A^b γρ. E: συνεὶς EJ   ³ ἢ post ἀπόφασις in mss. huc transp. Ross (qui coni. in app. οὐθὲν ἧττον ἡ ἀπόφασις ἢ)
⁴ ἀληθεύσεται A^b: ἀληθὲς ἔσται EJ

On the Identity of Opposites (R40–R41)

R40 (< T 152 Mouraviev) Arist. *Phys.* 1.2 185b19–25

ἀλλὰ μὴν εἰ τῷ λόγῳ ἓν τὰ ὄντα πάντα ὡς λώπιον καὶ ἱμάτιον, τὸν Ἡρακλείτου λόγον συμβαίνει λέγειν αὐτοῖς· ταὐτὸν γὰρ ἔσται ἀγαθῷ καὶ κακῷ εἶναι, καὶ ἀγαθῷ καὶ μὴ ἀγαθῷ εἶναι—ὥστε ταὐτὸν ἔσται ἀγαθὸν καὶ οὐκ ἀγαθόν, καὶ ἄνθρωπος καὶ ἵππος, καὶ οὐ

never possible for contradictory statements to be true about the same matters; but as it is, it was because he himself did not understand what he was saying that he adopted this view. And in general, if what he states is true, then this statement itself (I mean that the same thing can be and not be at one and the same time) would not be true. For just as if they are taken separately, the affirmation is no more true than the negation, in the same way if there is a single affirmation of their conjunction and combination, the negation will not be more true than the whole statement taken as an affirmation. And furthermore, if one cannot affirm anything truly, then this affirmation itself, according to which there is no such thing as a true affirmation, would be false. And if anything can be, then what those people say who raise this kind of objection and completely destroy discussion would be refuted.

On the Identity of Opposites (R40–R41)

R40 (≠ DK) Aristotle, *Physics*

If all things are one in their definition, as are clothing and dress, then it turns out that they [i.e. Parmenides and Melissus] are embracing Heraclitus' account: for the essence of the good and of the evil will be identical, as well as that of the good and the not good, so that good and not good will be identical, as well as human and horse, and

περὶ τοῦ ἓν εἶναι τὰ ὄντα ὁ λόγος ἔσται ἀλλὰ περὶ τοῦ μηδέν—καὶ τὸ τοιῳδὶ εἶναι καὶ τοσῳδὶ ταὐτόν.

R41 (< T 151 Mouraviev) Arist. *Top.* 8.5 159b30–33

διὸ καὶ οἱ κομίζοντες ἀλλοτρίας δόξας, οἷον ἀγαθὸν καὶ κακὸν εἶναι ταὐτόν, καθάπερ Ἡράκλειτός φησιν, οὐ διδόασι μὴ παρεῖναι ἅμα τῷ αὐτῷ τἀναντία, οὐχ ὡς οὐ δοκοῦν αὐτοῖς τοῦτο, ἀλλ' ὅτι καθ' Ἡράκλειτον οὕτω λεκτέον.

On Belief and Knowledge (R42)

R42 (< T 143 Mouraviev) Arist. *EN* 7.3 1146b26–30

ἔνιοι γὰρ τῶν δοξαζόντων οὐ διστάζουσιν, ἀλλ' οἴονται ἀκριβῶς εἰδέναι. [. . .] ἔνιοι γὰρ πιστεύουσιν οὐδὲν ἧττον οἷς δοξάζουσιν ἢ ἕτεροι οἷς ἐπίστασθαι· δηλοῖ δ' Ἡράκλειτος.

On the Soul (R43)

R43 (< A15) Arist. *An.* 1.2 405a25–26

καὶ Ἡράκλειτος δὲ τὴν ἀρχὴν εἶναί φησι ψυχήν, εἴπερ τὴν ἀναθυμίασιν, ἐξ ἧς τἆλλα συνίστησιν.

their statements will no longer bear on the fact that all things are one, but on nothing, and the same for being of such a kind and being in such a quantity.

R41 (≠ DK) Aristotle, *Topics*

That is why too those who cite others' opinions, for example that the good and the evil are the same thing, as Heraclitus said, do not concede that the contraries are not present at the same time in the same thing, not because this is not their own opinion, but because this is what one must say according to Heraclitus.

On Belief and Knowledge (R42)

R42 (≠ DK) Aristotle, *Nicomachean Ethics*

For some of those who have a certain opinion have no doubt, but think that they know exactly. [. . .] For certain people are not less convinced about their opinions than others are about their knowledge—[scil. the case of] Heraclitus shows this [cf. **P10a**].

On the Soul (R43)

R43 (< A15) Aristotle, *On the Soul*

Heraclitus too [scil. like Diogenes of Apollonia] says that the principle is the soul, since it is an evaporation, and out of this evaporation he composes everything else.

EARLY GREEK PHILOSOPHY III

Doxographies of Platonic-Peripatetic Inspiration (R44–R46)

A Systematization in Terms of Contraries (R44)

R44 (< 28 A46, 31 A86) Theophr. *Sens.* 1

περὶ δ' αἰσθήσεως αἱ μὲν πολλαὶ καὶ καθόλου δόξαι δύ' εἰσίν· οἱ μὲν γὰρ τῷ ὁμοίῳ ποιοῦσιν, οἱ δὲ τῷ ἐναντίῳ. Παρμενίδης μὲν καὶ Ἐμπεδοκλῆς καὶ Πλάτων τῷ ὁμοίῳ, οἱ δὲ περὶ Ἀναξαγόραν καὶ Ἡράκλειτον[1] τῷ ἐναντίῳ.

[1] καὶ Δημόκριτον malit Philippson

Two Systematizations in Terms of Physics (R45–R46)

R45 (> 22 A5, cf. 18.7) Simpl. *In Phys.*, p. 23.33–24.11 (< Theophr. Frag. 225 FHS&G)

Ἵππασος δὲ ὁ Μεταποντῖνος καὶ Ἡράκλειτος ὁ Ἐφέσιος ἓν καὶ οὗτοι καὶ κινούμενον καὶ πεπερασμένον, ἀλλὰ [24] πῦρ ἐποίησαν τὴν ἀρχὴν καὶ ἐκ πυρὸς ποιοῦσι τὰ ὄντα πυκνώσει καὶ μανώσει καὶ διαλύουσι πάλιν εἰς πῦρ, ὡς ταύτης μιᾶς οὔσης φύσεως τῆς ὑποκειμένης· πυρὸς γὰρ ἀμοιβὴν εἶναί φησιν Ἡράκλειτος πάντα. ποιεῖ δὲ καὶ τάξιν τινὰ καὶ[1] χρόνον ὡρισμένον τῆς τοῦ κόσμου μεταβολῆς κατά τινα εἱμαρμένην ἀνάγκην.[2] καὶ δῆλον ὅτι καὶ οὗτοι τὸ ζωο-

HERACLITUS

Doxographies of Platonic-Peripatetic Inspiration (R44–R46)
A Systematization in Terms of Contraries (R44)

R44 (‹ 28 A46, 31 A86) Theophrastus, *On Sensations*

With regard to perception, most general opinions are of two kinds: some people explain it by what is similar, others by what is contrary: Parmenides, Empedocles, and Plato by what is similar, those who follow Anaxagoras and Heraclitus by what is contrary.

Two Systematizations in Terms of Physics (R45–R46)

R45 (› 22 A5, cf. 18.7) Simplicius, *Commentary on Aristotle's* Physics

Hippasus of Metapontum [cf. **HIPPAS. D4**] and Heraclitus of Ephesus [scil. said like the other philosophers who admit a principle that is one and in motion, cf. **DOX. T14**] that it is one, in motion, and limited, but [24] they established fire as the principle and make beings come to be out of fire by condensation and rarefaction, and dissolve them again into fire, on the idea that this is the one nature that is a substrate. For Heraclitus says that all things are an exchange of fire [cf. **D87**]; and he establishes a certain order and a determinate period for the transformation of the world in conformity with a certain necessity that is fixed by destiny [cf. **D85**]. And it is clear that these too arrived at this opinion from having observed the genera-

---

¹ καί E^aF: περί D: παρά E   ² ἀνάγκην gloss. iud. Usener

EARLY GREEK PHILOSOPHY III

γόνον καὶ δημιουργικὸν καὶ πεπτικὸν καὶ διὰ πάντων χωροῦν καὶ πάντων ἀλλοιωτικὸν τῆς θερμότητος θεασάμενοι ταύτην ἔσχον τὴν δόξαν· οὐ γὰρ ἔχομεν ὡς ἄπειρον τιθεμένων αὐτῶν. ἔτι δὲ εἰ στοιχεῖον μὲν τὸ ἐλάχιστόν ἐστιν ἐξ οὗ γίνεται τὰ ἄλλα καὶ εἰς ὃ ἀναλύεται, λεπτομερέστατον δὲ τῶν ἄλλων τὸ πῦρ, τοῦτο ἂν εἴη μάλιστα στοιχεῖον.[3]

[3] *ἔτι δὲ . . . μάλιστα στοιχεῖον* transp. ed. Ald: post *λέγοντες τὸ στοιχεῖον* (p. 24.12) hab. mss.

R46 (< A1) Diog. Laert. 9. 7–11

a

[7] *ἐδόκει δὲ αὐτῷ καθολικῶς μὲν τάδε· ἐκ πυρὸς τὰ πάντα συνεστάναι καὶ εἰς τοῦτο ἀναλύεσθαι· πάντα δὲ γίνεσθαι καθ' εἱμαρμένην καὶ διὰ τῆς ἐναντιοτροπῆς*[1] *ἡρμόσθαι τὰ ὄντα· καὶ πάντα ψυχῶν εἶναι καὶ δαιμόνων πλήρη. εἴρηκε δὲ καὶ περὶ τῶν ἐν κόσμῳ συνισταμένων πάντων παθῶν, ὅτι τε ὁ ἥλιός ἐστι τὸ μέγεθος οἷος φαίνεται* [. . .].

[1] *ἐναντιοτροπῆς* mss.: *ἐναντιοτροπίας* Dindorf: *ἐναντιοδρομίας* Diels

b

[8] *καὶ τὰ ἐπὶ μέρους δὲ αὐτῷ ὧδε ἔχει τῶν δογμάτων· πῦρ εἶναι στοιχεῖον καὶ πυρὸς ἀμοιβὴν τὰ πάντα, ἀραιώσει καὶ πυκνώσει γινόμενα.*[1] *σαφῶς δὲ οὐδὲν*

tive, technical, and digestive properties of heat, its ability to pass through all things and to transform them all; for we have no information that they made it unlimited. Moreover, if an element is the smallest thing from which the others derive and into which they are dissolved, and if fire is the finest one of all, then it would be this one more than any other that would be the element.

R46 (< A1) Diogenes Laertius

a

[7] His opinions, speaking generally, are the following. All things are constituted out of fire and are dissolved into it [cf. **D85–D87**]. All things come about according to destiny [cf. **D63**], and the things that exist are fitted together thanks to the contrariety of their character [cf. **D47– D62**]. And everything is full of souls and divinities. He also spoke about everything that happens in the world, and that the sun is the size that it appears to be [cf. **D89**] [...].

b

[8] With regard to his detailed opinions, they are as follows. Fire is the element and all things are an exchange of fire [cf. **D87**], and they come about by rarefaction and condensation. But he does not explain anything clearly. All

---

¹ γινόμενα FP⁴: τὰ γιν- BP¹ Φh

ἐκτίθεται. γίνεσθαί τε πάντα κατ' ἐναντιότητα καὶ ῥεῖν τὰ ὅλα ποταμοῦ δίκην, πεπεράνθαι[2] τε τὸ πᾶν καὶ ἕνα εἶναι κόσμον· γεννᾶσθαί τε αὐτὸν ἐκ πυρὸς καὶ πάλιν ἐκπυροῦσθαι κατά τινας περιόδους ἐναλλὰξ τὸν σύμπαντα αἰῶνα· τοῦτο δὲ γίνεσθαι καθ' εἱμαρμένην. τῶν δὲ ἐναντίων τὸ μὲν ἐπὶ τὴν γένεσιν ἄγον καλεῖσθαι πόλεμον καὶ ἔριν, τὸ δ' ἐπὶ τὴν ἐκπύρωσιν ὁμολογίαν καὶ εἰρήνην. καὶ τὴν μεταβολὴν ὁδὸν ἄνω κάτω, τόν τε κόσμον γίνεσθαι κατ' αὐτήν. [9] πυκνούμενον γὰρ τὸ πῦρ ἐξυγραίνεσθαι συνιστάμενόν τε γίνεσθαι ὕδωρ, πηγνύμενον δὲ τὸ ὕδωρ εἰς γῆν τρέπεσθαι· καὶ ταύτην ὁδὸν ἐπὶ τὸ κάτω εἶναι. πάλιν τε αὖ τὴν[3] γῆν χεῖσθαι, ἐξ ἧς τὸ ὕδωρ γίνεσθαι, ἐκ δὲ τούτου τὰ λοιπά, σχεδὸν πάντα ἐπὶ τὴν ἀναθυμίασιν ἀνάγων τὴν ἀπὸ τῆς θαλάττης· αὕτη δέ ἐστιν ἡ ἐπὶ τὸ ἄνω ὁδός. γίνεσθαι δὲ ἀναθυμιάσεις ἀπό τε γῆς καὶ θαλάττης, ἃς μὲν λαμπρὰς καὶ καθαράς, ἃς δὲ σκοτεινάς. αὔξεσθαι δὲ τὸ μὲν πῦρ ὑπὸ τῶν λαμπρῶν, τὸ δὲ ὑγρὸν ὑπὸ τῶν ἑτέρων. τὸ δὲ περιέχον ὁποῖόν ἐστιν οὐ δηλοῖ· εἶναι μέντοι ἐν αὐτῷ σκάφας ἐπεστραμμένας κατὰ κοῖλον πρὸς ἡμᾶς, ἐν αἷς ἀθροιζομένας τὰς λαμπρὰς ἀναθυμιάσεις ἀποτελεῖν φλόγας, ἃς εἶναι τὰ ἄστρα. [10] λαμπροτάτην δὲ εἶναι τὴν τοῦ ἡλίου φλόγα καὶ θερμοτάτην. τὰ μὲν γὰρ ἄλλα ἄστρα πλεῖον ἀπέχειν ἀπὸ γῆς καὶ διὰ τοῦτο ἧττον λάμπειν καὶ θάλπειν, τὴν δὲ σελήνην προσγειοτέραν οὖσαν μὴ διὰ τοῦ καθαροῦ φέρεσθαι τόπου. τὸν μέντοι ἥλιον

HERACLITUS

things come about by contrariety and the totality of things flows like a river [cf. **D65–D66**]. The whole is limited and there is only one world [cf. **D85**]. It is generated out of fire and it burns up again [i.e. it becomes fire] according to certain periods [cf. **D85**], alternating, for the whole duration of time. And this comes about according to destiny. Of the contraries, the one that leads to generation is called war and strife [cf. **D63, D64**], the one that leads to the conflagration (*ekpurôsis*), agreement and peace [cf. **D48, D49**], and the changing is a way upward and downward [cf. **D51**], and it is according to this that the world comes about. [9] For as the fire becomes dense, it becomes moist, and when it collects together it becomes water, and when the water becomes solid it turns into earth [cf. **D86**]. And this is the downward way. But then in turn the earth spreads out and from it comes water [cf. **D86**], and from this comes everything else, since he derives almost everything from the evaporation from the sea; and this is the upward way. But there are evaporations that come from the earth and sea, some of them bright and pure, others dark. The fire increases because of the bright ones, the moisture because of the others. He does not explain what surrounds. But there are in it bowls turned over with their concave part facing us, in which bright evaporations that are pressed together produce flames, which are the heavenly bodies. [10] The brightest and hottest flame is that of the sun. For the other heavenly bodies are farther away from the earth and that is why they produce less light and heat; the moon is closer to the earth but does not move through the pure region. But the sun

---

² πεπεράνθαι Φh: πεπεράσθαι BP: -ᾶσθαι F   ³ αὐτὴν mss., corr. Reiske

ἐν διαυγεῖ καὶ ἀμιγεῖ κεῖσθαι[4] καὶ σύμμετρον ἀφ᾽ ἡμῶν ἔχειν διάστημα· τοιγάρτοι μᾶλλον θερμαίνειν τε καὶ φωτίζειν. ἐκλείπειν τε ἥλιον καὶ σελήνην, ἄνω στρεφομένων τῶν σκαφῶν· τούς τε κατὰ μῆνα τῆς σελήνης σχηματισμοὺς γίνεσθαι στρεφομένης ἐν αὑτῇ[5] κατὰ μικρὸν τῆς σκάφης. ἡμέραν τε καὶ νύκτα γίνεσθαι καὶ μῆνας καὶ ὥρας ἐτείους καὶ ἐνιαυτοὺς ὑετούς τε καὶ πνεύματα καὶ τὰ τούτοις ὅμοια κατὰ τὰς διαφόρους ἀναθυμιάσεις. [11] τὴν μὲν γὰρ λαμπρὰν ἀναθυμίασιν φλογωθεῖσαν ἐν τῷ κύκλῳ τοῦ ἡλίου ἡμέραν ποιεῖν, τὴν δὲ ἐναντίαν ἐπικρατήσασαν νύκτα ἀποτελεῖν· καὶ ἐκ μὲν τοῦ λαμπροῦ τὸ θερμὸν αὐξόμενον θέρος ποιεῖν, ἐκ δὲ τοῦ σκοτεινοῦ τὸ ὑγρὸν πλεονάζον χειμῶνα ἀπεργάζεσθαι. ἀκολούθως δὲ τούτοις καὶ περὶ τῶν ἄλλων αἰτιολογεῖ. περὶ δὲ τῆς γῆς οὐδὲν ἀποφαίνεται ποία τίς ἐστιν, ἀλλ᾽ οὐδὲ περὶ τῶν σκαφῶν. καὶ ταῦτα μὲν ἦν αὐτῷ τὰ δοκοῦντα.

[4] κεῖσθαι mss.: κινεῖσθαι Reiske [5] ἐν αὑτῇ Mouraviev: ἐν αὐτῇ BPF[2] Φh: ἐν αὐτοῖς F[1]: αὐτῆς Marcovich

Reports Reflecting a Platonic-Aristotelian
Appropriation (R47–R49)
Motion (R47)

R47 (A6) Aët. 1.23.7 (Ps.-Plut., cf. Stob.) [περὶ κινήσεως]

Ἡράκλειτος ἠρεμίαν μὲν καὶ στάσιν ἐκ τῶν ὅλων

HERACLITUS

lies in a diaphanous and unmixed [scil. region], and is at a proportionate distance from us; for that is why it gives more heat and light. Eclipses of the sun and moon occur when the bowls are turned upward; the monthly phases of the moon come about when the bowl turns around on itself little by little. Day, night, months, the seasons of the year, rainy years, winds, and similar phenomena come about because of different evaporations. [11] For the bright evaporation makes day when it is kindled in the circle of the sun, but when the contrary one prevails it produces night. And heat, increased by the bright one, makes summer, while moisture, made preponderant by the dark one, generates winter. He supplies the causes for other phenomena as well, along the same lines. But as for the earth, he does not explains what it is, nor about the bowls either. And these were his opinions.

Reports Reflecting a Platonic-Aristotelian Appropriation (R47–R49)
Motion (R47)

R47 (A6) Aëtius

Heraclitus abolishes immobility and rest from the uni-

ἀνῄρει· ἔστι γὰρ τοῦτο τῶν νεκρῶν· κίνησιν δ' ἀίδιον μὲν τοῖς ἀιδίοις, φθαρτὴν δὲ τοῖς φθαρτοῖς.[1]

[1] ἔστι . . . φθαρτοῖς Plut.: κίνησιν δὲ τοῖς πᾶσιν ἀπεδίδου Stob.

The Soul (R48)

R48

a (A15) Aët. 4.3.12 (Ps.-Plut.) [εἰ σῶμα ἡ ψυχὴ καὶ τίς ἡ οὐσία αὐτῆς]

Ἡράκλειτος τὴν μὲν τοῦ κόσμου ψυχὴν ἀναθυμίασιν ἐκ τῶν ἐν αὐτῷ ὑγρῶν, τὴν δ' ἐν τοῖς ζῴοις ἀπὸ τῆς ἐκτὸς καὶ τῆς ἐν αὐτοῖς ἀναθυμιάσεως, ὁμογενῆ.

b (cf. ad A17) Aët. 4.7.2 (Theod. 5.23) [περὶ ἀφθαρσίας ψυχῆς]

ὁ δὲ Ἡράκλειτος τὰς ἀπαλλαττομένας τοῦ σώματος εἰς τὴν τοῦ παντὸς ἀναχωρεῖν ψυχὴν ἔφησεν, οἷα δὴ ὁμογενῆ τε οὖσαν καὶ ὁμοούσιον.

c (T 782 Mouraviev) Macr. *In Somn.* 1.14.19

Heraclitus physicus scintillam stellaris essentiae.

verse, for these belong to corpses; and [scil. he attributes] an eternal motion to eternal things, and a perishable motion to perishable ones.

The Soul (R48)

R48

a (A15) Aëtius

Heraclitus: the soul of the world is an evaporation of the moisture it contains, and the one that is in animals, which derives from the external evaporation and from the one that is in them, is of the same kind.

b (cf. ad A17) Aëtius

Heraclitus said that the souls that leave the body return to the soul of the whole, since their genus and substance are of the same nature.

c (≠ DK) Macrobius, *Commentary on Cicero's* Dream of Scipio

Heraclitus, the natural philosopher, [scil. calls the soul] a spark of the stars' substance.

The Heavens (D49)

R49 (31 A62) (Ps.-?) Hippol. *Ref.* 1.4.3

καὶ ὥσπερ ὁ Ἐμπεδοκλῆς πάντα τὸν καθ' ἡμᾶς τόπον ἔφη κακῶν μεστὸν εἶναι καὶ μέχρι μὲν σελήνης τὰ κακὰ φθάνειν ἐκ τοῦ περὶ γῆν τόπου ταθέντα, περαιτέρω δὲ μὴ χωρεῖν, ἅτε καθαρωτέρου τοῦ ὑπὲρ τὴν σελήνην παντὸς ὄντος τόπου, οὕτω καὶ τῷ Ἡρακλείτῳ ἔδοξεν.

Stoics (R50–R66)
Stoic Appropriations (R50–R56)
Zeno (R50–R51)

R50 (< T 256 Mouraviev) Numen. in Eus. *PE* 14.5.11–12 (Frag. 25 Des Places)

[. . .] νυνὶ δὲ αὐτῷ λελογίσθω ὅτι καὶ Στίλπωνός τε μετέσχε καὶ τῶν λόγων τῶν Ἡρακλειτείων. ἐπεὶ γὰρ συμφοιτῶντες παρὰ Πολέμωνι ἐφιλοτιμήθησαν ἀλλήλοις, συμπαρέλαβον εἰς τὴν πρὸς ἀλλήλους μάχην ὁ μὲν Ἡράκλειτον καὶ Στίλπωνα ἅμα καὶ Κράτητα, ὧν ὑπὸ μὲν Στίλπωνος ἐγένετο μαχητής, ὑπὸ δὲ Ἡρακλείτου αὐστηρός, κυνικὸς δὲ ὑπὸ Κράτητος, ὁ δὲ Ἀρκεσίλαος [. . .] [cf. *SVF* 1.11].

HERACLITUS

The Heavens (D49)

R49 (31 A62) (Ps.-?) Hippolytus, *Refutation of All Heresies*

And as Empedocles said that the whole region near us is full of evils, and that evils spread as far as the moon, extending outward from the region around the earth, but do not go any farther, since the whole region beyond the moon is purer; this too was the view of Heraclitus [= **EMP. D142**].

Stoics (R50–R66)
Stoic Appropriations (R50–R56)
Zeno (R50–R51)

R50 (≠ DK) Numenius, *On the Infidelity of the Academy toward Plato,* in Eusebius, *Evangelical Preparation*

[. . .] Consider now that he [i.e. Zeno the Stoic] also had his share in Stilpo and the Heraclitean doctrines. For when they [i.e. Arcesilaus and Zeno] were fellow students of Polemon and became rivals, the one [i.e. Zeno] took as his allies in their struggle Heraclitus and Stilpo together with Crates: Stilpo made him a fighter, Heraclitus austere, and Crates a Cynic. As for Arcesilaus [. . .].

R51 (> B12) Ar. Did. in Eus. *PE* 15.20.2–3 (Frag. 39 Diels)

περὶ δὲ ψυχῆς Κλεάνθης μέν, τὰ Ζήνωνος δόγματα παρατιθέμενος πρὸς σύγκρισιν τὴν πρὸς ἄλλους φυσικούς, φησιν [*SVF* 1.141 et 519] ὅτι Ζήνων τὴν ψυχὴν λέγει αἰσθητικὴν[1] ἀναθυμίασιν, καθάπερ Ἡράκλειτος· βουλόμενος γὰρ ἐμφανίσαι, ὅτι αἱ ψυχαὶ ἀναθυμιώμεναι νοεραὶ ἀεὶ γίνονται, εἴκασεν αὐτὰς τοῖς ποταμοῖς λέγων οὕτως [. . . = **D65a**]· ἀναθυμίασιν μὲν οὖν ὁμοίως τῷ Ἡρακλείτῳ τὴν ψυχὴν ἀποφαίνει Ζήνων, αἰσθητικὴν δὲ αὐτὴν εἶναι [. . .] λέγει [. . .].

[1] αἴσθησιν ἢ mss., corr. Wellmann

Cleanthes (R52)

R52 (C4) Cleanth. in Stob. 1.1.12 [*SVF* 1. 537]

σοὶ δὴ πᾶς ὅδε κόσμος, ἑλισσόμενος περὶ γαῖαν,
πείθεται, ᾗ κεν ἄγῃς, καὶ ἑκὼν ὑπὸ σεῖο
   κρατεῖται·
τοῖον ἔχεις ὑποεργὸν ἀνικήτοις ἐνὶ χερσίν
ἀμφήκη, πυρόεντ᾽, αἰειζώοντα κεραυνόν·
5 τοῦ γὰρ ὑπὸ πληγῆς φύσεως πάντ᾽ ἐρρίγα⟨σιν⟩·
ᾧ σὺ κατευθύνεις κοινὸν λόγον, ὃς διὰ πάντων
φοιτᾷ, μιγνύμενος μεγάλοις μικροῖς τε φάεσσι.

1 δὲ ms., corr. Scaliger   2 σοῖο ms., corr. Ursinus
3 ἔχοις ms., corr. Ursinus   ἐνὶ Brunck: ὑπὸ ms.
4 πυρόεντα ἀειζώοντα ms., corr. Wachsmuth

HERACLITUS

R51 (> B12) Arius Didymus in Eusebius, *Evangelical Preparation*

Concerning the soul, Cleanthes, citing the doctrines of Zeno in order to establish a comparison with the other philosophers of nature, says that Zeno defines the soul as an evaporation endowed with sensation, like Heraclitus; for, wanting to show that the souls that come from an evaporation are always intelligent, he has compared them to rivers, when he says, [... = **D65a**]. Thus Zeno affirms, like Heraclitus, that the soul is an evaporation, and he says that it is endowed with sensation [...].

Cleanthes (R52)

R52 (C4) Stobaeus, *Anthology*

> It is to you [i.e. Zeus] that this whole world order,
>   whirling around the earth,
> Is obedient, wherever you lead it, and it is willingly
>   ruled by you—
> Such is the servant you hold in your invincible hands,
> The two-edged fiery ever-living lightning bolt:[1]
> For under its blow[2] all things in nature shudder;
> With it you make straight the account in common,
>   which through all things
> Proceeds,[3] mixing them with great lights and with
>   small ones.

[1] Cf. **D82.** [2] Cf. **D110.** [3] Cf. **D2, D82.**

---

5 πληγῆς ms., corr. Brunck   ἐρρίγασιν Ursinus: ἔρηγα spat. 10 litt. ms.   6 λόγον κοινόν ms., corr. Ursinus
7 μεγάλοις μικροῖς τε Brunck: μεγάλων μικροῖσι ms.

EARLY GREEK PHILOSOPHY III

Chrysippus (R53)

R53 (< T 262 Mouraviev) Philod. *Piet.* Col. 14 (p. 18 Henrichs)

[13] τὰ πα|ραπλήσια δὲ κἀν | τοῖς περὶ Φύσεως | γράφει [Chrysipp., *SVF* 2.636], μεθ᾽ ὧν εἴπα|μεν καὶ τοῖς Ἡρα|κλείτου συνοικειῶν. | [. . .] [21] ἐν δὲ | τῷ τρίτῳ [. . .] καὶ | τὸν πόλεμο[ν] καὶ | τὸν Δ[ί]α τὸν αὐτὸν | εἶν[αι, κα]θάπερ καὶ | τὸν [Ἡ]ράκλειτον λέ|γειν.

Marcus Aurelius (R54–R55)

R54 (> B71–74, B76) M. Aur. 4.46

ἀεὶ τοῦ Ἡρακλειτείου μεμνῆσθαι, ὅτι γῆς θάνατος ὕδωρ γενέσθαι καὶ ὕδατος θάνατος ἀέρα γενέσθαι καὶ ἀέρος πῦρ καὶ ἔμπαλιν. μεμνῆσθαι δὲ καὶ τοῦ ἐπιλανθανομένου ᾗ ἡ ὁδὸς ἄγει· καὶ ὅτι, ᾧ μάλιστα διηνεκῶς ὁμιλοῦσι, λόγῳ τῷ τὰ ὅλα διοικοῦντι, τούτῳ διαφέρονται, καὶ οἷς καθ᾽ ἡμέραν ἐγκυροῦσι, ταῦτα αὐτοῖς ξένα φαίνεται· καὶ ὅτι οὐ δεῖ ὥσπερ καθεύδοντας ποιεῖν καὶ λέγειν· καὶ γὰρ καὶ τότε δοκοῦμεν ποιεῖν καὶ λέγειν· καὶ ὅτι οὐ δεῖ ⟨ὡς⟩ παῖδας τοκεώνων[1] [= **D7**], τουτέστι κατὰ ψιλόν "καθότι παρειλήφαμεν."

[1] cf. app. ad **D7**

HERACLITUS

Chrysippus (R53)

R53 (≠ DK) Philodemus, *On Piety*

[13] He [i.e. Chrysippus] writes much the same things in his books *On Nature,* proceeding, after those we have discussed [i.e. Orpheus, Musaeus, Homer, Euripides, Cleanthes] to an assimilation with the doctrines of Heraclitus. [. . .] [21] In the third [scil. book, he says] that war and Zeus are the same thing, and that this is what Heraclitus says too [cf. **D64**].

Marcus Aurelius (R54–R55)

R54 (> B71–74, B76) Marcus Aurelius

To always remember what Heraclitus says, that death for the earth is to become water, death for water is to become air, and for air, to become fire; and inversely [cf. **D100**]. And to remember the man who has forgotten where the road leads [cf. **D104**]. And this too: that from what they most incessantly associate with, the reason that administers the universe, they are at variance, and what they encounter every day seems foreign to them [cf. **D3**]. And that we should not act and speak like people who are sleeping [cf. **D1**] (for then too we think we are acting and speaking); and that we should not [scil. act and speak] ⟨like⟩ the children of our parents [= **D7**], that is, in ordinary language, in conformity with what we have received from tradition.

R55 (B75) M. Aur. 6.42

τοὺς καθεύδοντας, οἶμαι, ὁ Ἡράκλειτος ἐργάτας εἶναι λέγει καὶ συνεργοὺς τῶν ἐν τῷ κόσμῳ γινομένων.

An Anonymous Paraphrase (R56)

R56 (B89) Ps.-Plut. *Superst.* 166C

ὁ Ἡράκλειτός φησι τοῖς ἐγρηγορόσιν ἕνα καὶ κοινὸν κόσμον εἶναι, τῶν δὲ κοιμωμένων ἕκαστον εἰς ἴδιον ἀποστρέφεσθαι.[1]

[1] ἀναστρέφεσθαι D

Some Characteristic Stoic Doctrines Linked with Heraclitus (R57–R66)
Various Subjects (R57)

R57 (T 270 Mouraviev) Clem. Alex. *Strom.* 5.105.1

[. . . = **R82**] παραπλήσια τούτῳ καὶ οἱ ἐλλογιμώτατοι τῶν Στωικῶν δογματίζουσι περί τε ἐκπυρώσεως διαλαμβάνοντες καὶ κόσμου διοικήσεως καὶ τοῦ ἰδίως ποιοῦ κόσμου τε καὶ ἀνθρώπου καὶ τῆς τῶν ἡμετέρων ψυχῶν ἐπιδιαμονῆς [SVF 2.590].

HERACLITUS

R55 (B75) Marcus Aurelius

I think that Heraclitus says that those who sleep are constructors and collaborators in what happens in the world.

An Anonymous Paraphrase (R56)

R56 (B89) Ps.-Plutarch, *On Superstition*

Heraclitus says that those who are awake have a world that is one and in common, but that each of those who are asleep turns aside into his own particular world [cf. **D2**].

Some Characteristic Stoic Doctrines Linked with Heraclitus (R57–R66)
Various Subjects (R57)

R57 (≠ DK) Clement of Alexandria, *Stromata*

[. . .] What the most illustrious Stoics profess concerning the conflagration (*ekpurôsis*), the administration of the world, the individuality of the world and of the human being, and the persistence of our souls, is very similar to this [i.e. Heraclitus' doctrine].

EARLY GREEK PHILOSOPHY III

Human Reason, Divine Reason (R58–R60)

R58 (A20) Calcid. *In Tim.* 251

Heraclitus vero consentientibus Stoicis [*SVF* 2.1198] rationem nostram cum divina ratione conectit regente ac moderante mundana: propter inseparabilem comitatum consciam decreti rationabilis factam, quiescentibus animis opere sensuum futura denuntiare; ex quo fieri ut appareant imagines ignotorum locorum simulacraque hominum tam viventium quam mortuorum. idemque asserit divinationis usum et praemoneri meritos instruentibus divinis potestatibus.

R59 (cf. A16) Sext. Emp. *Adv. Math.* 7.127–34

[127] [. . .] ἀρέσκει γὰρ τῷ φυσικῷ τὸ περιέχον ἡμᾶς λογικόν τε ὂν καὶ φρενῆρες. [. . .] [129] τοῦτον οὖν τὸν θεῖον λόγον καθ' Ἡράκλειτον δι' ἀναπνοῆς σπάσαντες νοεροὶ γινόμεθα, καὶ ἐν μὲν ὕπνοις ληθαῖοι, κατὰ δὲ ἔγερσιν πάλιν ἔμφρονες. ἐν γὰρ τοῖς ὕπνοις μυσάντων τῶν αἰσθητικῶν πόρων χωρίζεται τῆς πρὸς τὸ περιέχον συμφυΐας ὁ ἐν ἡμῖν νοῦς, μόνης τῆς κατὰ ἀναπνοὴν προσφύσεως σῳζομένης οἱονεί τινος ῥίζης, χωρισθείς τε ἀποβάλλει ἣν πρότερον εἶχε μνημονικὴν δύναμιν. [130] ἐν δὲ ἐγρηγόρσει πάλιν διὰ τῶν αἰσθητικῶν πόρων ὥσπερ διά τινων θυρίδων προσκύψας καὶ τῷ περιέχοντι συμβαλὼν λογικὴν ἐνδύεται δύναμιν. ὅνπερ οὖν τρόπον οἱ ἄνθρακες πλησιάσαντες τῷ πυρὶ κατ' ἀλλοίωσιν διάπυροι γίνονται, χωρι-

HERACLITUS

Human Reason, Divine Reason (R58–R60)

R58 (A20) Calcidius, *Commentary on Plato's* Timaeus

Heraclitus, with the approval of the Stoics, connects our reason with the divine reason that rules and governs the affairs of the world: being made conscious of the law of reason because of this inseparable connection, when our souls are resting it announces the future with the help of the senses. This is how it comes about that the images of unknown places and the likenesses of both living and dead men appear. And the same man defends the practice of divination and [scil. claims] that those who are deserving are forewarned by divine powers that instruct them.

R59 (cf. A16) Sextus Empiricus, *Against the Logicians*

[127] [. . .] this natural philosopher [i.e. Heraclitus] holds the view that the substance that surrounds us is rational and mindful. [. . .] [129] So according to Heraclitus, it is by inhaling this divine reason when we breathe that we become intelligent, and whereas we forget it when we sleep, we become mindful again when we are awake. For when we sleep, the channels of perception are closed and the mind within us is separated from its natural connection with what surrounds, and only the point of attachment, respiration, subsists like a kind of root, and when it is separated it loses the faculty of memory that it had before; [130] but then when it awakens, leaning toward the channels of perception as though toward windows and encountering what surrounds, it takes on the faculty of reason once again. In the same way as pieces of charcoal brought near to a fire are kindled according to a transformation but are extinguished when they are removed from

265

σθέντες δὲ σβέννυνται, οὕτω καὶ ἡ ἐπιξενωθεῖσα τοῖς ἡμετέροις σώμασιν ἀπὸ τοῦ περιέχοντος μοῖρα κατὰ μὲν τὸν χωρισμὸν σχεδὸν ἄλογος γίνεται, κατὰ δὲ τὴν διὰ τῶν πλείστων πόρων σύμφυσιν ὁμοιοειδὴς τῷ ὅλῳ καθίσταται. [131] τοῦτον δὴ τὸν κοινὸν λόγον καὶ θεῖον, καὶ οὗ κατὰ μετοχὴν γινόμεθα λογικοί, κριτήριον ἀληθείας φησὶν ὁ Ἡράκλειτος. ὅθεν τὸ μὲν κοινῇ πᾶσι φαινόμενον, τοῦτ᾽ εἶναι πιστόν (τῷ κοινῷ γὰρ καὶ θείῳ λόγῳ λαμβάνεται), τὸ δέ τινι μόνῳ προσπίπτον ἄπιστον ὑπάρχειν διὰ τὴν ἐναντίαν αἰτίαν. [132] ἐναρχόμενος γοῦν[1] τῶν Περὶ φύσεως ὁ προειρημένος ἀνήρ, καὶ τρόπον τινὰ δεικνὺς τὸ περιέχον, φησί· "**λόγου τοῦδε ἐόντος** [. . .] **ὅκωσπερ ὁκόσα εὕδοντες ἐπιλανθάνονται**" [= **D1**]. [133] διὰ τούτων γὰρ ῥητῶς παραστήσας, ὅτι κατὰ μετοχὴν τοῦ θείου λόγου πάντα πράττομέν τε καὶ νοοῦμεν, ὀλίγα προδιελθὼν ἐπιφέρει· διὸ δεῖ ἕπεσθαι τῷ κοινῷ (ξυνὸς γὰρ ὁ κοινός), "**τοῦ λόγου δ᾽ ἐόντος ξυνοῦ ζώουσιν οἱ πολλοὶ ὡς ἰδίαν ἔχοντες φρόνησιν**" [= **D2**]. ἡ δ᾽ ἔστιν οὐκ ἄλλο τι ἀλλ᾽ ἐξήγησις τοῦ τρόπου τῆς τοῦ παντὸς διοικήσεως [. . . = **R73**].

[1] οὖν mss., corr. Kayser

R60 (A16) Sext. Emp. *Adv. Math.* 8.286

καὶ μὴν ῥητῶς ὁ Ἡράκλειτός φησι τὸ μὴ εἶναι λογικὸν τὸν ἄνθρωπον, μόνον δ᾽ ὑπάρχειν φρενῆρες τὸ περιέχον.

it, so too the portion coming from what surrounds, which resides with our bodies, in the state of separation becomes almost irrational, but in the state of union by most of the channels it is restored to its affinity with the whole. [131] Heraclitus says that this reason, which is in common and divine, and by participation in which we become rational, is the criterion of the truth; this is why what appears to all in common is reliable (for it is apprehended by the reason that is common and divine), while what is evident to one man alone is unreliable, for the opposite reason. [132] For this is what the abovementioned man says at the beginning of his book *On Nature* [or: of his remarks about nature], when in a certain way he is indicating what surrounds: **"Of this account that is [. . .] just as they forget all they do while they are asleep"** [= **D1**]. [133] After he has indicated explicitly in these words that it is by participation in divine reason that we do and think everything, a little later he adds that therefore we ought to follow what is in common (for *xunos* [i.e. the Ionic term] means "in common"): **"But although the account is in common, most people live as though they had their own thought"** [= **D2**]. This is nothing other than an explanation of the way in which the whole is organized [. . .].

R60 (A16) Sextus Empiricus, *Against the Logicians*

And yet Heraclitus says explicitly that the human being is not rational, and that only what surrounds is endowed with intelligence.

EARLY GREEK PHILOSOPHY III

Cosmic Fire (R61–R63)

R61 (T 303 Mouraviev) Cic. *Nat. deor.* 3.14.35

sed omnia vestri, Balbe, solent ad igneam vim referre Heraclitum, ut opinor, sequentes, quem ipsum non omnes interpretantur uno modo, qui quoniam quid diceret intellegi noluit, omittamus [SVF 2.421].

R62 (T 260, T 940 Mouraviev) Simpl. *In Phys.*, p. 480.27–30

ἔλεγε γὰρ Ἡράκλειτος ἐκ πυρὸς πεπερασμένου πάντα εἶναι καὶ εἰς τοῦτο πάντα ἀναλύεσθαι. εἶεν δ᾽ ἂν καὶ οἱ Στωικοὶ ταύτης τῆς δόξης. ἡ γὰρ ἐκπύρωσις τοιοῦτόν τι αἰνίτεττται, καὶ πᾶν σῶμα πεπερασμένον εἶναι λέγουσιν [SVF 2.603].

R63 (cf. ad B30) Simpl. *In Cael.*, p. 294.4–7

καὶ Ἡράκλειτος δὲ ποτὲ μὲν ἐκπυροῦσθαι λέγει τὸν κόσμον, ποτὲ δὲ ἐκ τοῦ πυρὸς συνίστασθαι πάλιν αὐτὸν κατά τινας χρόνων περιόδους, ἐν οἷς φησι· "μέτρα ἁπτόμενος καὶ μέτρα σβεννύμενος" [cf. **D85**]. ταύτης δὲ τῆς δόξης ὕστερον ἐγένοντο καὶ οἱ Στωικοί [SVF 2.617].

HERACLITUS

Cosmic Fire (R61–R63)

R61 (≠ DK) Cicero, *On the Nature of the Gods*

But those [scil. Stoics] of yours, Balbus, have the habit of referring everything to the force of fire, following, I suppose, Heraclitus, whom they do not all interpret in the same way. But since he did not wish what he said to be understood, let us leave him aside.

R62 (≠ DK) Simplicius, *Commentary on Aristotle's Physics*

For Heraclitus said that all things come from a limited fire and that all things are resolved back into it. The Stoics too would be of this opinion. For the conflagration (*ekpurôsis*) makes an enigmatic allusion to something of this sort, and they say that every body is limited.[1]

[1] For a Latin poetic version of this interpretation of Heraclitus, see *Aetna* 537–40.

R63 (cf. ad B30), Simplicius, *Commentary on Aristotle's On the Heavens*

Heraclitus says that the world sometimes undergoes a conflagration and sometimes reconstitutes itself again out of the fire, following certain periods of time, when he says, **"kindled in measures and extinguished in measures"** [cf. **D85**]. Later, the Stoics too came to share this opinion.

EARLY GREEK PHILOSOPHY III

The Great Year (R64)

R64 (> A13) Aët. 2.32.3–4 (Ps.-Plut.) [περὶ ἐνιαυτοῦ, πόσος ἑκάστου τῶν πλανητῶν χρόνος καὶ τίς ὁ μέγας ἐνιαυτός]

[3] Ἡράκλειτος ἐκ μυρίων ὀκτακισχιλίων ἡλιακῶν.
[4] Διογένης ὁ Στωικὸς ἐκ πέντε καὶ ἑξήκοντα καὶ τριακοσίων ἐνιαυτῶν τοσούτων, ὅσων ὁ κατὰ Ἡράκλειτον ἐνιαυτός [SVF 2.603].

Evaporations (R65)

R65 (> A11) Aët. 2.17.4 (Ps.-Plut.) [πόθεν φωτίζονται[1] οἱ ἀστέρες]

Ἡράκλειτος καὶ οἱ Στωικοὶ τρέφεσθαι τοὺς ἀστέρας ἐκ τῆς ἐπιγείου ἀναθυμιάσεως [SVF 2.690].

[1] τρέφονται Mansfeld et Runia

Human Development (R66)

R66 (A18) Aët. 5.23 (Ps.-Plut.) [πότε ἄρχεται ὁ ἄνθρωπος τῆς τελειότητος]

Ἡράκλειτος καὶ οἱ Στωικοὶ ἄρχεσθαι τοὺς ἀνθρώπους τῆς τελειότητος περὶ τὴν δευτέραν ἑβδομάδα, περὶ ἣν ὁ σπερματικὸς κινεῖται ὀρρός [SVF 2.764].

HERACLITUS

The Great Year (R64)

R64 (> A13) Aëtius

[3] Heraclitus: [scil. the great year consists] of 10,800 solar years.
[4] Diogenes the Stoic: [scil. the great year consists] of 365 times the number of years of one [scil. great year] according to Heraclitus.

Evaporations (R65)

R65 (> A11) Aëtius

Heraclitus and the Stoics: the stars are nourished by the evaporation coming from the earth.

See also **R46b[9]**

Human Development (R66)

R66 (A18) Aëtius

Heraclitus and the Stoics: humans reach maturity in the second period of seven years, when the seminal fluid is set in motion.

EARLY GREEK PHILOSOPHY III

Epicurean Polemics (R67–R69)

R67 (T 279 Mouraviev) Diog. Laert. 10.6–8

καὶ μὴν καὶ Τιμοκράτης ἐν τοῖς ἐπιγραφομένοις Εὐφραντοῖς[1] [. . .] φησὶ [. . .] Ἡράκλειτόν τε κυκητὴν [. . .].

[1] εὐφραντοῖς FP[4]: εὐφάντοις BP[1]

R68 (cf. Nachtrag I, p. 491.37) Lucr. 1.635–44

635 quapropter qui materiem rerum esse putarunt
ignem atque ex igni summam consistere solo,
magno opere a vera lapsi ratione videntur.
Heraclitus init quorum dux proelia primus,
clarus ob obscuram linguam magis inter inanis
640 quamde gravis inter Graios qui vera requirunt.
omnia enim stolidi magis admirantur amantque
inversis quae sub verbis latitantia cernunt,
veraque constituunt quae belle tangere possunt
auris et lepido quae sunt fucata sonore.

HERACLITUS

Epicurean Polemics (R67–R69)

R67 (≠ DK) Diogenes Laertius

Timocrates in his book entitled *Pleasantries* [...] says [...] [scil. that Epicurus called] Heraclitus "*Kukêtês*" [i.e., "*Kukeôn*-drinker" or "Agitator"] [cf. **D59**].

R68 (cf. Nachtrag I, p. 491.37) Lucretius, *On the Nature of Things*

> That is why those people who have thought that the matter of things 635
> Is fire and that everything comes from fire alone
> Seem to have fallen very far from true reason.
> Among these, Heraclitus enters the fray as the first leader,
> Famous for his obscure language, more among the empty-headed
> Than among those serious Greeks who seek the truth; 640
> For foolish people admire and love everything
> That they perceive to lie hidden under words that conceal their meaning,
> And they consider true what can pleasantly touch
> Their ears and is adorned with a charming sound.[1]

[1] Lucretius goes on to provide criticisms of the idea that fire is the sole material principle for all things (1.645–711).

R69 (T 376 Mouraviev) Diog. Oen. Frag. 6, Col. 3 1–3, 7–14 Smith

[. . .] νυνεὶ δὲ [τοῖς] | εἰρημένοις ἀνδρά[σιν ἐν]|καλέσομεν [. . .] | [7] καὶ Ἡρακλείτῳ πρῶ[τον] | ἐπεὶ καὶ πρῶτος ἡμ[εῖν τέ]|τακται. κακῶς, Ἡρά[κλει]|τε, πῦρ εἶναι στοιχεῖ[ον λέ]|γεις· οὔτε γὰρ ἄφθα[ρτόν] | ἐστιν, ἐπεὶ φθειρόμ[ενον] | [13] ὁρῶμεν αὐτό, οὔτε δύν[α]|ται γεννᾶν τὰ πράγμ[ατα] | . . .

1–4 suppl. Usener   7–13 suppl. Cousin   14 πράγμ[ατα] Heberdey-Kalinka

Heraclitus Among the Skeptics (R70–R73)
Aenesidemus: Skepticism Leads to
Heraclitus (R70–R71)

R70 (< T 694 Mouraviev) Sext. Emp. *Pyrrh. Hyp.* 1.210

[. . . cf. **R72**] οἱ περὶ Αἰνησίδημον ἔλεγον ὁδὸν εἶναι τὴν σκεπτικὴν ἀγωγὴν ἐπὶ τὴν Ἡρακλείτειον φιλοσοφίαν, διότι προηγεῖται τοῦ τἀναντία περὶ τὸ αὐτὸ ὑπάρχειν τὸ τἀναντία περὶ τὸ αὐτὸ φαίνεσθαι, καὶ οἱ μὲν σκεπτικοὶ φαίνεσθαι λέγουσι τὰ ἐναντία περὶ τὸ αὐτό, οἱ δὲ Ἡρακλείτειοι ἀπὸ τούτου καὶ ἐπὶ τὸ ὑπάρχειν αὐτὰ μετέρχονται.

HERACLITUS

R69 (≠ DK) Diogenes of Oenoanda

Now we shall criticize the men that we have mentioned [. . .] and first of all Heraclitus, since he was put first by us. [. . .] You are wrong, Heraclitus, to say that fire is an element; for it is neither indestructible, since we see that it is destroyed, nor capable of generating things . . .

Heraclitus Among the Skeptics (R70–R73)
Aenesidemus: Skepticism Leads to
Heraclitus (R70–R71)

R70 (≠ DK) Sextus Empiricus, *Outlines of Pyrrhonism*

[. . .] Aenesidemus and his followers said that the Skeptical school was a path leading to Heraclitus' philosophy, because the thesis according to which, concerning the same thing, the opposites appear, precedes logically the thesis according to which, concerning the same thing, the opposites exist, and the Skeptics say that the opposites appear, concerning the same thing, and that the Heracliteans passed from this to their also existing.

R71 Tert. *An.*

a (< T 651 Mouraviev) 9.5

non, ut aer sit ipsa substantia eius, etsi hoc Aenesidemo visum est et Anaximeni, puto secundum quosdam et Heraclito [. . .].

b (cf. ad B67a) 14.5

non longe hoc exemplum est a Stratone et Aenesidemo et Heraclito; nam et ipsi unitatem animae tuentur, quae in totum corpus diffusa et ubique ipsa, velut flatus in calamo per cavernas [. . .].

Sextus Empiricus: Heraclitus Was Not a Skeptic (R72–R73)

R72 (< T 694 Mouraviev) Sext. Emp. *Pyrrh. Hyp.* 1.210, 212 [ὅτι διαφέρει ἡ σκεπτικὴ ἀγωγὴ τῆς Ἡρακλείτου φιλοσοφίας]

[210] ὅτι μὲν οὖν αὕτη διαφέρει τῆς ἡμετέρας ἀγωγῆς, πρόδηλον· ὁ μὲν γὰρ Ἡράκλειτος περὶ πολλῶν ἀδήλων ἀποφαίνεται δογματικῶς, ἡμεῖς δ᾽ οὐχί. [. . .] ἐπεὶ δὲ οἱ περὶ Αἰνησίδημον ἔλεγον ὁδὸν εἶναι τὴν σκεπτικὴν ἀγωγὴν ἐπὶ τὴν Ἡρακλείτειον φιλοσοφίαν [. . . = **R70**], φαμὲν πρὸς τούτους,[1] ὅτι τὸ τὰ ἐναντία περὶ τὸ αὐτὸ φαίνεσθαι οὐ δόγμα ἐστὶ τῶν σκεπτικῶν ἀλλὰ πρᾶγμα οὐ μόνον τοῖς σκεπτικοῖς ἀλλὰ καὶ τοῖς ἄλ-

HERACLITUS

R71 (≠ DK) Tertullian, *On the Soul*

a (≠ DK)

Not that air itself is the substance of it [i.e. the soul], even if this was the view of Aenesidemus and Anaximenes, and I think also of Heraclitus, according to some people [...].

b (cf. ad B67a)

This example [i.e. of a water organ] is not very remote from Strato, Aenesidemus, and Heraclitus: for these too preserve the unity of the soul, which is diffused throughout the whole body and yet everywhere is itself, like the breath in a reed instrument throughout its cavities [...].

Sextus Empiricus: Heraclitus Was Not a Skeptic (R72–R73)

R72 (≠ DK) Sextus Empiricus, *Outlines of Pyrrhonism* [That the Skeptical school differs from Heraclitus' philosophy.]

[210] The fact that it differs from our school is obvious. For Heraclitus makes dogmatic assertions about many unclear matters, while we do not. [...] But since Aenesidemus and his followers said that the Skeptical school was a path leading to Heraclitus' philosophy [...], we reply to them that the thesis according to which, concerning the same thing, the opposites appear, is not a doctrine of the Skeptics but a datum of experience, not only for the Skep-

---

¹ τούτους ML: αὐτοὺς EAB

λοις φιλοσόφοις καὶ πᾶσιν ἀνθρώποις ὑποπίπτον·
[. . .] [212] μήποτε δὲ οὐ μόνον οὐ συνεργεῖ πρὸς τὴν
γνῶσιν τῆς Ἡρακλειτείου φιλοσοφίας ἡ σκεπτικὴ
ἀγωγή, ἀλλὰ καὶ ἀποσυνεργεῖ, εἴγε ὁ σκεπτικὸς πάντα τὰ ὑπὸ τοῦ Ἡρακλείτου δογματιζόμενα ὡς προ-
πετῶς λεγόμενα διαβάλλει, ἐναντιούμενος μὲν τῇ ἐκ-
πυρώσει, ἐναντιούμενος δὲ τῷ τὰ ἐναντία περὶ τὸ αὐτὸ
ὑπάρχειν, καὶ ἐπὶ παντὸς δόγματος τοῦ Ἡρακλείτου
τὴν μὲν δογματικὴν προπέτειαν διασύρων, τὸ δὲ "οὐ
καταλαμβάνω"[2] καὶ τὸ "οὐδὲν ὁρίζω" ἐπιφθεγγόμενος,
ὡς ἔφην ἔμπροσθεν· ὅπερ μάχεται τοῖς Ἡρακλειτείοις. ἄτοπον δέ ἐστι τὸ τὴν μαχομένην ἀγωγὴν ὁδὸν
εἶναι λέγειν τῆς αἱρέσεως ἐκείνης ᾗ μάχεται· ἄτοπον
ἄρα τὸ τὴν σκεπτικὴν ἀγωγὴν ἐπὶ τὴν Ἡρακλείτειον
φιλοσοφίαν ὁδὸν εἶναι λέγειν.

[2] οὐ καταλαμβάνω Stephanus: οὐχ ὑπολαμβάνω mss.

R73 (< A16) Sext. Emp. *Adv. Math.* 7.126–27, 133–34

[126] ὁ δὲ Ἡράκλειτος, ἐπεὶ πάλιν ἐδόκει δυσὶν
ὠργανῶσθαι ὁ ἄνθρωπος πρὸς τὴν τῆς ἀληθείας
γνῶσιν, αἰσθήσει τε καὶ λόγῳ, τούτων τὴν ⟨μὲν⟩[1]
αἴσθησιν παραπλησίως τοῖς προειρημένοις φυσικοῖς
ἄπιστον εἶναι νενόμικεν, τὸν δὲ λόγον ὑποτίθεται κριτήριον. ἀλλὰ τὴν μὲν αἴσθησιν ἐλέγχει λέγων κατὰ
λέξιν, [. . . = **D33**], ὅπερ ἴσον ἦν τῷ[2] βαρβάρων ἐστὶ
ψυχῶν ταῖς ἀλόγοις αἰσθήσεσι πιστεύειν. [127] τὸν δὲ
λόγον κριτὴν τῆς ἀληθείας ἀποφαίνεται οὐ τὸν ὁποι-

HERACLITUS

tics but also for all other philosophers and for all human beings [. . .]. [212] But perhaps the Skeptical school not only does not make a contribution to the knowledge of Heraclitus' philosophy, but it even leads away from it, since the Skeptic rejects all of Heraclitus' dogmatic affirmations as rash and opposes the conflagration (*ekpurôsis*), opposes the thesis that, concerning the same thing, the contraries exist, disparages the dogmatic rashness of all of Heraclitus' doctrines, and asserts "I do not apprehend" and "I define nothing," as I said earlier. All of this is opposed to the Heracliteans. And it is absurd to say that an opposing school is a path leading to the very doctrine that it opposes; so that it is absurd to say that the Skeptical school is a path leading to Heraclitus' philosophy.

R73 (< A16) Sextus Empiricus, *Against the Logicians*

[126] Since Heraclitus for his part thought that the human being is equipped with two instruments with a view toward knowledge of the truth, perception and reason (*logos*), he held the view, much like the natural philosophers I discussed earlier, that of these two perception is untrustworthy, and he establishes reason as the criterion. But he refutes perception, saying in his own words, [. . . = **D33**], which doubtless means the same thing as, "It belongs to barbarian souls to trust irrational perceptions." [127] But the reason that he indicates as judge of the truth is not just

---

[1] ⟨μὲν⟩ Bekker   [2] τῷ Bekker: τὸν mss.

ονδήποτε, ἀλλὰ τὸν κοινὸν καὶ θεῖον. τίς δ' ἐστὶν
οὗτος, συντόμως ὑποδεικτέον. [. . . = cf. **R59**] [133] [. . .]
διὸ καθ' ὅ τι ἂν αὐτοῦ τῆς μνήμης κοινωνήσωμεν,
ἀληθεύομεν, ἃ δὲ ἂν ἰδιάσωμεν, ψευδόμεθα. [134] νῦν
γὰρ ῥητότατα καὶ ἐν τούτοις τὸν κοινὸν λόγον κριτήριον ἀποφαίνεται, καὶ τὰ μὲν κοινῇ φησι[3] φαινό-
μενα πιστὰ ὡς ἂν τῷ κοινῷ κρινόμενα λόγῳ, τὰ δὲ
κατ' ἰδίαν ἑκάστῳ ψευδῆ.

[3] φησι Bekker: φασι mss.: πᾶσι Natorp

*Philo: Heraclitus' Doctrines Derive from the
Hebrew Bible (R74–R76)*

R74 (cf. Nachtrag I, p. 491.42) Phil. *Quaest. Gen.* 3.5,
p. 178.11–25 Aucher

Բայց պարտ է գիտել, զի եւ մասունքն աշխարհիս ընդ
երկու հաստեալն են, եւ ‹ընդ›դէմ ընդդէմ հաստատեալ
են։ Երկիրըʼ ի լեռնային եւ ի դաշտային վայրսն։ Եւ
չուր ի քաղցր եւ յաղտաղտուկ. քաղցրն ըմպելին է՝ զոր
մատուցանեն աղբերք եւ գետք. եւ աղտաղտուկ
ծովային։ Եւ աղʼ ի ձմեռն եւ յամառն, եւ դարձեալ ի
զարունն եւ յաշունն։ Եւ աստուստ Հերակլիտոս
դիմեալʼ զյաղագս բնութեանն գիրս գրեաց. զոր
իմացեալ յաստուածաբանէն զյաղագս ընդդիմակացն
վարկս, եւ յաւելեալ անբաւութիւն աշխատելի
ձեռնարկութեանցն ի նմա։

280

any one, but the one that is in common and divine. What this is must be indicated briefly [. . .]. [133] [. . .] That is why, to the extent that we have in common the memory of this [scil. of divine reason] we are in the truth, while wherever we are in particularity we are in error. [134] For here too it is explicitly asserted that reason in common is the criterion, and he says that the things that appear in common are reliable, since they are discerned by reason in common, while the things that are particular to each individual are erroneous.

Philo: Heraclitus' Doctrines Derive from the Hebrew Bible (R74–R76)

R74 (cf. Nachtrag I, p. 491.42) Philo, *Questions on Genesis*

But one must know that the parts of this world are divided into two as well, and established as opposites. The earth [scil. is divided] into mountainous areas and flat ones. And water into sweet and salt; the sweet is the potable one, which springs and rivers bring forth; and the salt is seawater. And the weather into winter and summer, and again into spring and autumn. And starting from this, Heraclitus wrote the book on nature; which [scil. he wrote] having learned from the theologian [i.e. Moses] the ideas about the opposites, and having added to it an infinity of laborious arguments.[1]

[1] Translated by Irene Tinti.

R75

a (T 339 Mouraviev) Phil. *Quaest. Gen.* 4.152, pp. 359.34–360.6 Aucher

Ճառդ եւ ոչ մի ինչ ունի խնդիր. բայց բնականագոյն ի մէջ առնլի է, եւ հատուցանեւ պատասխանի զայն, զի մարդոյս մահ՝ կեանք ոգւոյ է, իւր իսկ ոգւոյն զանմարմին կեանս կեցեալ։ Զորմէ եւ Հերակլիտոս գողաբար ի բաց գերծեալ ի Մովսիսէ զաղէնս եւ զկարծիս՝ ասէ, եթէ կեամք զնոցայն մահն, եւ մեռաք զնոցայն կեանս. առակելով, զի մարդովս կեանք՝ մահ ոգւոյ է. իսկ որ մահ ասի, կեանք բարեփառագոյն առաջին՝ ոգւոյն։

b (T 338 Mouraviev) Phil. *Leg. alleg.* 1.33.107–8

[107] ὅπου δ' ἂν λέγῃ "θανάτῳ ἀποθανεῖν," παρατήρει ὅτι θάνατον τὸν ἐπὶ τιμωρίᾳ παραλαμβάνει, οὐ τὸν φύσει γινόμενον· φύσει μὲν οὖν ἐστι, καθ' ὃν χωρίζεται ψυχὴ ἀπὸ σώματος, ὁ δὲ ἐπὶ τιμωρίᾳ συνίσταται, ὅταν ἡ ψυχὴ τὸν ἀρετῆς βίον θνῄσκῃ, τὸν δὲ κακίας ζῇ μόνον. [108] εὖ καὶ ὁ Ἡράκλειτος κατὰ τοῦτο Μωυσέως ἀκολουθήσας τῷ δόγματι, φησὶ γάρ· "ζῶμεν τὸν ἐκείνων θάνατον, τεθνήκαμεν δὲ τὸν ἐκείνων βίον" [cf. **D70**], ὡς νῦν μέν, ὅτε ζῶμεν, τεθνηκυίας τῆς ψυχῆς καὶ ὡς ἂν ἐν σήματι τῷ σώματι ἐντετυμβευμένης, εἰ δὲ ἀποθάνοιμεν, τῆς ψυχῆς ζώσης τὸν ἴδιον βίον καὶ ἀπηλλαγμένης κακοῦ καὶ νεκροῦ συνδέτου τοῦ σώματος.

HERACLITUS

R75

a (≠ DK) Philo, *Questions on Genesis*

The literal meaning [scil. of this verse, Gen. 25:8] does not cause any difficulty; but it is necessary to consider it in a more natural sense and give the following answer, namely that the death of this body is the life of the soul, since the soul lives its own incorporeal life. On this topic Heraclitus too, stealing the law and the opinion from Moses, like a thief, says, "We live their death and die their life" [cf. **D70**], thus suggesting that the life in this body is the death of the souls, while what is called 'death' is the most glorious and primary life, that of the soul.[1]

[1] Translated by Irene Tinti.

b (≠ DK) Philo, *Allegories of the Sacred Laws*

[107] When he [i.e. Moses] says, "to die by death" [cf. Gen. 2:17], notice that he is taking death as a punishment, not as the one that happens by nature; the one that happens by nature is the one by which the soul is separated from the body, whereas the one that is a punishment happens when the soul dies for the life of virtue and lives only for the life of vice. [108] And Heraclitus did well to follow the doctrine of Moses on this point, for he says, "we live their death and we die their life" [cf. **D70**], on the idea that now, while we are alive, our soul has died and is buried in the body as though in a tomb, but that if we die, then the soul lives its own life and is freed from the evil, dead body to which it was attached.

R76 (cf. Nachtrag I, p. 491.39) Phil. *Her.* 213–14

[213] παγκάλως οὖν ὁ τῶν τῆς φύσεως ἑρμηνεὺς[1] πραγμάτων,[2] τῆς ἀργίας καὶ ἀμελετησίας ἡμῶν λαμβάνων οἶκτον ἑκάστοτ'[3] ἀφθόνως[4] ἀναδιδάσκει, καθὰ καὶ νῦν, τὴν ἀντιπρόσωπον ἑκάστων θέσιν οὐχ ὁλοκλήρων, ἀλλὰ τμημάτων ὑπαρχόντων· ἓν γὰρ τὸ ἐξ ἀμφοῖν τῶν ἐναντίων, οὗ τμηθέντος γνώριμα τὰ ἐναντία. [214] οὐ τοῦτ' ἐστίν, ὅ φασιν Ἕλληνες τὸν μέγαν καὶ ἀοίδιμον παρ' αὐτοῖς Ἡράκλειτον κεφάλαιον τῆς αὐτοῦ προστησάμενον φιλοσοφίας αὐχεῖν ὡς ἐφ' εὑρέσει καινῇ; παλαιὸν γὰρ εὕρεμα Μωυσέως ἐστὶ τὸ ἐκ τοῦ αὐτοῦ τὰ ἐναντία τμημάτων λόγον ἔχοντα ἀποτελεῖσθαι [. . .].

[1] ἑρμηνεὺς pap.: ἑρμηνευτὴν mss.   [2] πραγμάτων pap. (Mangey): γραμμάτων mss.   [3] ἑκάστοτ' Wendland: ἕκαστον mss.   [4] ἀφθόνως Wendland: αφονως pap.: ἀφανῶς mss.: ἐμφανῶς coni. Mangey

Christian Appropriations and Polemics (R77–R87)
Justin Martyr (R77)

R77 (T 601 Mouraviev) Just. M. *Apol.* 1.46.2–3

τὸν Χριστὸν πρωτότοκον τοῦ θεοῦ εἶναι ἐδιδάχθημεν καὶ προεμηνύσαμεν Λόγον ὄντα, οὗ πᾶν γένος ἀνθρώπων μετέσχε. καὶ οἱ μετὰ Λόγου βιώσαντες Χριστιανοί ἦσαν,[1] κἂν ἄθεοι ἐνομίσθησαν, οἷον ἐν Ἕλλησι μὲν Σωκράτης καὶ Ἡράκλειτος καὶ οἱ ὅμοιοι αὐτοῖς, ἐν βαρβάροις δὲ Ἀβραὰμ [. . .].

R76 (cf. Nachtrag I, p. 491.39) Philo, *Who is the Heir of Divine Things?*

[213] Magnificently, then, the interpreter of the things of nature, feeling pity for our sloth and carelessness, teaches us generously every time, as he does now, the antithetical position of each of the things that are deprived of wholeness and result from divisions: for what is one is formed out of one and the other of contraries, and it is by its division that the contraries are known. [214] Is this not what the Greeks say that the great Heraclitus, much besung among them, put forward as the chief point of his philosophy and boasted as though it were a new discovery? Yet in fact it is a very ancient discovery by Moses that the contraries have come from the same thing and have the status of things divided [. . .].

Christian Appropriations and Polemics (R77–R87)
Justin Martyr (R77)

R77 (≠ DK) Justin Martyr, *Apology*

We have been taught that Christ is the firstborn son of God, and we indicated earlier that he is the Word, of which the whole human race has received a share. And those people who have lived with the Word were Christians, even if they were considered to be atheists, as for example, among the Greeks, Socrates, Heraclitus, and those men similar to them, and, among the barbarians, Abraham [. . .].

---

[1] ἦσαν Ashton: εἰσι A

EARLY GREEK PHILOSOPHY III

Tatian (R78)

R78 (T 604 Mouraviev) Tat. *Or.* 3

τὸν γὰρ Ἡράκλειτον οὐκ ἂν ἀποδεξαίμην, "ἐμαυτὸν ἐδιδαξάμην"[1] [cf. **D36**] εἰπόντα, διὰ τὸ αὐτοδίδακτον εἶναι καὶ ὑπερήφανον. οὔτ᾽ ἂν ἐπαινέσαιμι κατακρύψαντα τὴν ποίησιν ἐν τῷ τῆς Ἀρτέμιδος ναῷ μυστηριωδῶς ὅπως ὕστερον ἡ ταύτης ἔκδοσις γένηται· καὶ γὰρ οἷς μέλον ἐστὶ περὶ τούτων φασὶν Εὐριπίδην τὸν τραγῳδοποιόν, κατιόντα καὶ ἀναγινώσκοντα, διὰ μνήμης κατ᾽ ὀλίγον τὸ Ἡρακλείτου σκότος σπουδαίως παραδεδωκέναι. τούτου μὲν οὖν τὴν ἀμαθίαν ὁ θάνατος διήλεγξεν· ὕδρωπι γὰρ συσχεθείς, καὶ τὴν ἰατρικὴν ὡς φιλοσοφίαν ἐπιτηδεύσας, βολβίτοις τε περιπλάσας ἑαυτόν, τῆς κόπρου κρατυνθείσης, συνολκάς τε τοῦ παντὸς ἀπεργασαμένης σώματος, σπασθεὶς ἐτελεύτησε.

[1] ἐδιζησάμην Heraclitus

Clement of Alexandria (R79–R85)

R79 (> B22) Clem. Alex. *Strom.* 4.4.1–2

ἔστω δὲ ἡμῖν[1] τὰ ὑπομνήματα, ὡς πολλάκις εἴπομεν διὰ τοὺς ἀνέδην ἀπείρως ἐντυγχάνοντας ποικίλως,[2] ὡς αὐτό που τοὔνομά φησι, διεστρωμένα, ἀπ᾽ ἄλλου εἰς ἄλλο συνεχὲς μετιόντα, καὶ ἕτερον μέν τι κατὰ τὸν εἱρμὸν τῶν λόγων μηνύοντα, ἐνδεικνύμενα δὲ ἄλλο τι.

HERACLITUS

Tatian (R78)

R78 (≠ DK) Tatian, *Oration to the Greeks*

I would not accept Heraclitus, who says, "I have taught myself" [cf. **D36**], because he is self-taught and arrogant; and I would not praise him either for having mysteriously hidden his poem in the temple of Artemis so that it would be published only later [cf. **P13**]. For those people who study these matters say that the tragedian Euripides went there and read it, and, having memorized it little by little, eagerly transmitted Heraclitus' obscurity [cf. **R5a**]. Death confuted this man's ignorance: for when he came down with a dropsy, he practiced medicine like philosophy and smeared himself with cow dung; and when the dung hardened and caused contractions in his whole body, he died in convulsions [cf. **P16–P17**].

Clement of Alexandria (R79–R85)

R79 (> B22) Clement of Alexandria, *Stromata*

These notices of ours, as we have often said for the sake of those who, without experience, read them freely, may well be a variegated patchwork, as their very title [scil. *Stromata*] indicates, one that passes constantly from one topic to another, revealing one thing in virtue of its series of the arguments, but signifying something else. [2] For

---

¹ ἡμῖν Hervet: ὑμῖν ms.   ² ποικίλως Mayor: ποικίλα ms.: ποικίλα ‹καὶ› Hiller

[2] "χρυσὸν γὰρ οἱ διζήμενοι," φησὶν Ἡράκλειτος, "γῆν πολλὴν ὀρύσσουσι καὶ εὑρίσκουσιν ὀλίγον" [= **D39**], οἱ δὲ τοῦ χρυσοῦ ὄντως γένους τὸ συγγενὲς μεταλλεύοντες εὑρήσουσι τὸ πολὺ ἐν ὀλίγῳ.

R80 (T 643b Mouraviev) Clem. Alex. *Strom.* 6.27.1

σιωπῶ δὲ Ἡράκλειτον τὸν Ἐφέσιον, ὃς παρ' Ὀρφέως τὰ πλεῖστα εἴληφεν.

R81 (> B18) Clem. Alex. *Strom.* 2.17.3–4

εἰ τοίνυν ἡ πίστις οὐδὲν ἄλλο ἢ πρόληψίς ἐστι διανοίας περὶ τὰ λεγόμενα καὶ τοῦτο ὑπακοή τε εἴρηται σύνεσίς τε καὶ πειθώ, οὐ μὴ[1] μαθήσεταί τις ἄνευ πίστεως, ἐπεὶ μηδὲ ἄνευ προλήψεως. [4] ἀληθὲς δ' οὖν ὂν παντὸς[2] μᾶλλον ἀποδείκνυται τὸ ὑπὸ τοῦ προφήτου εἰρημένον· "ἐὰν μὴ πιστεύσητε, οὐδὲ μὴ συνῆτε." τοῦτο καὶ Ἡράκλειτος ὁ Ἐφέσιος τὸ λόγιον παραφράσας εἴρηκεν· "ἐὰν μὴ ἔλπηται ἀνέλπιστον, οὐκ ἐξευρήσει, ἀνεξερεύνητον ἐὸν καὶ ἄπορον" [= **D37**].

[1] μὴ Mayor: μὴν ms.   [2] παντὸς Dindorf: πάντως ms.

R82 (> B30, B31) Clem. Alex. *Strom.* 5.104.1–105.1 (et al.)

[104.1] σαφέστατα ⟨δ'⟩[1] Ἡράκλειτος ὁ Ἐφέσιος ταύ-

[1] ⟨δ'⟩ Stählin ex Eus. *PE* 13.13.31

Heraclitus says, **"Those who search for gold dig up much earth and find little"** [= **D39**], but those who, really belonging to the golden race, quarry what is akin to them, will find much in little.[1]

[1] Cf. Clem. Alex, *Strom.* 5.14.140.4.

R80 (≠ DK) Clement of Alexandria, *Stromata*

I pass over in silence Heraclitus of Ephesus, who took over most [scil. of his doctrines] from Orpheus.

R81 (> B18) Clement of Alexandria, *Stromata*

If faith is nothing other than the apprehension by thought of what is said, and if this is called obedience, understanding, and persuasion, then no one will ever learn without faith, since it is not possible either without apprehension. [4] So that what has been said by the prophet—"if you do not have faith, neither will you ever understand" (Isa. 7:9)—is revealed to be absolutely true. And this is also what Heraclitus of Ephesus, paraphrasing this verse, said: **"If one does not expect the unexpected one will not find it** (*exeurein*), **for it cannot be searched out** (*anexereunêton*) **nor arrived at** (*aporon*)" [= **D37**].

R82 (> B30, B31) Clement of Alexandria, *Stromata*

[104.1] But it is Heraclitus of Ephesus [scil. rather than Empedocles] who is most clearly of this opinion [scil. that

της ἐστὶ τῆς δόξης, τὸν μέν τινα κόσμον ἀίδιον εἶναι δοκιμάσας, τὸν δέ τινα φθειρόμενον, τὸν κατὰ τὴν διακόσμησιν εἰδὼς οὐχ ἕτερον ὄντα ἐκείνου πως ἔχοντος. [2] ἀλλ' ὅτι μὲν ἀίδιον τὸν ἐξ ἁπάσης τῆς οὐσίας ἰδίως[2] ποιὸν κόσμον ᾔδει, φανερὸν ποιεῖ λέγων οὕτως· "*κόσμον τὸν[3] αὐτὸν ἁπάντων* [. . .] *ἁπτόμενον μέτρα καὶ ἀποσβεννύμενον μέτρα*"[4] [= **D85**]. [3] ὅτι δὲ καὶ γενητὸν καὶ φθαρτὸν αὐτὸν εἶναι ἐδογμάτιζεν, μηνύει τὰ ἐπιφερόμενα· "*πυρὸς τροπαὶ πρῶτον θάλασσα,* [. . .] *τὸ δὲ ἥμισυ πρηστήρ*"[5] [= **D86**]. [4] δυνάμει γὰρ λέγει, ὅτι πῦρ ὑπὸ τοῦ διοικοῦντος λόγου καὶ θεοῦ τὰ σύμπαντα δι' ἀέρος τρέπεται εἰς ὑγρὸν τὸ ὡς σπέρμα τῆς διακοσμήσεως, ὃ καλεῖ θάλασσαν· ἐκ δὲ τούτου αὖθις γίνεται γῆ καὶ οὐρανὸς καὶ τὰ ἐμπεριεχόμενα. [5] ὅπως δὲ πάλιν ἀναλαμβάνεται καὶ ἐκπυροῦται, σαφῶς διὰ τούτων δηλοῖ· "*θάλασσα διαχέεται* [. . .] *γενέσθαι γῆ*"[5] [cf. **D86**]. ὁμοίως καὶ περὶ τῶν ἄλλων στοιχείων τὰ αὐτά [. . . = **R57**].

[2] ἰδίως Bernays: ἀιδίως ms. Heraclitus   [3] κόσμον τόνδε τὸν
[4] app. cf. ad **D85**   [5] app. cf. ad **D86**

R83 (> B28) Clem. Alex. *Strom.* 5.9.2–4

διὰ τοῦτο καὶ ὁ ἀπόστολος παρακαλεῖ, "ἵνα ἡ πίστις ἡμῶν μὴ ᾖ ἐν σοφίᾳ ἀνθρώπων" τῶν πείθειν ἐπαγγελλομένων, "ἀλλ' ἐν δυνάμει θεοῦ," τῇ μόνῃ καὶ ἄνευ τῶν ἀποδείξεων διὰ ψιλῆς τῆς πίστεως σῴζειν δυναμένῃ. [3] "*δοκεόντων γὰρ ὁ δοκιμώτατος γινώσκει*"

HERACLITUS

there will someday be a transformation of all things into fire]: he believes that there exists one world that is eternal and another one that is perishable, even though he knows that the one that results from the organization of the world (*diakosmêsis*) is not different from the other one, which is in a particular condition. [2] But he makes it clear that he knew that the world that is constituted from the totality of substance and endowed with a particular quality is eternal, for he says, **"The world order, the same for all,** [. . .] **kindled in measures and extinguished in measures"** [= **D85**]. [3] And the fact that he taught that this one is generated and perishable is indicated by the following words: **"Turnings of fire: first sea** [. . .] **and the other half, lightning storm"** [= **D86**]. [4] For he is saying potentially that fire, under the effect of Reason and God who directs the totality of things, turns, passing through air, into moisture which is like the seed of the organization of the world, which he calls the sea; and out of this then comes the earth, the heavens, and everything that it encompasses. [5] But the fact that it is regenerated and undergoes conflagration he shows clearly in the following words: **"It spreads out as sea** [. . .] **it became earth"** [= cf. **D86**]. The same applies in a similar way to the other elements.

R83 (> B28) Clement of Alexandria, *Stromata*

It is for this reason that the apostle calls upon us "so that our faith not be in the wisdom of men," who proclaim that they use persuasion, "but in the power of God," the only one that is capable of saving by faith alone, even without proofs [1 Cor. 2:5]. [3] For **"of those who have opinions,**

[= **D19**], φυλάσσει·[1] καὶ μέντοι καὶ "*δίκη καταλήψεται ψευδῶν τέκτονας καὶ μάρτυρας*" [= **D28**], ὁ Ἐφέσιός φησιν. [4] οἶδεν γὰρ καὶ οὗτος ἐκ τῆς βαρβάρου φιλοσοφίας μαθὼν τὴν διὰ πυρὸς κάθαρσιν τῶν κακῶς βεβιωκότων, ἣν ὕστερον ἐκπύρωσιν ἐκάλεσαν οἱ Στωικοί [*SVF* 2.630].

[1] φυλάσσει Schleiermacher: φυλάσσειν mss.: Heraclito saepe trib. edd.

R84 (cf. B62) Clem. Alex. *Paed.* 3.1.5–2.1

ὁ δὲ ἄνθρωπος ἐκεῖνος, ᾧ σύνοικος ὁ λόγος, οὐ ποικίλλεται, οὐ πλάττεται, μορφὴν ἔχει τὴν τοῦ λόγου, ἐξομοιοῦται τῷ θεῷ, καλός ἐστιν, οὐ καλλωπίζεται· κάλλος ἐστὶ τὸ ἀληθινόν, καὶ γὰρ ὁ θεός ἐστιν· θεὸς δὲ ἐκεῖνος ὁ ἄνθρωπος γίνεται, ὅτι βούλεται ὃ[1] θεός· ὀρθῶς ἄρα εἶπεν Ἡράκλειτος· "*ἄνθρωποι θεοί, θεοὶ ἄνθρωποι*" [cf. **D70**], λόγος γὰρ ωὑτός·[2] μυστήριον ἐμφανές· θεὸς ἐν ἀνθρώπῳ, καὶ ὁ ἄνθρωπος θεός, καὶ τὸ θέλημα τοῦ πατρὸς ὁ μεσίτης ἐκτελεῖ· μεσίτης γὰρ ὁ λόγος ὁ κοινὸς ἀμφοῖν, θεοῦ μὲν υἱός, σωτὴρ δὲ ἀνθρώπων, καὶ τοῦ μὲν διάκονος, ἡμῶν δὲ παιδαγωγός.

[1] ὁ ms., corr. Bernays   [2] ωὑτός ms.: ὁ αὐτός Bernays

R85 (cf. B26) Clem. Alex. *Strom.* 4.139.4–141.4

[139.4] διὰ τοῦτό τοι καὶ ὁ Κύριος ἐγρηγορέναι παραγ-

it is the man who enjoys the highest opinion who knows" [= **D19**], preserves; and indeed **"Justice will seize hold of those who fabricate lies and of those who bear witness to them"** [= **D28**], says the Ephesian. [4] For he too knew, from having learned about it from the barbarian philosophy, of the purification by fire of those who have lived in evil—what the Stoics later called "conflagration" (*ekpurôsis*).

R84 (cf. B62) Clement of Alexandria, *Pedagogue*

That man in whom the *Logos* is indwelling does not transform himself, he does not put on appearances, he possesses the form of the *Logos,* he is assimilated to God, he is beautiful, he is not beautified by cosmetics: he is beautiful in truth, for God is too. That man becomes God because he wants what God wants. So Heraclitus was right to say, **"Immortals mortals, mortals immortals"** [cf. **D70**]: for the *Logos* is the same.[1] A manifest mystery: God in a man, and the man God, and the mediator accomplishes the will of the Father. For the mediator is the *Logos* which is in common for both, the Son of God, but also the Savior of mankind, a servant of the former and a pedagogue for us.

[1] This last phrase is doubtless a commentary by Clement.

R85 (cf. B26) Clement of Alexandria, *Stromata*

[139.4] For this reason the Lord too calls upon us to stay

γέλλει, ὥστε μηδὲ ὄναρ ἡμῶν παθαίνεσθαί ποτε τὴν ψυχήν, ἀλλὰ καὶ τῆς νυκτὸς τὴν πολιτείαν ὡς ἐν ἡμέρᾳ ἐνεργουμένην καθαρὰν καὶ ἀκηλίδωτον διαφυλάττειν προστάττει [. . .]. [140.2] "ἆρ' οὖν μὴ καθεύδωμεν ὡς οἱ λοιποί, ἀλλὰ γρηγορῶμεν καὶ νήφωμεν. οἱ γὰρ καθεύδοντες νυκτὸς καθεύδουσι καὶ οἱ μεθυσκόμενοι νυκτὸς μεθύουσιν· ἡμεῖς δὲ ἡμέρας ὄντες νήφωμεν, ἐνδυσάμενοι θώρακα πίστεως καὶ ἀγάπης καὶ περικεφαλαίαν ἐλπίδα σωτηρίου." [141.1] ὅσα δ' αὖ περὶ ὕπνου λέγουσι, τὰ αὐτὰ χρὴ καὶ περὶ θανάτου ἐξακούειν. ἑκάτερος γὰρ δηλοῖ τὴν ἀπόστασιν τῆς ψυχῆς, ὁ μὲν μᾶλλον, ὁ δὲ ἧττον, ὅπερ ἐστὶ καὶ παρὰ Ἡρακλείτου λαβεῖν· [2] **"ἄνθρωπος ἐν εὐφρόνῃ** [. . .] **ἐγρηγορὼς ἅπτεται εὕδοντος"**[1] [= **D71**]. [3] μακάριοι γὰρ οἱ "εἰδότες τὸν καιρόν,"[2] κατὰ τὸν ἀπόστολον, "ὅτι ὥρα ὑμᾶς ἤδη ἐξ ὕπνου ἐγερθῆναι· νῦν γὰρ ἐγγύτερον ἡμῶν ἡ σωτηρία ἢ ὅτε ἐπιστεύσαμεν. ἡ νὺξ προέκοψεν, ἡ δὲ ἡμέρα ἤγγικεν. ἀποθώμεθα οὖν τὰ ἔργα τοῦ σκότους, ἐνδυσώμεθα δὲ τὰ ὅπλα τοῦ φωτός." [4] ἡμέραν δὲ τὸν υἱὸν ἀλληγορεῖ καὶ φῶς, τάς τε αὖ παραγγελίας ὅπλα φωτὸς μεταφορικῶς.

[1] cf. app. ad **D71**   [2] καιρόν Rom. 13:11: κύριον ms.

(Ps.-?) Hippolytus (R86)

R86 (cf. B1, B50–67) (Ps.-?) Hippol. *Ref.* 9.7–8, 9.9–10

[7.1] γεγένηταί τις ὀνόματι Νοητός, τῷ γένει Σμυρ-

awake [cf. Matt. 24:42], so that our soul not be disturbed by passion even in a dream, but he ordains that we keep our constitution at night in an activity pure and immaculate as during the day [. . .]. [140.2] "So let us not sleep like the others but let us stay awake and sober. For those who sleep sleep at night, and those who get drunk get drunk at night. But we, who belong to the day, let us stay sober, having donned the corselet of faith and love and as a helmet the hope of salvation" [1 Thess. 5:6–8]. [141.1] And the same things as they say about sleep must also be understood about death. For both indicate the departure of the soul, the latter more, the former less—which can also be seen in Heraclitus. [2] **"A human being, in the night, [. . .] awake he touches on a sleeping man"** [= **D71**]. [3] For "blessed are those who know the right moment," according to the Apostle, "for it is time for you to awaken from your sleep; for our salvation is now closer than it was when we acquired our faith. The night is far gone, the day is near. So let us put aside the works of darkness, and let us don the weapons of light" [Rom. 13:11–12]. [4] By "day" and "light" he is allegorically indicating the Son, and by "the weapons of light" he is metaphorically indicating the precepts.

(Ps.-?) Hippolytus (R86)

R86 (cf. B1, B50–67) (Ps.-?) Hippolytus, *Refutation of All Heresies*

[7.1] There was a man named Noetus, originally from

ναῖος. οὗτος εἰσηγήσατο αἵρεσιν ἐκ τῶν Ἡρακλείτου δογμάτων· [. . .].
[8.1] [. . .] δοκεῖ λοιπὸν καὶ τῶν δογμάτων τὴν κακοδιδασκαλίαν ἐκθέσθαι, πρότερον ⟨μὲν⟩[1] τὰ Ἡρακλείτῳ τῷ σκοτεινῷ δόξαντα παραθεμένους, ἔπει⟨τα δὲ⟩[2] καὶ τὰ τούτων μέρη Ἡρακλείτεια ὄντα φανερώσαντας,[3] ἃ τυχόντες[4] οἱ νῦν προστάται τῆς αἱρέσεως οὐκ ἴσασιν ὄντα τοῦ σκοτεινοῦ, νομίζοντες εἶναι Χριστοῦ. [2] οἷς εἰ ἐνέτυχον, κἂν οὕτω δυσωπηθέντες παύσαιντ᾽ ἂν[5] τῆς ἀθέου δυσφημίας. [. . .]

[1] ⟨μὲν⟩ Marcovich [2] ἔπειτα Miller, δὲ add. Marcovich: ἐπεὶ ms. [3] φανερώσαντας Marcovich: φανερῶσαι ms.
[4] ἃ τυχὸν Cruice: ⟨οἷς οὐκ⟩ ἐντυχόντες Marcovich [5] παύσαιντ᾽ ἂν Diels: παύσονται ms.

[9.1] Ἡράκλειτος μὲν οὖν φησιν εἶναι τὸ πᾶν διαιρετὸν ἀδιαίρετον, γενητὸν ἀγένητον, θνητὸν ἀθάνατον, λόγον αἰῶνα, πατέρα υἱόν, θεὸν δίκαιον. "οὐκ ἐμοῦ ἀλλὰ τοῦ δόγματος ἀκούσαντας ὁμολογεῖν σοφόν ἐστιν, ἓν πάντα εἶναι"[1] [cf. **D46**], ὁ Ἡράκλειτός φησι· [2] καὶ ὅτι τοῦτο οὐκ ἴσασιν πάντες οὐδὲ ὁμολογοῦσιν, ἐπιμέμφεται ὧδέ πως· "οὐ ξυνιᾶσιν ὅκως διαφερόμενον ἑωυτῷ ὁμολογέει· παλίντροπος ἁρμονίη ὅκωσπερ τόξου καὶ λύρης"[2] [= **D49**]· [3] ὅτι δὲ λόγος ἐστὶν ἀεὶ τὸ πᾶν καὶ διὰ παντὸς ὤν, οὕτως λέγει· "τοῦ δὲ λόγου τοῦδ᾽ ἐόντος [. . .] φράζων ὅπως ἔχει"[3] [cf. **D1**]. [4] ὅτι δέ ἐστι παῖς τὸ πᾶν καὶ δι᾽ αἰῶνος αἰώνιος βασιλεὺς τῶν ὅλων, οὕτως λέγει· "αἰὼν παῖς

Smyrna. He introduced a heresy based on the doctrines of Heraclitus. [...]

[8.1] [...] it seems that it remains for us to set out the evil teaching of his doctrines, first citing the opinions of Heraclitus the Obscure, and then demonstrating the Heraclitean character of those parts which the current leaders of the heresy know without knowing that they belong to the Obscure, but thinking that they belong to Christ; [2] but if they encountered them [i.e. Heraclitus' doctrines], they would be so ashamed that they would stop their atheist blasphemy. [...]

[9.1] Well then, Heraclitus says that the whole is divisible indivisible, generated ungenerated, mortal immortal, *logos* eternity, father son, a just god: **"After you have listened not to me but to** the doctrine,[1] **it is wise to agree that all things are one"** [cf. **D46**], says Heraclitus. [2] And the fact that not all people know this or agree about it, he criticizes as follows: **"They do not comprehend how, diverging, it accords with itself: a backward-turning fitting-together, as of a bow and a lyre"** [= **D49**]. [3] The fact that the *Logos* is always, being the whole and for all of time, he says in the following way: **"And of this account that is** [...] **indicate how it is"** [cf. **D1**]. [4] The fact that the whole is a child and is the eternal king of the universe throughout eternity, he says

---

[1] (Ps.-?) Hippolytus probably substitutes 'doctrine' (*dogma*) for 'account' (*logos*).

---

[1] app. cf. ad **D46**   [2] app. cf. ad **D49**   [3] app. cf. ad **D1**

EARLY GREEK PHILOSOPHY III

ἐστι παίζων, πεσσεύων· παιδὸς ἡ βασιληίη"⁴ [= **D76**]. ὅτι δέ ἐστιν ὁ πατὴρ πάντων τῶν γεγονότων γενητὸς⁵ ἀγένητος, κτίσις δημιουργός, ἐκείνου λέγοντος ἀκούομεν· "πόλεμος πάντων μὲν πατήρ ἐστι [. . .] τοὺς δὲ ἐλευθέρους" [= **D64**]. [5] ὅτι δέ ἐστιν ‹. . .›⁶ "ἁρμονίη ὅκωσπερ τόξου καὶ λύρης" [cf. **D49**]. ὅτι δέ ἐστιν⁷ ἀφανὴς⁸ ἀόρατος ἄγνωστος ἀνθρώποις, ἐν τούτοις λέγει· "ἁρμονίη ἀφανὴς φανερῆς κρείττων" [= **D50**]· ἐπαινεῖ ‹γὰρ›⁹ καὶ προθαυμάζει πρὸ τοῦ γινωσκομένου τὸ ἄγνωστον αὐτοῦ καὶ ἀόρατον τῆς δυνάμεως. ὅτι δέ ἐστιν ὁρατὸς ἀνθρώποις καὶ οὐκ ἀνεξεύρετος ἐν τούτοις λέγει· "ὅσων ὄψις ἀκοὴ μάθησις, ταῦτα ἐγὼ προτιμέω"¹⁰ [= **D31**], φησί, τουτέστι τὰ ὁρατὰ τῶν ἀοράτων. ‹ταὐτὸ δὲ καὶ›¹¹ ἀπὸ τῶν τοιούτων αὐτοῦ λόγων κατανοεῖν ῥᾴδιον· [6] "ἐξηπάτηνται, φησίν, οἱ ἄνθρωποι πρὸς τὴν γνῶσιν τῶν φανερῶν [. . .] ὅσα δὲ οὔτε εἴδομεν οὔτ' ἐλάβομεν, ταῦτα φέρομεν"¹² [= **D22**].

⁴ app. cf. ad **D76**   ⁵ γενητῶν ms., corr. Bernays
⁶ lac. sign. Miller   ⁷ ἐ(στιν) ms., ut videtur: ὁ θεὸς Wendland
⁸ ὁ post ἀφανὴς del. Wendland   ⁹ ‹γὰρ› Marcovich: ‹ἐν οἷς› ἐπαινεῖ Diels   ¹⁰ app. cf. ad **D31**   ¹¹ add. Wendland
¹² app. cf. ad **D22**

[10.1] οὕτως Ἡράκλειτος ἐν ἴσῃ μοίρᾳ τίθεται καὶ τιμᾷ τὰ ἐμφανῆ τοῖς ἀφανέσιν, ὡς ἕν τι τὸ ἐμφανὲς καὶ τὸ ἀφανὲς ὁμολογουμένως ὑπάρχον. ‹ἔσ›τι¹ γάρ, φησίν, "ἁρμονίη ἀφανὴς φανερῆς κρείττων"²

in this way: **"Eternity is a child playing, playing checkers: the kingship belongs to a child"** [= **D76**].[2] And the fact that the father of everything that has come about is generated ungenerated, creation creator, we hear him say it: **"War is the father of all [. . .] and the others free"** [= **D64**]. [5] But the fact that ‹. . .› **"fitting-together, as of a bow and a lyre"** [cf. **D49**].[3] The fact that he is invisible, unseen, unknown to humans, he says in these words: **"Invisible fitting-together, stronger than a visible one"** [= **D50**]. For he praises and admires, more than what is known, the unknown and unseen character of his power. But the fact that he is seen by humans and is not impossible to find, he says in these words: **"All the things of which there is sight, hearing, and knowledge I honor most"** [= **D31**],[4] he says, that is, what is visible more than what is invisible. It is easy to know ‹the same thing also› from statements of his of this sort: [6] he says, **"Regarding the knowledge of things that are evident, humans are fooled [. . .] the ones we do not see or grasp, we take away"** [= **D22**].

[2] We translate what seems to be (Ps.-?) Hippolytus' understanding of the original sentence. [3] The sentence has a lacuna. [4] We translate what seems to be (Ps.-?) Hippolytus' understanding of the original sentence.

[10.1] This is how Heraclitus, in a coherent way, considers and values as being equal what is visible and what is invisible, on the idea that the visible and the invisible, according together, are only one thing: for he says that **"Invisible fitting-together** is **stronger than a visible one"**

---

[1] ‹ἔσ›τι Miller: τίς ms.: τί Bernays   [2] app. cf. ad **D50**

[= **D50**], καὶ "ὅσων ὄψις ἀκοὴ μάθησις"—τουτέστι τὰ ὄργανα—, "ταῦτα," φησίν, "ἐγὼ προτιμέω"[3] [= **D31**], οὐ τὰ ἀφανῆ προτιμήσας. [2] τοιγαροῦν οὐδὲ σκότος οὐδὲ φῶς, οὐδὲ πονηρὸν οὐδὲ ἀγαθὸν ἕτερόν φησιν εἶναι ὁ Ἡράκλειτος, ἀλλὰ ἓν καὶ τὸ αὐτό. ἐπιτιμᾷ γοῦν Ἡσιόδῳ, ὅτι ἡμέραν καὶ νύκτα ⟨οὐκ⟩[4] οἶδεν· ἡμέρα γάρ, φησί, καὶ νύξ ἐστιν ἕν, λέγων ὧδέ πως· "διδάσκαλος δὲ πλείστων Ἡσίοδος [. . .] ἔστι γὰρ ἕν"[5] [= **D25a**].

[3] app. cf. ad **D31**   [4] ⟨οὐκ⟩ Schneidewin-Duncker
[5] app. cf. ad **D25a**

[3] καὶ ἀγαθὸν καὶ κακόν· "οἱ γοῦν ἰατροί," φησὶν ὁ Ἡράκλειτος, "τέμνοντες, καίοντες,"—πάντῃ βασανίζοντες κακῶς τοὺς ἀρρωστοῦντας—"ἐπαιτιῶνται μηδέν' ἄξιον μισθὸν λαμβάνειν παρὰ τῶν ἀρρωστούντων, ταῦτα ἐργαζόμενοι, †τὰ ἀγαθὰ καὶ τὰς νόσους†"[1] [= **D57**]. [4] καὶ εὐθὺ δέ, φησίν, καὶ στρεβλὸν τὸ αὐτό ἐστι. "γνάφων, φησίν, ὁδὸς εὐθεῖα καὶ σκολιή"[2] [= **D52**]—ἡ τοῦ ὀργάνου τοῦ καλουμένου κοχλίου ἐν τῷ γναφείῳ[3] περιστροφὴ εὐθεῖα καὶ σκολιή· ἄνω γὰρ ὁμοῦ καὶ κύκλῳ περιέρχεται[4]—"μία ἐστί," φησί, "καὶ ἡ αὐτή" [cf. **D51**]. καὶ τὸ ἄνω καὶ τὸ κάτω ἕν ἐστι καὶ τὸ αὐτό· "ὁδὸς ἄνω κάτω μία καὶ ὠυτή" [= **D51**]. [5] καὶ τὸ μιαρόν φησιν καὶ τὸ καθαρὸν ἓν καὶ ταὐτὸν

[1] app. cf. ad **D57**   [2] app. cf. ad **D52**   [3] γραφείῳ
ms., corr. Bernays   [4] περιέρχεται Roeper: περιέχεται ms.

[= **D50**], and again he says, **"All the things of which sight and hearing are knowledge"**—that is, the organs of perception—**"I honor most"** [= **D31**],[1] not honoring more the invisible ones. [2] That is why Heraclitus says that neither darkness nor light, neither bad nor good are different from one another, but that they are one and the same thing. In any case he criticizes Hesiod, for he did ⟨not⟩ know day and night: for, he says, day and night are one—this is what he says: **"The teacher of the most people is Hesiod [. . .] for they are one"** [= **D25a**].

[1] Perhaps this repetition of two of Heraclitus' sentences that have already been cited derives from a marginal note.

[3] and good and bad: **"Doctors,"** Heraclitus says, **"cutting, cauterizing,** badly mistreating their patients in every way, **complain that they do not receive an adequate payment from their patients—and are producing the same effects,** †benefits and diseases†" [= **D57**]; [4] and, he says, the straight and the twisted are the same thing: he says, **"The way of carding-combs: straight and crooked"** [= **D52**]—the rotation of the instrument called the screw in the carding-comb is straight and crooked, for while it turns in a circle, at the same time it moves up—he says it is **"one and the same"** [cf. **D51**].[1] And up and down are one and the same: **"The road upward and downward: one and the same"** [= **D51**]. [5] And he says that the polluted and the pure are one and the

[1] Perhaps this is an anticipation of the following sentence, or a marginal note.

εἶναι, καὶ τὸ πότιμον καὶ τὸ ἄποτον ἓν καὶ τὸ αὐτὸ εἶναι· "**θάλασσα,**" φησίν, "**ὕδωρ καθαρώτατον καὶ μιαρώτατον, ἰχθύσι μὲν πότιμον καὶ σωτήριον, ἀνθρώποις δὲ ἄποτον καὶ ὀλέθριον**" [= **D78**].

[6] λέγει δὲ ὁμολογουμένως τὸ ἀθάνατον εἶναι θνητὸν καὶ τὸ θνητὸν ἀθάνατον διὰ τῶν τοιούτων λόγων· "**ἀθάνατοι θνητοί, θνητοὶ ἀθάνατοι· ζῶντες τὸν ἐκείνων θάνατον, τὸν δὲ ἐκείνων βίον τεθνεῶτες**" [= **D70**]. λέγει δὲ καὶ σαρκὸς ἀνάστασιν ταύτης ⟨τῆς⟩[1] φανερᾶς, ἐν ᾗ γεγενήμεθα, καὶ τὸν θεὸν οἶδε ταύτης τῆς ἀναστάσεως αἴτιον οὕτως λέγων· "**ἔνθα δ' ἐόντι ἐπανίστασθαι καὶ φύλακας γίνεσθαι ἐγερτὶ ζώντων καὶ νεκρῶν**"[2] [= **D123**]. [7] λέγει δὲ καὶ τοῦ κόσμου κρίσιν καὶ πάντων τῶν ἐν αὐτῷ διὰ πυρὸς γίνεσθαι· "**πάντα γάρ, φησί, τὸ πῦρ ἐπελθὸν κρινεῖ καὶ καταλήψεται**"[3] [= **D84**]. λέγει δὲ καὶ φρόνιμον τοῦτο εἶναι τὸ πῦρ καὶ τῆς διοικήσεως τῶν ὅλων αἴτιον, λέγων οὕτως· "**τάδε πάντα οἰακίζει**"—τουτέστι κατευθύνει— "**κεραυνός**"[4] [= **D82**], κεραυνὸν τὸ πῦρ λέγων τὸ αἰώνιον.[5] καλεῖ[6] δὲ αὐτὸ "**χρησμοσύνην καὶ κόρον**" [= **D88**]· χρησμοσύνη δέ ἐστιν ἡ διακόσμησις κατ' αὐτόν, ἡ δὲ ἐκπύρωσις κόρος. [8] ἐν δὲ τούτῳ τῷ κεφαλαίῳ πάντα ὁμοῦ τὸν ἴδιον νοῦν ἐξέθετο, ἅμα δὲ καὶ τὸν τῆς Νοητοῦ αἱρέσεως, ⟨ὃν⟩[7]

---

[1] ⟨τῆς⟩ Diels   [2] app. cf. ad **D123**

[3] πάντα . . . καταλήψεται post ἐκπύρωσις κόρος ms., transp. Marcovich post Fränkel

[4] κεραυνός, τουτέστι κατευθύνει ms., transp. Marcovich

HERACLITUS

same thing, and the drinkable and the undrinkable are one and the same thing: he says, **"The sea, the purest water and the foulest: for fish it is drinkable and life-giving, but for humans undrinkable and deadly"** [= **D78**].
[6] He says, in a coherent way, that the immortal is mortal and the mortal immortal, in statements like the following: **"Immortals mortals, mortals immortals, living the death of these, dying the life of those"** [= **D70**]. He also speaks of the resurrection of this visible flesh, in which we have been born, and he knew that God is the cause of this resurrection, when he speaks as follows: **"For the one who is there they rise up and become wakeful guardians of the living and of the dead"** [= **D123**].
[7] He also says that the judgment of the world and of everything in it takes place by fire: for he says, **"When the fire has come upon all things, it will judge them and seize hold of them"** [= **D84**]. He also says that this fire is intelligent and the cause for the organization of the universe, when he speaks as follows: **"All these things the thunderbolt steers"** [= **D82**]—that is, directs, calling the eternal fire "thunderbolt." And he calls this **"shortage and satiety"** [= **D88**]: for according to him the organization of the world is shortage and the conflagration (*ekpurôsis*) is satiety. [8] In this chapter he has expounded all together his own thought and at the same time that of Noetus' heresy, about whom I demonstrated briefly that

---

⁵ λέγων οὕτως (ante **D82**) . . . τὸ αἰώνιον post διὰ πυρὸς γίνεσθαι [7 line 2] ms., transp. Marcovich post Fränkel

⁶ καλεῖς ms., corr. Miller

⁷ ⟨ὃν⟩ Schneidewin-Duncker

δι' ὀλίγων ἐπέδειξα[8] οὐκ ὄντα Χριστοῦ ἀλλὰ Ἡρακλείτου μαθητήν. τὸν γὰρ ποιητὸν[9] κόσμον αὐτὸν δημιουργὸν καὶ ποιητὴν ἑαυτοῦ γινόμενον οὕτω λέγει· "ὁ θεὸς ἡμέρη εὐφρόνη, χειμὼν θέρος, πόλεμος εἰρήνη, κόρος λιμός"—τἀναντία ἅπαντα· οὗτος ὁ νοῦς—"ἀλλοιοῦται δὲ ὅκωσπερ ⟨πῦρ⟩, ὁκόταν συμμιγῇ θυώμασιν, ὀνομάζεται καθ' ἡδονὴν ἑκάστου"[10] [= **D48**].

[8] ἐπεδείξω Mouraviev   [9] π(ρ)ῶτον ms., corr. Bernays
[10] app. cf. ad **D48**

[9] φανερὸν δὲ πᾶσι τοὺς ⟨ἀ⟩νοήτους[1] Νοητοῦ διαδόχους καὶ τῆς αἱρέσεως προστάτας, εἰ καὶ Ἡρακλείτου λέγοις ἂν αὐτοὺς[2] μὴ γεγονέναι ἀκροατάς, ἀλλά γε τὰ[3] Νοητῷ δόξαντα αἱρουμένους ἀναφανδὸν ταὐτὰ ὁμολογεῖν. λέγουσι γὰρ οὕτως· ἕνα καὶ τὸν αὐτὸν θεὸν εἶναι πάντων δημιουργὸν καὶ πατέρα, εὐδοκήσαντα δὲ πεφηνέναι[4] τοῖς ἀρχῆθεν δικαίοις ὄντα ἀόρατον· [10] ὅτε μὲν γὰρ οὐχ ὁρᾶται, ἦν[5] ἀόρατος, ⟨ὅτε δὲ ὁρᾶται, ὁρατός· καὶ⟩[6] ἀχώρητος δὲ ὅτε μὴ χωρεῖσθαι θέλει, χωρητὸς δὲ ὅτε χωρεῖται· οὕτως κατὰ τὸν αὐτὸν λόγον ἀκράτητος καὶ κρατητός,[7] ἀγέν⟨ν⟩ητος[8] ⟨καὶ γεννητός⟩,[9] ἀθάνατος καὶ θνητός. πῶς ⟨οὖν⟩[10] οὐχ Ἡρακλείτου οἱ τοιοῦτοι δειχθήσονται μαθηταί, μὴ ⟨αὐ⟩τῇ δὴ τῇ λέξει[11] ⟨ἰ⟩δίᾳ ⟨δὲ⟩ φθάσας[12] ἐφιλοσόφησεν ὁ σκοτεινός;

[1] νοητοὺς ms., corr. Bernays   [2] λέγοισαν ἑαυτοὺς ms., corr. Bernays   [3] τῷ ms., corr. Miller

he was a disciple not of Christ but of Heraclitus. For this is how he says that the created world is the craftsman and creator of itself: **"God: day night, winter summer, war peace, satiety hunger."** (all the contraries, this is the meaning) **"He changes just as ⟨fire⟩, when it is mixed together with incense, is named according to the scent of each one"** [= **D48**].

[9] It is clear to all that even if you were to say that Noetus' thoughtless (*anoêtous*) successors and the heads of his heresy were not pupils of Heraclitus themselves, nonetheless by embracing Noetus' doctrines they were evidently subscribing to these same theses. For this is what they say: that one and the same god is the craftsman and the father of all things, and that, although invisible, he consented in the beginning to reveal himself to the just. [10] For when he is not seen, he is invisible; ⟨when he is seen, he is visible;⟩ immobile when he does not wish to move, but mobile when he moves; thus in the same way invincible and vanquished, ungenerated ⟨and generated⟩, immortal and mortal. How ⟨then⟩ will men of this sort not reveal themselves to be disciples of Heraclitus, even if the Obscure, the first man to have adopted this philosophy, did not express himself in this way, but in his own words?

---

⁴ πεφηκέναι ms., corr. Miller   ⁵ ἦν ms.: ἐστιν Cruice
⁶ add. Marcovich post Schneidewin-Duncker
⁷ ἀκράτητος ms., corr. Bernays   ⁸ ἀγένητος ms., corr. Schneidewin-Duncker   ⁹ add. Schneidewin-Duncker
¹⁰ ⟨οὖν⟩ Wendland   ¹¹ μὴ ⟨αὐ⟩τῇ τῇ λέξει Miller et δὴ Marcovich: μὴ δὲ (τῇ suprasc.) λέξει (τῇ suprasc.) ms.: ⟨εἰ καὶ⟩ μὴ τῇδε τῇ λέξει Wendland   ¹² ⟨ἰ⟩δίᾳ ⟨δὲ⟩ φθάσας Wendland: διαφθάσας ms.

305

Theodoret (R87)

R87 (cf. B24, B25, B27) Theod. *Cur.* 8.39–41

ὁ δέ γε Ἡράκλειτος καὶ τοὺς ἐν τοῖς πολέμοις ἀναιρεθέντας πάσης ἀξίους ὑπολαμβάνει τιμῆς· "ἀρηιφάτους" γάρ φησιν, "οἱ θεοὶ τιμῶσι καὶ ἄνθρωποι" [= **D122a**], καὶ πάλιν· "μόνοι γὰρ μείζονες μείζονος μοίρας λαγχάνουσιν" [= **D122b**]. [40] ἀλλὰ τόνδε τὸν λόγον ἔγωγε οὐ προσίεμαι· πλεῖστοι γὰρ δὴ παμπόνηρον ἀσπασάμενοι βίον τὸν βίαιον ὑπέμειναν θάνατον. [. . .] [41] [. . .] οὔκουν πάντας ʽἀρηιφάτουςʼ κατὰ τὸν Ἡράκλειτον τιμητέον, ἀλλ' ἐκείνους, οἳ τὸν ὑπὲρ τῆς εὐσεβείας ἀσπασίως κατεδέξαντο θάνατον· ἐκεῖνοι γὰρ ἀληθῶς, κατά γε τοῦτον αὐτόν, μόνοι μείζονες. οὗ δὴ ἕνεκα καὶ μείζονος ἀπολαύουσι μοίρας, καὶ νῦν τὸ παρὰ πάντων ἀνθρώπων κομιζόμενοι γέρας καὶ τοὺς αἰωνίους στεφάνους προσμένοντες. ἐκεῖνο δὲ τοῦ Ἡρακλείτου μάλα θαυμάζω, ὅτι "μένει τοὺς ἀνθρώπους ἀποθνήσκοντας, ὅσα οὐκ ἔλπονται οὐδὲ δοκέουσιν" [= **D120**].

Neoplatonic Appropriations (R88–R92)
Plotinus (R88–R89)

R88 (cf. B84a–b) Plot. 4.8.1.11–17

ὁ μὲν γὰρ Ἡράκλειτος, ὃς ἡμῖν παρακελεύεται ζητεῖν τοῦτο, ἀμοιβάς τε ἀναγκαίας τιθέμενος ἐκ τῶν ἐναν-

HERACLITUS

Theodoret (R87)

R87 (cf. ad B24, B25, B27) Theodoret, *Cure of the Greek Maladies*

Heraclitus maintains that those who have been killed in war are worthy of being fully honored: for he says, **"Gods and humans honor those men whom Ares has slain"** [= **D122a**]; and again: **"Greater deaths [*moroi*] obtain greater portions [*moirai*]"** [= **D122b**]. [40] But I myself do not accept this idea: for very many people have lived a depraved life and then suffered a violent death. [. . .] [41] [. . .] So it is not all those "whom Ares has slain" who ought to be honored according to Heraclitus, but only those who have joyously accepted death in the service of piety; for in truth it is only they, according to him, who are the "greater" ones. And because of this they enjoy "greater portions," those who not only receive honors from all human beings in this life but also await eternal garlands. And I admire greatly this other saying of Heraclitus: **"What awaits humans after they have died is everything that they do not expect nor suppose"** [= **D120**].

Neoplatonic Appropriations (R88–R92)
Plotinus (R88–R89)

R88 (cf. B84a–b) Plotinus, *Ennead*

For Heraclitus, who bids us investigate this question [scil. that of the descent of the soul into the body], when he established the necessary exchanges between the oppo-

τίων, "ὁδὸν τε ἄνω καὶ κάτω" εἰπὼν [cf. **D51**] καὶ "μεταβάλλον ἀναπαύεται" [= **D58**] καὶ "κάματός ἐστι τοῖς αὐτοῖς μοχθεῖν καὶ ἄρχεσθαι" [= **D109**] εἰκάζειν ἔδωκεν ἀμελήσας σαφῆ ἡμῖν ποιῆσαι τὸν λόγον, ὡς δέον ἴσως παρ' αὐτῷ ζητεῖν, ὥσπερ καὶ αὐτὸς ζητήσας εὗρεν.

R89 (cf. B96) Plot. 5.1.2.38–42

καὶ πολὺς ὢν ὁ οὐρανὸς καὶ ἄλλος ἄλλῃ ἕν ἐστι τῇ ταύτης δυνάμει καὶ θεός ἐστι διὰ ταύτην ὁ κόσμος ὅδε. ἔστι δὲ καὶ ἥλιος θεός, ὅτι ἔμψυχος, καὶ τὰ ἄλλα ἄστρα, καὶ ἡμεῖς, εἴπερ τι, διὰ τοῦτο· **νέκυες γὰρ κοπρίων ἐβλητότεροι** [= **D119**].

Porphyry (R90)

R90 Porph. *Antr.*

a (B77) 10

ὅθεν καὶ Ἡράκλειτον ψυχῇσι φάναι τέρψιν μὴ[1] θάνατον ὑγρῇσι γενέσθαι, τέρψιν δὲ εἶναι αὐταῖς τὴν εἰς τὴν γένεσιν πτῶσιν, καὶ ἀλλαχοῦ δὲ φάναι ζῆν ἡμᾶς τὸν ἐκείνων θάνατον καὶ ζῆν ἐκείνας τὸν ἡμέτερον θάνατον.

[1] ἢ Diels, καὶ Kranz

sites and asserted, **"The road upward and downward"** [cf. **D51**] and **"Changing, it remains at rest"** [= **D58**] and **"It is wearisome to work hard for the same ones and to be ruled by them"** [= **D109**], seems to proceed by images and neglects to make his account (*logos*) clear, perhaps thinking that we have to seek within ourselves, just as he himself had sought and then found [cf. **D36**].

R89 (cf. B96) Plotinus, *Ennead*

And although the heavens are multiple and different in different places, they are also one by the power of this [scil. the soul], and this world here is a god by virtue of this. The sun too is a god, for it has a soul, as well as the other heavenly bodies, and above all we too for the following reason: **"Corpses are more to be thrown out than manure"** [= **D119**].

Porphyry (R90)

R90 Porphyry, *On the Cave of the Nymphs in the* Odyssey

a (B77)

[. . .] that is why [scil. probably according to Numenius] Heraclitus also says that for souls it is a pleasure, and not death, to become moist [cf. **D101**] and that the fall into becoming is a pleasure for them, and he says elsewhere that we live their death and they live our death [cf. **D70**].

b (cf. ad B51) 29

ἀρξαμένης γὰρ τῆς φύσεως ἀπὸ ἑτερότητος πανταχοῦ τὸ δίθυρον αὐτῆς πεποίηνται σύμβολον. ἢ γὰρ διὰ νοητοῦ ἡ πορεία ἢ δι' αἰσθητοῦ· καὶ τοῦ αἰσθητοῦ ἢ διὰ τῆς ἀπλανοῦς ἢ διὰ τῆς τῶν πεπλανημένων, καὶ πάλιν ἢ διὰ τῆς ἀθανάτου ἢ διὰ τῆς θνητῆς πορείας. καὶ κέντρον τὸ μὲν ὑπὲρ γῆν, τὸ δ' ὑπόγειον, καὶ τὸ μὲν ἀνατολικόν, τὸ δὲ δυτικόν, καὶ τὰ μὲν ἀριστερά, τὰ δὲ δεξιά, νύξ τε καὶ ἡμέρα· καὶ διὰ τοῦτο **παλίντονος** ἡ ἁρμονία καὶ τοξεύει[1] διὰ τῶν ἐναντίων.

[1] παλίντροπος ἁρμονίη ὅκωσπερ τόξου καὶ λύρης Heraclitus **D49**

Iamblichus (R91)

R91 (cf. Nachtrag I, p. 494.15) Iambl. *An.* in Stob. 1.49.39 (I, p. 378.19–25 Wachsmuth)

ἀπὸ μὲν δὴ τοσούτων καὶ οὕτω διαφερόντων μερῶν γίγνεσθαι διαφερούσας τὰς τῇδε καθόδους, αὐτοὺς δὲ τοὺς τρόπους διίστασθαι πολυειδῶς. Ἡράκλειτος μὲν γὰρ ἀμοιβὰς ἀναγκαίας τίθεται ἐκ τῶν ἐναντίων [cf. **D87**], ὁδόν τε ἄνω καὶ κάτω διαπορεύεσθαι τὰς ψυχὰς ὑπείληφε [cf. **D51**] καὶ τὸ μὲν τοῖς αὐτοῖς ἐπιμένειν κάματον εἶναι, τὸ δὲ μεταβάλλειν φέρειν ἀνάπαυσιν [cf. **D58**].

b (cf. ad B51)

Since nature begins everywhere from difference, they [scil. the ancients] have given everywhere as a symbol for it the two-gated entrance. For the way passes either by the intelligible or by the perceptible; and regarding the intelligible, either through the sphere of fixed stars or through that of the planets, and again either through the immortal passage or through the mortal one. And there is one center above the earth, another below it, and one to the east, and another to the west; and some things are to the left, others to the right, and there is night and day. And that is why **the fitting-together is backward-stretching** and it [scil. the bow?] shoots arrows through the opposites [cf. **D49**].

Iamblichus (R91)

R91 (< Nachtrag I, p. 494.15) Iamblichus, *On the Soul*

The descents [scil. of the souls] derive their difference from the great number of the parts [scil. of the world], which are different themselves, from which they come, and the modes [scil. of the descents] also differ from one another in many ways. For Heraclitus posits necessary exchanges between the opposites [cf. **D87**], he thought that the souls travel along the road upward and downward [cf. **D51**], and that to remain in the same place is toil, whereas to be transformed brings repose [cf. **D58**].

EARLY GREEK PHILOSOPHY III

Proclus (R92)

R92 (T 901 Mouraviev) Procl. *In Tim.* 1 ad 20d (1.76.17–21 Diehl)

οἳ δὲ γεγονέναι μὲν ταῦτα τοῦτον τὸν τρόπον οὐκ ἀπογινώσκουσι, παραλαμβάνεσθαι δὲ νῦν ὡς εἰκόνας τῶν ἐν τῷ παντὶ προουσῶν ἐναντιώσεων· **πόλεμον** γὰρ εἶναι τῶν **πάντων πατέρα** καὶ κατὰ τὸν Ἡράκλειτον [cf. **D64**].

Invective, Praise, and Variations on Heraclitean Themes in Greek Poetry and Literature (R93–R99)
Scythinus of Teos (R93)

R93

a (< A1) Diog. Laert. 9.16

Ἱερώνυμος δέ φησι [Frag. 46 Wehrli] καὶ Σκυθῖνον τὸν τῶν ἰάμβων ποιητὴν ἐπιβαλέσθαι τὸν ἐκείνου λόγον διὰ μέτρου ἐκβάλλειν.

b (< C3.1) Plut. *Pyth. orac.* 16 402A

ἣν ἁρμόζεται
Ζηνὸς εὐειδὴς Ἀπόλλων πᾶσαν, ἀρχὴν καὶ τέλος
συλλαβών, ἔχει δὲ λαμπρὸν πλῆκτρον ἡλίου
φάος.

HERACLITUS

Proclus (R92)

R92 (≠ DK) Proclus, *Commentary on Plato's* Timaeus

Other people do not reject the idea that these events [scil. the story of Atlantis] happened in this way, but [scil. they think] that they are to be understood now as images of the oppositions existing previously in the universe, for **"War is the father of all,"** according to Heraclitus too [cf. **D64**].

Invective, Praise, and Variations on Heraclitean Themes in Greek Poetry and Literature (R93–R99) Scythinus of Teos (R93)

R93

a (< A1) Diogenes Laertius

Hieronymus says that Scythinus too, the iambic poet, undertook to put his [i.e. Heraclitus'] account into verse.

b (< C3.1) Scythinus in Plutarch, *On the Pythian Oracles*

which well-shaped Apollo,
Zeus' son, fits together as a whole [scil. the lyre, cf. **D49**], taking together
Beginning and end [cf. **D54**]; and he holds the sun's light as a gleaming plectrum.

Timon of Phlius (R94)

R94 (< A1) Diog. Laert. 9.6

τοῦτον δὲ καὶ ὁ Τίμων ὑπογράφει λέγων· [Frag. 43 Di Marco]

τοῖς δ' ἔνι κοκκυστής, ὀχλολοίδορος Ἡράκλειτος,
αἰνικτὴς ἀνόρουσε.

Epigrams (R95–R98)
Theodoridas (R95)

R95 (T 294 Mouraviev) *Anth. Gr.* 7.479 (Theodoridas)

πέτρος ἐγὼ τὸ πάλαι γυρὴ καὶ ἄτριπτος ἐπιβλής
  τὴν Ἡρακλείτου ἔνδον ἔχω κεφαλήν·
αἰών μ' ἔτριψεν κροκάλαις ἴσον· ἐν γὰρ ἁμάξῃ
  παμφόρῳ αἰζηῶν εἰνοδίη τέταμαι.
ἀγγέλλω δὲ βροτοῖσι, καὶ ἄστηλός περ ἐοῦσα,
  θεῖον ὑλακτητὴν δήμου ἔχουσα κύνα.

R96 (cf. ad B74) *Anth. Gr.* 7.79 (Meleagrus?)

ὤνθρωφ', Ἡράκλειτος ἐγώ, σοφὰ μοῦνος ἀνευρεῖν
  φαμί.—"τὰ δ' ἐς πάτραν κρέσσονα καὶ
  σοφίας."

1 ἀνευρών ms., corr. Headlam

HERACLITUS

Timon of Phlius (R94)

R94 (< A1) Diogenes Laertius

This man [i.e. Heraclitus] Timon too sketches when he says,

> Among these the crower, the mob-reviler, Heraclitus
> The enigmatic, arose.

Epigrams (R95–R98)
Theodoridas (R95)

R95 (≠ DK) *Greek Anthology* (Theodoridas)

> I, a stone—once a round and unworn cover—
>   I now contain Heraclitus' head within myself.
> But time has worn me down like the seashore; for I lie
>   In a public wayfare, on the path of vigorous men.
> I announce to mortals, even though I am without my stele,
>   That I possess the divine dog that barked at the common people.

R96 (cf. ad B74) *Greek Anthology* (Meleager?)[1]

> "Oh you, human being, I say that I, Heraclitus, am
>   the only man to have discovered wisdom."

---

[1] The text of this poem and the distribution of the utterances between the two speakers are uncertain; the manuscript's attribution of it to Meleager has often been doubted.

EARLY GREEK PHILOSOPHY III

—λὰξ γὰρ καὶ τοκεῶνας, ἰὼ ξένε, δύσφρονας
   ἄνδρας
ὑλάκτευν.—"λαμπρὰ θρεψαμένοισι χάρις."
5 —οὐκ ἀπ᾽ ἐμεῦ;—"μὴ τρηχύς, ἐπεὶ τάχα καὶ σύ
   τι πεύσῃ
τρηχύτερον."—πάτρας χαῖρε σὺ δ᾽ ἐξ Ἐφέσου.

3 λὰξ] δὰξ Jacobs   τοκέων ἀσίωι ms., corr. Headlam
5–6 interp. Gullo

Anonymous Epigrams (R97–R98)

R97 (< A1) Diog. Laert. 9.16

Ἡράκλειτος ἐγώ· τί μ᾽ ἄνω κάτω ἕλκετ᾽, ἄμουσοι;
οὐχ ὑμῖν ἐπόνουν, τοῖς δέ μ᾽ ἐπισταμένοις.
εἷς ἐμοὶ ἄνθρωπος τρισμύριοι, οἱ δ᾽ ἀνάριθμοι
οὐδείς. ταῦτ᾽ αὐδῶ καὶ παρὰ Φερσεφόνῃ.

1 τί μ᾽ ἄνω Meineke: τιμαίω vel τί με ὦ vel τί με ὦν vel τί με mss.

R98 (< A1) Diog. Laert. 9.16

μὴ ταχὺς Ἡρακλείτου ἐπ᾽ ὀμφαλὸν εἴλεε βύβλον
τοὐφεσίου· μάλα τοι δύσβατος ἀτραπιτός.
ὄρφνη καὶ σκότος ἐστὶν ἀλάμπετον· ἢν δέ σε
   μύστης
εἰσαγάγῃ, φανεροῦ λαμπρότερ᾽ ἠελίου.

HERACLITUS

"But what is done for one's fatherland is even
   greater than wisdom."
"Yes, I barked savagely at my own parents, oh
   stranger, those evil-minded people."
   "Illustrious gratitude toward those who raised
      you!"
"Won't you go away?" "Enough of your rudeness, for   5
   soon you too will hear
   Something even ruder." "Farewell, you, from my
      fatherland Ephesus!"

Anonymous Epigrams (R97–R98)

R97 (< A1) Diogenes Laertius

I am Heraclitus. Why do you drag me upward and
   downward, you boors? [cf. **D59**]
   I labored not for you but for those who
      understand me.
For me one man is thirty thousand [cf. **D12**], the
   countless multitude
   Are no one. This I declare even in Persephone's
      domain.

R98 (< A1) Diogenes Laertius

Do not hasten to reach the end of the book of
   Heraclitus
   Of Ephesus: the path is not easy to traverse.
There is gloom and lightless obscurity: but if a mystic
   initiate
   Leads you in, it is brighter than the shining sun.

A Parody (R99)

R99 (> C5) Luc. *Vit. auct.* 14

[ΑΓ.] σὺ δὲ τί κλάεις, ὦ βέλτιστε; πολὺ γὰρ οἶμαι κάλλιον σοι προσλαλεῖν.

[ΗΡ.] ἡγέομαι γάρ, ὦ ξεῖνε, τὰ ἀνθρωπήια πρήγματα ὀιζυρὰ καὶ δακρυώδεα καὶ οὐδὲν αὐτέων ὅ τι μὴ ἐπικήριον· τὸ δὴ οἰκτείρω τε σφέας καὶ ὀδύρομαι, καὶ τὰ μὲν παρεόντα οὐ δοκέω μεγάλα, τὰ δ' ἐν ὑστέρῳ χρόνῳ ἐσόμενα πάμπαν ἀνιηρά, λέγω δὴ τὰς ἐκπυρώσιας καὶ τὴν τοῦ ὅλου συμφορήν· ταῦτα δὲ ὀδύρομαι καὶ ὅτι ἔμπεδον οὐδέν, ἀλλά κως ἐς κυκεῶνα τὰ πάντα συνειλέονται καί ἐστι τὠυτὸν τέρψις ἀτερψίη, γνῶσις ἀγνωσίη, μέγα μικρόν, ἄνω κάτω, περιχωρέοντα καὶ ἀμειβόμενα ἐν τῇ τοῦ αἰῶνος παιδιῇ.

[ΑΓ.] τί γὰρ ὁ αἰών ἐστιν;

[ΗΡ.] παῖς παίζων, πεσσεύων, ‹συμφερόμενος,›[1] διαφερόμενος.

[ΑΓ.] τί δὲ ἄνθρωποι;

[ΗΡ.] θεοὶ θνητοί.

[ΑΓ.] τί δὲ θεοί;

[ΗΡ.] ἄνθρωποι ἀθάνατοι.

[ΑΓ.] αἰνίγματα λέγεις, ὦ οὗτος, ἢ γρίφους συντίθης; ἀτεχνῶς γὰρ ὥσπερ ὁ Λοξίας οὐδὲν ἀποσαφεῖς.

[ΗΡ.] οὐδὲν γάρ μοι μέλει ὑμέων.

[ΑΓ.] τοιγαροῦν οὐδὲ ὠνήσεταί σέ τις εὖ φρονῶν.

[1] add. Diels

HERACLITUS

A Parody (R99)

R99 (> C5) Lucian, *Philosophies for Sale*

[A buyer:] But you there [i.e. Heraclitus], poor fellow, why are you weeping? For I think it is much better to speak with you [scil. than with Democritus].

[Heraclitus:] It is because I think, stranger, that human affairs deserve only pity and tears and that there is not one of them that is not perishable; that is why I pity them and feel grief [cf. **P12**], and I think that the present is of no importance, but that what will happen in the future is completely upsetting—I am talking about the conflagrations and the destruction of the whole. I grieve over these things and because nothing is stable but all things are pressed together as in a *kukeôn* [cf. **D59**], and that pleasure and displeasure, knowledge and ignorance, big and little, up and down, are the same thing, moving around and changing places in the game of eternity.

[A buyer:] And what is eternity?

[Heraclitus:] A child playing, playing checkers [cf. **D76**], ‹converging,› diverging [cf. **D49**].

[A buyer:] What are human beings?

[Heraclitus:] Mortal gods [cf. **D70**].

[A buyer:] What are gods?

[Heraclitus:] Immortal human beings [cf. **D70**].

[A buyer:] Are you telling riddles, fellow, or constructing enigmas? Quite frankly, you do not say anything clearly, just like Apollo [cf. **D41**].

[Heraclitus:] That is because I care nothing at all about you.

[A buyer:] Then no one who has any sense will buy you.

[HP.] ἐγὼ δὲ κέλομαι πᾶσιν ἡβηδὸν οἰμώζειν, τοῖσιν ὠνεομένοισι καὶ τοῖσιν οὐκ ὠνεομένοισι.

[ΑΓ.] τουτὶ τὸ κακὸν οὐ πόρρω μελαγχολίας ἐστιν. οὐδέτερον δὲ ὅμως αὐτῶν ἔγωγε ὠνήσομαι.

The Text of Heraclitus: Some Examples of Multiple Versions of the Same Phrase (R100–R102)

R100 "φύσις κρύπτεσθαι φιλεῖ." (= **D35**)

a (< T 326 Mouraviev) Phil. *Quaest. Gen.* 4.1, p. 237.4–6 Aucher

Օառ ըստ Հերակլիտեայ բնութիւնս մեր՝ հաւէլ եւ թաքչել սիրէ:

b (< T 328 Mouraviev) Phil. *Somn.* 1.6

ἐμοὶ τοίνυν δοκεῖ σύμβολον εἶναι τὸ φρέαρ ἐπιστήμης· οὐ γάρ ἐστιν ἐπιπόλαιος αὐτῆς ἡ φύσις, ἀλλὰ πάνυ βαθεῖα· οὐδ' ἐν φανερῷ πρόκειται, ἀλλ' ἐν ἀφανεῖ που κρύπτεσθαι φιλεῖ.

c (T 327 Mouraviev) Phil. *Spec. leg.* 4.51

χρόνῳ δὲ παντάπασιν ὀλίγῳ διακαλύπτεται τὰ τοιαῦτα στρατηγήματα, τῆς φύσεως οὐκ ἀεὶ κρύπτεσθαι φιλούσης, ἀλλ' ὁπόταν καιρὸς ᾖ τὸ ἴδιον κάλλος ἀναφαινούσης ἀηττήτοις δυνάμεσιν.

HERACLITUS

[Heraclitus:] I tell everyone to lament, young and old, those who are buying and those who are not buying.
[A buyer:] This man's trouble is not very far from melancholia [cf. **P11**]. I am not going to buy either of the two of them.

The Text of Heraclitus: Some Examples of Multiple Versions of the Same Phrase (R100–R102)

R100 "A nature tends to hide." (= ***D35***)

a (≠ DK) Philo, *Questions on Genesis*

The tree [i.e. the great tree of Mambre mentioned in Gen. 18:1] according to Heraclitus is our nature: it likes to hide itself.[1]

[1] Based on an unidentified glossary quoted by Aucher (1826: 237, note 2), the similarity asserted between the tree and our nature might refer to the roots, which are hidden underground. Note and translation by Irene Tinti.

b (≠ DK) Philo, *On Dreams*

The well seems to me a symbol of knowledge. For its nature is not on the surface, but very deep: and it does not lie in front of us in a manifest way, but it likes in some way to hide in invisibility.

c (≠ DK) Philo, *The Special Laws*

But in a very short time these kinds of stratagems are discovered, for nature, which does not like to hide forever, at the right moment reveals its own beauty by its undefeated powers.

d (T 330 Mouraviev) Phil. *Fuga et inv.* 179

οἱ μὲν οὖν ἀλληγορίας καὶ φύσεως τῆς κρύπτεσθαι φιλούσης ἀμύητοι τὴν εἰρημήνην εἰκάζουσι πηγὴν τῷ Αἰγυπτίῳ ποταμῷ [. . .].

e (T 329 Mouraviev) Phil. *Mut. nom.* 6

[. . .] πάνθ' ὅσα μὴ τὸ εὐπρεπὲς ἐν λόγῳ διασῴζειν δοκεῖ σύμβολα φύσεως τῆς ἀεὶ κρύπτεσθαι φιλούσης ὑπάρχοντα [. . .].

f (> B123) Them. *Orat.* 5

φύσις δὲ καθ' Ἡράκλειτον κρύπτεσθαι φιλεῖ καὶ πρὸ τῆς φύσεως ὁ τῆς φύσεως δημιουργός [. . .].

g (cf. ad B123, < T 736 Mouraviev) Procl. *In Remp.* 2, p. 107.5

[. . .] καὶ ὅτι τὸ πλασματῶδες τοῦτο κατὰ φύσιν πώς ἐστιν, διότι καὶ ἡ φύσις κρύπτεσθαι φιλεῖ καθ' Ἡράκλειτον [. . .].

h (< T 772 Mouraviev) Jul. *Or.* 7 216C

φιλεῖ γὰρ ἡ φύσις κρύπτεσθαι, καὶ τὸ ἀποκεκρυμμένον τῆς τῶν θεῶν οὐσίας οὐκ ἀνέχεται γυμνοῖς εἰς ἀκαθάρτους ἀκοὰς ῥίπτεσθαι ῥήμασιν.

HERACLITUS

d (≠ DK) Philo, *On Flight and Finding*

Those who are uninitiated in allegory and in nature, which tends to hide, liken the source we have mentioned to the river of Egypt [. . .].

e (≠ DK) Philo, *On the Change of Names*

[. . .] all the expressions that seem not to preserve decorum in language but are symbols of nature, which always tends to hide [. . .].

f (> B123) Themistius, *Oration*

Nature, according to Heraclitus, tends to hide, and, more even than nature, the craftsman of nature [. . .].

g (cf. ad B123) Proclus, *Commentary on Plato's* Republic

[. . .] and that this fiction is in a certain way in accordance with nature, since nature too tends to hide, according to Heraclitus [. . .].

h (≠ DK) Julian, *Oration*

For nature tends to hide, and what of the substance of the gods is hidden does not tolerate being cast with naked words to unpurified listeners.

R101 "αὔη ψυχή, σοφωτάτη καὶ ἀρίστη." (= **D103**)

a (< T 358 Mouraviev, cf. B118) Mus. Ruf. in Stob. 3.17.42

[. . .] οὕτω δ' ἂν καὶ τὴν ψυχὴν ἡμῶν ὑπάρχειν καθαράν τε καὶ ξηράν, ὁποία οὖσα ἀρίστη καὶ σοφωτάτη εἴη ἄν, καθάπερ Ἡρακλείτῳ δοκεῖ λέγοντι οὕτως· "αὐγὴ[1] ξηρὴ ψυχὴ σοφωτάτη καὶ ἀρίστη."

[1] αὐγη (sic) S M(d) A[1]: αὔη A[2]

b (< T 818 Mouraviev, cf. B118) Stob. 3.5.6–8

Ἡρακλείτου. [. . .] αὐγὴ ξηρὴ[1] ψυχὴ σοφωτάτη καὶ ἀρίστη.

[1] αὔη scripsit et ξηρὴ lineola induxit A[2]

c (< T 342 Mouraviev, cf. B118) Phil. *Prov.* 2.67 Colson ap. Eus. *PE* 8.14.67

[. . .] Ἡράκλειτος οὐκ ἀπὸ σκοποῦ φησιν· αὐγὴ ξηρὴ ψυχὴ σοφωτάτη καὶ ἀρίστη.

d (< T 510 Mouraviev, cf. B118) Plut. *Esu carn.* 995E

"αὐγὴ ξηρὴ ψυχὴ σοφωτάτη" κατὰ τὸν Ἡράκλειτον.

e (< T 509 Mouraviev, cf. B118) Plut. *Def. orac.* 432F

"αὕτη" γὰρ "ξηρὰ ψυχή," καθ' Ἡράκλειτον.

HERACLITUS

R101 "A dry soul: wisest and best." (= *D103*)

a (cf. B118) Musonius Rufus in Stobaeus, *Anthology*

[. . .] and thus our soul too would be pure and dry, and being like this it would be best and wisest, in conformity with the opinion of Heraclitus, who says, "dry light-beam, the wisest and best soul."

b (cf. B118) Stobaeus, *Anthology*

Of Heraclitus: "Dry light-beam, the wisest and best soul."

c (cf. B118) Philo of Alexandria, *On Providence*

Heraclitus does not miss the mark when he says, "Dry light-beam, the wisest and best soul."

d (cf. B118) Plutarch, *On the Eating of Flesh*

"Dry light-beam, the wisest soul," according to Heraclitus.

e (cf. B118) Plutarch, *The Obsolescence of Oracles*

For "this is a dry soul," according to Heraclitus.

f (< T 511 Mouraviev, cf. B118) Plut. *Rom.* 28.7

"αὕτη" γὰρ "ψυχὴ ξηρὴ καὶ ἀρίστη" καθ᾽ Ἡράκλειτον [. . .].

g (< T 623 Mouraviev, cf. B118) Clem. Alex. *Paed.* 2.29.3

οὕτω δ᾽ ἂν καὶ ἡ ψυχὴ ἡμῶν ὑπάρξαι καθαρὰ καὶ ξηρὰ καὶ φωτοειδής, "αὐγὴ δὲ ψυχὴ ξηρὰ σοφωτάτη καὶ ἀρίστη."

h (< T 578 Mouraviev, cf. B118) Gal. *Quod animi mores*, p. 786

[. . .] ἀλλ᾽ οὐ[1] καὶ ξηρότητα συγχωρήσομεν αἰτίαν εἶναι συνέσεως ⟨ὥσπερ⟩ οἵ γ᾽ ἀμφ᾽[2] Ἡρακλείτον; καὶ γὰρ καὶ οὗτος εἶπεν, "αὐγὴ ξηρὴ ψυχὴ σοφωτάτη" [. . .].

[1] οὐ Müller: εἰ mss. [2] ⟨ὥσπερ⟩ οἵ γ᾽ ἀμφ᾽ Müller: οἵ γε μὴν ἀμφ᾽ mss.

i (< T 290 Mouraviev, cf. B118) Herm. *In Phaedr.* (p. 29.27–29 Lucarini-Moreschini).

ἐπιτήδειον δὲ καὶ τὸ θέρος καὶ ἡ μεσημβρία πρὸς ἀναγωγὴν καὶ κατὰ τὸν Ἡράκλειτον, ὅς φησιν· "αὐγὴ ξηρὴ ψυχὴ σοφωτάτη."

f (cf. B118) Plutarch, *Romulus*

For "this soul is dry and best" according to Heraclitus [. . .].

g (cf. B118) Clement of Alexandria, *Pedagogue*

And thus our soul would be pure and dry and luminous: "dry light-beam, the wisest and best soul."

h (cf. B118) Galen, *That the Faculties of the Soul Follow the Mixtures of the Body*

[. . .] but we will not concede that dryness is the cause of intelligence, as those who follow Heraclitus say; for he said, "dry light-beam, the wisest soul" [. . .].

i (cf. B118) Hermias, *Commentary on Plato's* Phaedrus

Both summer and noon are appropriate for the elevation of the soul according to Heraclitus too, who says, "dry light-beam, the wisest soul."

j (< T 591 Mouraviev, cf. B118) Arist. Quint. *Mus.* 2.17

λέγει [. . .] Ἡράκλειτος [. . .] "ψυχὴ αὐγὴ ξηρὴ σοφωτάτη" [. . .].

k (< T 735 Mouraviev) Porph. *Sent.* 29.40

ὅταν δὲ μελετήσῃ ἀφίστασθαι φύσεως, αὐγὴ ξηρὰ γίνεται, ἄσκιος καὶ ἀνέφελος.

l (< T 734 Mouraviev, cf. B118) Porph. *Antr.* 11

αὐτὸς δέ φησιν Ἡράκλειτος "ξηρὰ ψυχὴ σοφωτάτη."

R102 "*ἀμαθίην ἄμεινον κρύπτειν.*" (= ***D113***)

a (< T 479 Mouraviev) Plut. *An virt.* 439D

"ἀμαθίην" γὰρ, Ἡράκλειτός φησι, "κρύπτειν ἄμεινον."

b (< T 478 Mouraviev) Plut. *De aud.* 43D

τάχα μὲν γὰρ οὐδὲ "ἀμαθίην κρύπτειν ἄμεινον," ὥς φησιν Ἡράκλειτος, ἀλλ' εἰς μέσον τιθέναι καὶ θεραπεύειν.

c (> B95) Plut. *Quaest. conv.* 3.1 644F

"ἀμαθίην" γὰρ "ἄμεινον," ὥς φησιν Ἡράκλειτος, "κρύπτειν," ἔργον δ' ἐν ἀνέσει καὶ παρ' οἶνον.

HERACLITUS

j (cf. B118) Aristides Quintilian, *On Music*

Heraclitus [. . .] says, "soul, dry light-beam, the wisest" [. . .].

k (≠ DK) Porphyry, *Sentences*

Whenever it [scil. the soul] trains itself in removing itself from nature, it becomes a dry light-beam, without shadow or cloud.

l (cf. B118) Porphyry, *On the Cave of the Nymphs in the Odyssey*

Heraclitus himself says, "dry soul, the wisest."

R102 "It is better to hide one's ignorance." (= *D113*)

a (≠ DK) Plutarch, *Can Virtue Be Taught?*

For Heraclitus says, "it is better to hide one's ignorance."

b (≠ DK) Plutarch, *How to Listen*

But perhaps it is not "better to hide one's ignorance," as Heraclitus says, but to make it public and cure it.

c (> B95) Plutarch, *Table Talk*

For, as Heraclitus says, "it is better to hide one's ignorance"; but this is hard to do when one is relaxing and drinking wine.

d (< T 481 Mouraviev) Plut. in Stob. 3.18.31

ἀμαθίην, ὥς φησιν Ἡράκλειτος, καὶ ἄλλως κρύπτειν ἔργον ἐστίν, ἐν οἴνῳ δὲ χαλεπώτερον.

e (< B95) Stob. 3.1.174–75

Ἡρακλείτου. [. . .] κρύπτειν ἀμαθίην κρέσσον ἢ ἐς τὸ μέσον φέρειν.

Doubtful and Pseudepigraphic Texts (R103–R117)
Variations of Heraclitean Aphorisms Attributed to
Democrates or Democritus (R103–R107)

R103 (68 B64) Stob. 3.4.81 (= Democrates 29)

πολλοὶ πολυμαθέες νοῦν οὐκ ἔχουσιν.

R104 (68 B65) Democrates 30

πολυνοίην, οὐ πολυμαθίην ἀσκέειν χρή.

R105 (68 B98) Democrates 64

ἑνὸς φιλίη ξυνετοῦ κρέσσων ἀξυνέτων πάντων.

R106 (68 B236) Stob. 3.20.56

θυμῷ μάχεσθαι μὲν χαλεπόν· ἀνδρὸς δὲ τὸ κρατέειν εὐλογίστου.

HERACLITUS

d (≠ DK) Plutarch in Stobaeus

To hide one's ignorance, as Heraclitus says, is hard work under any circumstances, but it is even more difficult when one is drinking wine.

e (< B95) Stobaeus, *Anthology*

Of Heraclitus: To hide one's ignorance is better than to make it public.

Doubtful and Pseudepigraphic Texts (R103–R117)
Variations of Heraclitean Aphorisms Attributed to Democrates or Democritus (R103–R107)

R103 (68 B64) Democrates

Many people who possess much learning do not have intelligence [= **ATOM. D307**] [cf. **D20**].

R104 (68 B65) Democrates

One should practice having much intelligence, not much learning [cf. **D20**].

R105 (68 B98) Democrates

The friendship of one intelligent man is better than that of all the unintelligent ones [cf. **D12**].

R106 (68 B236) Stobaeus, *Anthology*

To fight against an ardor is hard; but it is the mark of a rational man to dominate over it [= **ATOM. D296**] [cf. **D116**].

R107 (68 B147) Clem. Alex. *Protr.* 10.92.4 (et al.)

"ὕες" γάρ, φησίν, "ἥδονται βορβόρῳ μᾶλλον ἢ καθαρῷ ὕδατι" καὶ "ἐπὶ φορυτῷ μαργαίνουσιν" κατὰ Δημόκριτον.

Other Doubtful Aphorisms (R108–R116)

R108 (B46) Diog. Laert. 9.7

τήν τ' οἴησιν ἱερὰν νόσον ἔλεγε καὶ τὴν ὅρασιν ψεύδεσθαι.

R109 (B131) *Gnomol. Par.* 209

ὁ δέ γε Ἡράκλειτος ἔλεγε τὴν οἴησιν προκοπῆς ἐγκοπήν.

R110 (B132) *Gnomol. Vat.* 743 n. 312

τιμαὶ θεοὺς καὶ ἀνθρώπους καταδουλοῦνται.

R111 (B133) *Gnomol. Vat.* 743 n. 313

ἄνθρωποι κακοὶ ἀληθινῶν ἀντίδικοι.

R112 (B134) *Gnomol. Vat.* 743 n. 314

Ἡράκλειτος τὴν παιδείαν ἕτερον ἥλιον εἶναι τοῖς πεπαιδευμένοις ἔλεγεν.

HERACLITUS

R107 (68 B147) Clement of Alexandria, *Protreptic*

For he [scil. probably Heraclitus] says, "pigs take greater pleasure in mire than in pure water" [cf. **D80**] and "they go mad for rubbish" according to Democritus [= **ATOM. D250**].

Other Doubtful Aphorisms (R108–R116)

R108 (B46) Diogenes Laertius

He said that opinion is the holy disease [i.e. epilepsy] and that vision is deceptive.

R109 (B131) Paris Gnomology

He said that opinion is an obstacle to progress.

R110 (B132) Vatican Gnomology

Honors enslave gods and men.

R111 (B133) Vatican Gnomology

Wicked men are the adversaries of genuine ones.

R112 (B134) Vatican Gnomology

Heraclitus said that education is a second sun for people who have been educated.

R113 (B135) *Gnomol. Vat.* 743 n. 315

ὁ αὐτὸς συντομωτάτην ὁδὸν ἔλεγεν εἰς εὐδοξίαν τὸ γενέσθαι ἀγαθόν.

R114 (< B125a) Tzetz. *In Aristoph. Plut.* 88

"μὴ ἐπιλίποι ὑμᾶς πλοῦτος," ἔφη, "Ἐφέσιοι, ἵν' ἐξελέγχοισθε πονηρευόμενοι."

R115 (T 1044 Mouraviev) Ps.-Max. Conf. *Loc. comm.* 8.65

Ἡρακλείτου φυσικοῦ. ἡ εὔκαιρος χάρις, λιμῷ καθάπερ τροφὴ ἁρμόττουσα, τὴν τῆς ψυχῆς ἔνδειαν ἰᾶται.

R116 (B130) *Gnomol. Mon. Lat.* 1.19

non convenit ridiculum esse ita, ut ridendus ipse videaris. Heraclitus dixit.

Selections from an Apocryphal
Correspondence (R117)

R117 (T 705 Mouraviev) Diog. Laert.

a 9.13–14

Βασιλεὺς Δαρεῖος πατρὸς Ὑστάσπεω Ἡράκλειτον Ἐφέσιον σοφὸν ἄνδρα προσαγορεύει χαίρειν.

[13] καταβέβλησαι λόγον Περὶ φύσεως δυσνόητόν τε καὶ δυσεξήγητον. ἔν τισι μὲν οὖν ἑρμηνευόμενος

R113 (B135) Vatican Gnomology

He said that the shortest path to attaining fame is to be a good man.

R114 (< B125a) Tzetzes, *Commentary on Aristophanes'* Wealth

"May your wealth never abandon you," he said, "men of Ephesus, so that your wickedness can be proven."

R115 (≠ DK) Ps.-Maximus the Confessor, *Florilegium*

Of Heraclitus, the natural philosopher: "Gratitude at the right moment, like appropriate food for hunger, heals the neediness of the soul."

R116 (B130) Munich Gnomology

"It is unseemly to be so funny that you yourself become ridiculous." Heraclitus said it.

Selections from an Apocryphal Correspondence (R117)[1]

[1] There are several other apocryphal letters.

R117 (≠ DK) Diogenes Laertius

a

King Darius, the son of Hystaspes, sends greetings to Heraclitus of Ephesus, the wise man.

[13] "You have written down an account *On Nature,* hard to understand and hard to explain. In some passages, when it is interpreted literally, it seems to me to exhibit a

κατὰ λέξιν σὴν δοκεῖ δύναμίν τινα περιέχειν θεωρίας κόσμου τε τοῦ σύμπαντος καὶ τῶν ἐν τούτῳ γινομένων, ἅπερ ἐστὶν ἐν θειοτάτῃ κείμενα κινήσει· τῶν δὲ πλείστων ἐποχὴν ἔχοντα, ὥστε καὶ τοὺς ἐπὶ πλεῖστον μετεσχηκότας συγγραμμάτων διαπορεῖσθαι τῆς ὀρθῆς δοκούσης γεγράφθαι παρὰ σοὶ διηγήσεως.[1] βασιλεὺς οὖν Δαρεῖος Ὑστάσπου βούλεται τῆς σῆς ἀκροάσεως μετασχεῖν καὶ παιδείας Ἑλληνικῆς. ἔρχου δὴ συντόμως πρὸς ἐμὴν ὄψιν καὶ βασίλειον οἶκον. [14] Ἕλληνες γὰρ ἐπὶ τὸ πλεῖστον ἀνεπισήμαντοι σοφοῖς ἀνδράσιν ὄντες παρορῶσι τὰ καλῶς ὑπ' αὐτῶν ἐνδεικνύμενα πρὸς σπουδαίαν ἀκοὴν καὶ μάθησιν. παρ' ἐμοὶ δ' ὑπάρχει σοι πᾶσα μὲν προεδρία, καθ' ἡμέραν δὲ καλὴ καὶ σπουδαία προσαγόρευσις καὶ βίος εὐδόκιμος σαῖς παραινέσεσιν.

[1] διηγήσεως mss.: ἐξηγήσεως Cobet

b 9.14

Ἡράκλειτος Ἐφέσιος βασιλεῖ Δαρείῳ πατρὸς Ὑστάσπεω χαίρειν.

ὁκόσοι τυγχάνουσιν ὄντες ἐπιχθόνιοι τῆς μὲν ἀληθείης καὶ δικαιοπραγμοσύνης ἀπέχονται, ἀπληστίῃ δὲ καὶ δοξοκοπίῃ προσέχουσι κακῆς ἕνεκα ἀνοίης. ἐγὼ δὲ ἀμνηστίην ἔχων πάσης πονηρίης καὶ κόρον φεύγων παντὸς[1] οἰκειούμενον φθόνῳ[2] καὶ διὰ τὸ περιίστασθαι ὑπερηφανίην[3] οὐκ ἂν ἀφικοίμην εἰς Περσῶν χώρην, ὀλίγοις ἀρκεόμενος κατ' ἐμὴν γνώμην.

certain capacity for knowing the whole universe and the phenomena that occur in it and that remain in a perfectly divine motion. But most of it seems to suspend judgment, with the result that even those who are most familiar with your writings are at a loss regarding the correct explanation of what you have written. That is why King Darius, son of Hystaspes, wishes to participate in your teaching and in Greek education. Come at once to my presence and to the royal palace. [14] For the Greeks, who most often do not know how to distinguish wise men, neglect everything that they indicate so well with a view toward serious study and learning. But at my court you will benefit from every form of privileged treatment, and every day you will receive a fine and serious greeting and your life will become celebrated by virtue of your exhortations."

b

Heraclitus of Ephesus sends greetings to King Darius son of Hystaspes.

"All men who live on this earth are remote from truth and justice, and they devote themselves to greediness and desire for popularity because of their evil stupidity. But because I myself do not recollect ever having committed any kind of wickedness, and shun the surfeit that dwells with every man's envy, and also because I avoid arrogance, I do not wish to come to the land of the Persians, for I am satisfied with little, in accordance with my thought."

---

^{1} πάντως Cobet ^{2} φθόνῳ rec.: φθόνου BPF
^{3} ὑπερηφανίην Cobet: ὑπερηφανίας mss.